What Happy Families Are Doing

What Happy Families Are Doing

Eric G. Stephan
Judith Stephan Smith

Deseret Book Company
Salt Lake City, Utah
1981

©1981 Deseret Book Company
All rights reserved
Printed in the United States of America
First printing October 1981

Library of Congress Cataloging in Publication Data
Stephan, Eric G.
    What happy families are doing.

    Includes index.
    1. Family home evenings (Mormon Church) I. Smith,
Judith Stephan, 1935-   . II. Title.
BX8643.F3S73   249   81-15151
ISBN 0-87747-877-5   AACR2

To our parents
Martin Stephan and Paula Alma Adam
and to the students, loved ones, and friends who
were able to share these experiences because they follow
the counsel of the prophets (and to all of us
who may be having a little difficulty
through various ages and stages in finding
joy in our posterity!)

Contents

Introduction

As we experience the great highs and the not-so-great lows in our families from week to week, questions arise: "What makes the difference between our mountaintop moments and our valley skirmishes? Since family time together is a priority, how can I make it effective more of the time? Am I alone in my problems? What are happy families doing?"

This book was not designed to be a general lecture or essay on how to think or feel as a parent—it was written to answer your questions. It contains personal experiences—shared by Latter-day Saint families in varied locations and circumstances—and instructional material. It gives specific help on how to build family unity, resist harmful outside influences, solve family problems, teach without preaching, hold successful family activities, and many other skills. A list of one hundred things families are doing is also included; it provides ideas you can try in your own family. The Family Checkup Quiz will give a quick profile of your family and help you pinpoint areas needing improvement and areas of success. By studying and applying these materials, you will learn how to use many successful ideas in your own family. What you achieve is limited only by the extent of your application and exertion.

Part 1
Benefits of
Family Home
Evening

1
Why Hold Family Home Evening?

As members of the Church living in the 1980s and enjoying the fullness of the Restoration, it is difficult for us to realize that there was a time when the concept of family home evening was first introduced in the Church. It occurred in an era when submarine attacks, poison gas, women's suffrage, and President Woodrow Wilson were in the headlines. World War I had just begun. It was 1915.

President Joseph F. Smith presided over the Church with its membership of 466,238. During that year a letter from the First Presidency was sent out to the membership: "We advise and urge the inauguration of a 'Home Evening' throughout the Church, at which time fathers and mothers may gather their boys and girls about them in the home and teach them the word of the Lord. . . ." With the introduction of the principle came the promise: "If the Saints obey this counsel, we promise that great blessings will result. Love at home and obedience to parents will increase. Faith will be developed in the hearts of the youth of Israel, and they will gain power to combat the evil influences and temptations which beset them." (*Improvement Era*, June 1915, pp. 733–34.)

Since the inauguration of family home evening, evil

3

influences have manifested themselves increasingly, with devastating effects on families.

From 1915 to 1980, the divorce rate in the United States increased five hundred percent. About one family in five is now guided and maintained by a single parent. The pace and pressure of our society have increased, and correspondingly the amount of time parents are spending with their children has decreased. Through all of these changing circumstances, six successive prophets have continued to raise their voices, pleading for our attention. "Oh, brothers and sisters, *families can be forever!* Do not let the lures of the moment draw you away from them! *Divinity, eternity,* and *family*—they go together, hand in hand, and so must we!" (Spencer W. Kimball, *Ensign,* Nov. 1980, p. 5.)

As members and nonmembers throughout the world learn and accept the counsel of the prophets to strengthen their families by holding family home evening, their activities vary widely. The experiences in this book are from typical families throughout the Church who struggle to obey counsel, couples who are yet childless, missionaries who teach families, and servicemen and students who are isolated from their families. As you read each of their experiences, see what answers you can find to the question, "What are the benefits of family home evening?"

A Heavenly Pattern Continued

Perhaps the most memorable family home evening I can recall occurred while I was serving as a missionary in the Philippine Islands. We had made an appointment with a wonderful Filipino family to teach them the program. In our first visit, we planned the time together so that everyone knew what they would be doing and could make some preparation.

A few days later, we returned, and the father called his wife and children together. As we gathered I sensed a real feeling of excitement. We began by teaching them a

4

well-known Latter-day Saint hymn, "Love at Home." The oldest daughter was very good with the guitar and picked up the tune and played along. Everyone sang, and I have to admit we sounded pretty good! My companion offered the opening prayer and blessed the family that they would remember this special occasion and the spirit there. Next, the whole family participated in one way or another. The youngest recited a poem about a little yellow bird. The youngest daughter sang a song she had learned, and the two oldest daughters sang a popular Filipino folk song. I then gave a simple lesson about love in the family and how holding family home evening would cause them to grow closer together.

The most memorable part of the whole evening was the message by the father. He thanked us for explaining this special program to his family. He said he had no idea his children were so talented, and it was the first time he had heard such beautiful music in his family. He then expressed his love to each of his children and his wife. When he finished, we asked each family member how they felt. Each one responded that they felt very happy. The mother said she had never realized how much her family meant to her. Tears filled her eyes as she told her children and husband how much she loved them. I then told the family that the feeling they were experiencing was from God, and that we had a message that would teach them how to have this kind of love lastingly and bring their family together forever.

If Only Two Are Gathered

My wife and I were in a peaceful, thoughtful mood. I had spent much of the day pondering the goals I had set for myself for the next year. I felt that we needed some emphasis on establishing a Zion home, and went to the *Ensign* for an article on that subject. After studying that article, I asked my wife to play the piano, and together we sang a song. It brought such a sweet feeling

5

that I felt somewhat like we were singing to the angels. We prayed, and then I introduced our need and the topic. Together we discussed the steps outlined in the article and built each other up as we went. One principle discussed was that of fidelity. I felt so good to bear to my sweetheart the witness that I was and wanted always to be loyal to her. We planned and talked and grew closer together in our family home evening for two.

Encouraging Each Other

It was only the second time we had met as a "family" at Brigham Young University, and we didn't know our new "brothers" and "sisters" very well. Our group leader passed out papers and pencils. We were to put our name at the top and then pass the papers around the circle. Each person was to write something good they noticed about the person whose name appeared at the top of the paper. At the conclusion, our leader would read the comments from each paper, and we would try to guess who was being described.

My paper was read last, and as I heard the comments I sat shocked, ready to cry. I had always had a rather negative self-image, but here were people telling me that I was a "happy," "pleasant," "pretty" person. I managed to get out a "thank you" and was very moved. Later, I put the paper in my journal, and whenever I became discouraged or down on myself, I would get out the paper, read it, and think about it. Soon my outlook would brighten and the negative feelings disperse.

Later in the semester, after getting to know each other better, we did this exercise again, and again people saw good things in me that I had never dreamed existed.

These family home evening experiences showed me how a Latter-day Saint gives spiritual and emotional support. (My family has no other Church members.) Because of this support, I was able to improve my social relations with others and most of all my relationship with my Heavenly Father.

Servicemen and Orphans

In November of 1974, I was stationed in Takhli, Thailand, with the United States Air Force. Our Latter-day Saint servicemen's group consisted of twelve brethren, active Church members on full-time military duty. On this evening we decided to visit an orphanage seven miles away from the base. Most of the children there were Indian, Thai, and Malaysian. We sang songs and performed little acts and skits. Then we passed out goodies to these, God's little ones, who had been deprived of a home or whose parents had abandoned them. None of the men were able to hold back their tears as we came to the climax of our family home evening.

Following Counsel

On a special night some years ago, my mother made an attempt to gather her family together for the family home evening that the Church leaders and our home teachers had counseled us to hold.

My older sister was away in Utah at Brigham Young University at the time. My brother was in Korea with the army. My father was off drunk somewhere, and my little sister was sick. It seemed foolish to me that my mother would attempt to hold a family home evening with just her and me alone on a frosty winter night in Maine—but she insisted.

We started off with a song. It was an eerie, lonesome thing to me as a young boy to hear just my voice and my mother's singing in the night. I don't even remember what the song was, but I do remember that before it was over both mother and I were in tears. The air felt thick and heavy around us, full of depression and loss of hope. But I remember feeling closer to my mother on that night than I ever had before. We prayed together and talked together, and on that cold night together we discovered new hope and the will to go on.

7

Scripture Reading

One of the best family home evening experiences I have had occurred when I was about fifteen years old. I remember that the members of my family were very involved in outside activities at that time. It was hard to get together. On this particular evening, my father simply announced that we were going to hold a family night. My friend Clint, who was visiting me, was also invited to participate. Because it was the first time in a long time that my whole family was together, I felt a good feeling just seeing us there.

We had a very short, simple home evening lesson. We all searched through the house and gathered up every copy of the New Testament that we could find. There were enough for each of us to have one. My father then asked us to open to the book of Matthew, and he started reading aloud. After reading the first column on the page, he turned to my mother and asked her to read the next column. For the next forty-five minutes, each of us, including my friend, took our turns reading aloud one column from the book of Matthew.

For some reason I don't fully understand, the words of the book sank deeper into my soul than they ever had before. I can still clearly remember those first few pages of Matthew that we read that night and the principles that I learned from them. Even my friend Clint said that he had never had such a great experience, and he was going to try to encourage the reading of the Bible in his family.

Creating Wholesome Fun

My companion and I were at a member's home in Holland. There were seven children in the family, and they had invited three of their nonmember friends. The ages ranged from about seven to twenty. They all waited patiently as my companion and I arranged chairs and some things we had brought for games for this family home evening together.

8

After we opened with prayer, our desire was to get each one of these children involved. We paired them off and tied a long string around the waist of one partner in each pair. Then we tied a ball of wadded-up paper about an inch in diameter on the end of each string. The object of the game was for this first partner to stand above a cup of water (which we had placed on the floor), bend over it until the ball got wet in the cup, and then run across the room to where his partner held a four-inch candle burning, and without using hands try to put out the flame with the wet ball.

There were cheers as each struggled to get enough water on the ball to put out the candle. Each one traded turns in this game and others, and each time the group reacted or laughed it seemed somehow to draw closer everyone involved. We drew back quietly and watched. We saw joy and unity and a lot of shared happiness. Later, we talked together as we ate refreshments. There was a good spirit there. In a world where iniquity abounds, from the magazine racks to the school playgrounds, we felt joy in being able to create for this family some good, wholesome fun—the kind that would be enjoyed and remembered.

Turning Our Hearts to Each Other

There was always Monday night football, the tiredness left from a day's work, or something else to interfere with our home evening. But we tried, and the trying paid off.

I remember one evening in particular. I was about ten, my brothers were eight and eighteen, and my sister (who had planned the lesson) was sixteen. The questions during the lesson were directed toward my parents, and gradually, with promptings and memory-joggers from my sister, my parents began to talk about their early lives and *their* parents.

Mom and dad hadn't talked much about their younger days, or perhaps we children had just never asked, but it was fascinating to hear stories about the

9

jobs they had had and the situations they had encountered, and to have these experiences related so clearly that we could almost see our parents in those funny, sometimes touching scenes.

As the evening went on, my grandparents seemed more like real people to me than just relatives. With tears in his eyes, my father told about his father and expressed his love for him as he related incidents of his faithfulness. His words made a deep impression on my mind. I found myself looking with new respect at my grandpa, and at all of my grandparents.

I know it meant a lot to my parents to have the opportunity to go back in time for a few minutes. We ended with a very close-knit feeling. Memories had been shared and explained, and understanding was clearer and sweeter. This family night strengthened the ties between three generations. It has always meant a great deal to me.

Becoming an Eternal Family

It seems to me that the basic idea of the Church is that the children are taught under the leadership of mom and dad. In my family, things have not fit that general pattern. My mother and father were inactive for many years, while my brother and I were active. I remember vividly the times we sat together as a family, and my brother and I taught my mother and father the doctrines of the Church. It was exciting to be able to answer their questions and help them understand the principles of the gospel. I hoped that we were able to make up in some small degree for all they had given and done for us. (Since that time, our parents have become active and have been to the temple—and we are on our way to becoming an eternal family!)

10

In the foregoing personal experiences, we hope you discovered several reasons for holding family home evenings. Note that even though some of the circumstances were discouraging and could have prevented the families from holding their family home evenings, they persisted. Every effort we make to obey counsel will be recognized and rewarded by our Father in Heaven. Obedience in itself is sweet.

Notice that some of the home evenings were being held in non-traditional "families"—servicemen away from home, students away at school—all organized themselves into family groups. This search for strength in association with others and the desire to relate to others in the gospel setting seem almost innate. Indeed, family life, family councils, and family home evenings are earthly reflections of eternal realities. We hold our home evenings to continue this heavenly pattern, and by doing so we sustain each other in our struggles, we learn to follow the counsel of the prophets, we have fun together, and we help each other on our way to becoming families forever.

2
Building Family Unity

The crowning blessing in the restoration ... is the authority to seal both on earth and in heaven, husbands and wives and children to parents. (Joseph Fielding Smith, The Restoration of All Things *[Salt Lake City: Deseret News Press, 1945], p. 252.)*

Our joyful expectation as families is to develop our relationships with each other so that nothing can mar or diminish the love and devotion we share. We call this goal family unity, and many families are reaching it. Husbands and wives are standing side by side in their efforts to build a united family—one with great bonds of friendship, love, and loyalty. Children are seeking advice and support from their parents and each other, and in return are giving encouragement and time to each other.

Unfortunately, not all families rise to this ideal. On the sad side of this picture are thousands of families who suffer daily disappointment and unhappiness. Some parents don't get along well with each other and present weak leadership roles for children to emulate. Some children are bitter at being dominated and regulated by

12

their parents, so they choose not to become close or intimate with anyone in the family.

How can families be brought to a satisfying unity? Is it possible to bind the hearts of the parents to the children and the children to each other and the parents?

The answer to these questions is an emphatic and resounding *Yes, if*... There is a way to achieve unity and closeness in any family. It is to meet together often (for a variety of activities) and make each activity together a happy experience.

Yes, families can grow in unity and love *if* they share many activities and *if* they do so in a supportive, happy atmosphere. Though these two principles seem self-evident, it is amazing how few families consistently apply them. To increase family effectiveness in this area, consider the following ideas.

Meet together often. President Spencer W. Kimball has said, "We must spend more time with the children and less in clubs, bowling alleys, banquets and social gatherings. Fathers and Mothers, we must 'come back home.'" (*The Miracle of Forgiveness* [Salt Lake City: Bookcraft, 1969], p. 256.)

Building unity in our families requires that we spend time together. Children also need to spend time with brothers and sisters, as well as with mother and father, in order to understand each other's interests and achievements. By doing as many things as possible together, family members open the door for increasing their love and understanding of each other.

It is true that children often express the wish to "do more fun things together." It is also a fact that all of us are busily running hither and yon from one commitment or obligation to another. Perhaps the solution is to run *together* to as many activities as is appropriate. In this way the whole family offers its support to each individual family member. They all go to each other's recitals, athletic events, plays, and school or Church programs. And when the whole family can't attend an activity, maybe most of them can.

13

Family friends can also be encouraged to join in family activities so that the parents and the children's friends become better acquainted. Most wise parents realize that sometimes the only way a child will participate happily in a family activity is if he can invite a friend.

The more a family works together, plays together, learns together, and worships together, the closer the members feel toward each other. Have the children ever been to visit dad's place of work or seen him in action during the day? Has the family ever peeked in on mom while she is conducting Primary? Have you ever all waited together for the bus that brought a family member home from camp, and listened to the endless songs and experiences pouring out of his brimming heart? The more we really know about and share in each other's activities, the more our appreciation and love for each other grow.

Take time. Plan vacations, share hobbies, enjoy family games, cooperate on home improvement projects, create many little outings together. Whatever effort it may take, if you want to strengthen the ties that bind families together, plan to meet together often.

Make each activity together a happy experience. Imagine now that we have brought our family together and have planned an outing to foster greater unity among us. Somehow, during the outing, individuals begin arguing, finding fault with each other, and criticizing the activity. By the end of this time together everyone is tired, a bit irritable, and eager to return home. Eyes didn't sparkle. Love was not strengthened. And while the children tell each other how "boring" family activities are, mother and father look at each other quizzically and ask, "What went wrong?"

What went wrong is that family members forgot to avoid negative criticism about each other and the activity. They forgot to look for the good traits in each other and the nice things about the outing and to tell each other about them. They even missed hearing the song of the stream, drinking in the freshness of the mountain air,

14

and "tasting" little Erica's homemade (mud and pebbles) chocolate pudding with raisins!

Probably the worst communication habit we have in the American culture is negative criticism. "Stupid!" "Did you leave your brain at home with your wallet?" "Did you just eat a piece of cake? Your face sure looks crumby."

We hear it on the streets, in the schools, and even in some of our homes. We all know what it feels like to be on the sharp end of negative judgments. It hurts—and sometimes for quite a long time. When we are criticized we want to defend ourselves and to argue back. Conversely, when someone praises us, we feel good, and we like the person who gives us the compliment.

If we want to create happy family experiences, we must learn to avoid negative criticism and arguments. To help accomplish this we suggest two rules: (1) Use family activities as a time to practice giving only compliments. (2) If someone doesn't like something, he should avoid negative comments and arguing, and instead ask questions about it. Suppose that little Vicki has prepared a special game for family night called "Button, button, who has the button?" If her older brother says, "What a stupid game," that negative comment will probably hurt Vicki as well as start an argument. The older brother should have praised Vicki for taking the time to prepare a family night game, and if he didn't particularly like the game he could have asked, "How did you happen to think about this game?" "What other games do they play at school?" Become an expert at asking questions instead of making negative judgments.

Certainly it will not be easy to change past habits overnight. But if every family member is instructed in what to do and how to do it (possibly in a family home evening) and then is reminded before each family activity, before long everyone will catch on to the two rules. Keeping them almost becomes a game, and wise parents will set the example and give lots of positive comments on progress.

15

More peace, more love, and greater unity can be brought into our families if we do things together often and work together to make each activity a happy experience. When we try to accomplish righteousness in our home by meeting together often, the Lord promises, "Verily, verily, I say unto you, as I said unto my disciples, where two or three are gathered together in my name, as touching one thing, behold, there will I be in the midst of them—even so am I in the midst of you." (D&C 6:32.)

3
Resisting Harmful Outside Influences

We find that we Latter-day Saints are also vulnerable to the destructive forces of evil that are all about us in this sin-sick world. Of the greatest concern in this day are those evils which tear at the fabric of the home and family. (Spencer W. Kimball, Ensign, May 1979, p. 4.)

Most of us feel quite comfortable when we have our families gathered around us and are holding a family home evening. It seems easy, for a few minutes, to live the gospel, to support each other, and to be happily involved in a lesson or activity. Our main difficulty occurs when family members must leave the home to attend school, go to work, or play with friends. Then influences change. Outside the home, we are often exposed to a glittering array of temptations ranging from lying, using profane language, and cheating to acts of stealing, destruction of property, and various immoral behaviors.

Inside the home, children find little cause to practice immoral living, tell off-color stories, or even dress immodestly. The home is a place to practice righteous living. If we could lock the doors, close the windows, and keep the worldly temptations out, we would all rejoice in peace. Unfortunately, such simple protective measures are ineffective. Adverse influences sometimes steal in through television, radio, newspapers, magazines, and people. And outside the home, exposure to harmful influences is almost constant as we move from school to playground and from work to places of recreation.

What, then, must we do to defend our families against the onslaught of evils that surround and influence us? How can we fortify our homes to withstand the destructive forces that seem to besiege us on every side? And is there a way to immunize our children against evil?

President Kimball admonishes us to teach and train our children in the "way of the Lord." The way of the Lord versus the way of the world—perhaps our families must be brought to realize that some ideas taught in the world are not true. They should know that though love and trust may change and deteriorate outside of our homes, there are eternal relationships within the home that will not change.

Let us consider four ways to help immunize children against harmful temptations.

1. *Stimulate a defense.* To help your sons and daughters resist the arguments and temptations placed before them, help them develop strong counterarguments. Simply warning them to "be careful" or "do what is right" may not provide them with enough resistance to ward off the highly attractive temptations placed before them. Immunization requires that a small dose of the disease be given to the individual in order for him to build up resistance to it. You can do this for your child by feigning several very mild attacks on his viewpoint, similar to the ones he would receive from people who would tempt him. Then let your child refute these attacks, point by point.

For example, suppose that at school several young people have started using drugs. They will probably tempt your son or daughter to follow their example by

18

saying, "It will be fun" and "There is nothing in this drug that can possibly hurt you." The key to successful immunization is to present your child with these same arguments *before* someone else does. In the security of your own home, let the child develop a defense for his beliefs by refuting specifically the "fun" and "can't hurt you" arguments.

If the family is involved in this discussion, other members should initially refrain from giving their ideas; that would rob the individual of the chance to think through his own defenses. Most young people can develop counterarguments and defenses that are much more powerful and specific than those you might anticipate for them. If a child uses your answers instead of his own, he generally is less able to stand firmly against persuasive attacks. After the child has made his best defense, the knowledge of older brothers and sisters may be useful. They can support the young family member with the practical ideas and suggestions they have gained by already having passed through such temptations.

Most temptations can be anticipated—the tempting candy bar at the store when mom has already said no; the invitations to try alcohol, drugs, or cigarettes; the put-down for refusing physical intimacy; the use of profane language; or the pornographic movie. Discuss these with your children individually and with the whole family. Let your children develop counterarguments as you mildly attack their ideas and standards with the kinds of comments and persuasions that you know they will meet outside of the home. Allow them to make righteous decisions *before* they face the temptations, and to find arguments and evidence to support their position. This is one of the most important things you can do to immunize your children against evil.

2. *Tie beliefs together.* It is more difficult to change several beliefs than to change one. You can increase your child's resistance to persuasion by linking several of his beliefs together. You can help your daughter remember

that she believes in the prophet, and that he has pointed out the harmful effects of drugs; she believes in the Doctrine and Covenants, and it warns and forewarns against the evils and designs of conspiring men in the last days (89:4); she believes in the ward member who is a chemist, and he has described the harmful effects of drugs on the body; and she has a testimony of prayer, the promptings of the Spirit, and the restoration of the gospel. Then help her tie these beliefs together to form a strong foundation against adverse suggestions. An attack on one belief becomes an attack on many strong beliefs, and the child's resistance increases.

You can help your son resist temptation by relating his beliefs to a worthy goal that he is trying to reach or to people he admires. Ask questions such as: "Would that behavior affect your plans for a mission? If you chose to do that, would it better your performance in gymnastics? Would your best friend still be your best friend? What would the coach think of you?" A child will resist an adverse suggestion if it gets in the way of his goals or interferes with a great relationship.

3. *Evaluate the source.* We tend to be most influenced by people we consider to be knowledgeable and trustworthy. Sometimes children are led into forbidden paths because they fail to recognize that the person doing the leading is not giving them all the facts and, in fact, is really being dishonest. Another way, then, to decrease the influence of an idea on a child is to examine the credibility of the source of the message. Don't be afraid to ask your child where the other person got his information. And never hesitate to question why the other person is failing if that information or point of view is supposed to be correct. Many young people brag about skipping church meetings, staying out late at night, using drugs, and engaging in sexual activities. These young people then try to influence others to do the same. However, when they are approached about their knowledge of the effects of drugs, or the emotional disturbances that arise from premarital sex, they are very

20

often ignorant and uninformed. They also tend to be dishonest about the benefits and rewards of these activities, and many lie about the penalties that they have already experienced. If by raising questions about these matters, you can help your child understand that the information source is not very credible, the child is less likely to be influenced.

4. *Announce your position.* We strengthen our commitment to a position when we make it known in public. Sincere prayer and bearing testimony both witness publicly our belief about something. It would be difficult for someone to declare that a magnificent blessing came because he paid his tithing and then to go on his way and never pay tithing again. If a child identifies with a visible project that "announces" his belief, he is less likely to change that belief. A teenager who writes a series of articles for the school paper summarizing the psychological and physiological complications of drug abuse increases his own ability to resist that temptation. Young people assigned to present a fireside on using courteous language strengthen their resistance to profanity. Ex-smokers reinforce their commitment to refrain from smoking when they publicly display "I QUIT" buttons on their clothing. Even the four-year-old's poster, scrawled with his own hand and taped to his bedroom door, announces to the world his intentions: "I hate cigarettes. I love my friends."

So another reason for holding family home evenings is to fortify and immunize our family against harmful outside influences. We must train our children to resist temptation. Prayerful and inspired effort on our part will bring us the help of the Creator himself, for it was he who said, "I pray not that thou shouldest take them out of the world, but that thou shouldest keep them from the evil." (John 17:15.)

4

Solving Family Problems

Behold, I say unto you, that you must study it out in your mind; then you must ask me if it be right, and if it is right I will cause that your bosom shall burn within you; therefore, you shall feel that it is right. (D&C 9:8.)

It is impossible to have a family without also having problems to solve, choices to make, and conflicts to resolve. Problems and conflicts are natural, and they are solvable. We are expected to use every means and talent that we possess to solve our problems; then we are to seek with great effort the confirmation of the Spirit.

A good place to begin practicing these skills might be to examine how you presently handle conflicts and challenges. Consider these five areas in particular:

1. *Communication.* This involves a closer look at how well individuals in the family communicate their thoughts and feelings to each other. When you and a member of your family work on a project together, what do you talk about? What are the subjects and feelings that the other person expresses or tries to shift away from?

2. *General issues.* Which general concerns are repeatedly brought up? Perhaps money, morality, school, and family are subjects that are aired from week to week.

Are these subjects dealt with only in the abstract or is there an attempt to discuss specifics?

3. *Ups and downs.* All families and individuals travel over emotional hills and valleys. Births, deaths, sicknesses, changes in employment and school, accidents, and personal disappointments all contribute to tremendous stress and tension in families. Ask yourself, "How easily do we talk to each other during the pressure periods?" When family members sever communications, it becomes most difficult for them to make decisions and solve problems. Families need to be reminded about the ups and downs of daily living, particularly when stress and tension strike, and realize the importance of striving to keep communication open during these times.

4. *Emotional connections.* A significant deterrent to effective problem-solving is the walling in of feelings. When this happens emotional stresses are bottled up inside family members. How open and available are you to your children or your spouse when they want to share some emotional outpouring?

5. *Expect differences.* The only way that individuals can be individuals is to be different. Families have to expect differences and conflict because each member of the family is an individual. An awareness of the similarities and differences among the family members will help you approach problems on a specific and individual basis. If you can do this, you will avoid hasty generalizations about the whole family and blanket solutions that really don't fit the problem.

Let's consider a three-step problem-solving formula that provides a logical and spiritual approach to handling conflicts and differences. *Step 1.* Get a clear definition of the problem, goal, task, challenge, or conflict. *Step 2.* Consider *many* solutions. *Step 3.* Don't stop until you actually implement a solution. Sounds fairly simple, doesn't it! Stop and think for a moment. How do you get a clear definition of a problem? In the face of a difficult problem, do family members become upset and emotional, and then make snap decisions? When a decision

23

is made, does anyone take the time to figure out the best ways to implement it? And who finds the solution to a problem? Is it always the parent? If it is, do parents try to force the solution onto the child? Or do they help the child solve the problem because they know the three basic steps to the process?

The essential first step is to define as precisely as possible the problem to be solved. The more specifically the problem is stated, the easier it is to find solutions. This is the step that is most often overlooked by parents as they attempt to solve perplexing situations in their families. When you are able to develop a clear statement of the problem, you are more than halfway to a solution.

Consider this example. Two children have started to argue and yell at each other. Mother rushes in and asks, "What is going on here?" Immediately one child says that the problem is Danny. Too often, the mother will assume that the problem *is* Danny and will say to him, "You are the older and should know better. If you can't play together quietly, then find something else to do." Notice that in this example the mother did not define the problem; she assumed the problem was Danny, thus failing to pinpoint the specific trouble. The mother also made a snap judgment about a solution: "Find something else to do."

This mother could have done several things to specifically define the problem. The easiest thing to do is to remain calm and ask: "What is the problem?" If you are given a general answer, "Danny is the problem," then ask, "What is the problem with Danny?" Or you might ask: "Why is that a problem?" And if the answer is vague, ask again, "Why is *that* a problem?" You might also ask for a specific example or instance of the problem. If everything fails and you still can't figure out the specific problem, you can simply ask for suggestions about what the ideal solution would be: "*How* would you like to play together?" "How would you like to share the bike?" "How can you divide the dessert fairly?" Unless you cut a problem down to something manageable, you will find

24

great difficulty in discovering an effective solution. The more specifically the problem is stated, the easier it is to find solutions. The secret to problem-solving success is to spend more time pinpointing the problem.

The second step in the problem-solving process is to consider many solutions. Our minds and the minds of our children are filled with knowledge and experiences. We need only to take the time to stimulate those minds into creative activity.

The easiest approach to finding solutions is to brainstorm. Ask yourself and your children, "What are all the possible ways that we could solve that problem?" "How have other people solved that problem?" "Do we have a book that talks about that problem?" "Who could we ask that knows something about that problem?" "Are there some suggestions in the scriptures or in conference talks?"

Getting a clear definition of the problem and arriving at a solution are two ways to "study it out" in our minds; then when we are ready, we can ask the Lord. The Lord will speak to us through his Spirit, as he did with Enos: "And while I was thus struggling in the spirit, behold, the voice of the Lord came into my mind ..." (Enos 1:10.) The word of the Lord will come into our minds and hearts.

The third step: Don't stop solving the problem until you actually implement a solution. Be just as specific and creative in implementing a solution as you were in defining the problem and finding solutions. If it's an important solution and involves a great expenditure of time and money, then find out how that idea or one like it has been successfully implemented in the past. Almost everything you decide to do has been tried by someone before—starting a family business, building a go-cart, adding a room to the house, or campaigning for a student-body office. Ask an expert; read a book; find out what was successful and what failed.

If the problem is a simple conflict in the family, let the children suggest how they would like to implement the solution. Brainstorm together, but be sure that at some point you: (1) identify the specific steps to be taken, (2) plan for any resources that will be required, (3) define individual responsibilities, (4) provide for emergencies or an alternative procedure if something goes wrong, and (5) be sure to evaluate and reward the implementation.

Family home evenings and other family times together provide splendid opportunities for learning how to solve problems and make decisions. Be willing to take the time to give each child many opportunities to make decisions. Teach by example and use loving guidance in helping the children decide how they will act. President Joseph F. Smith said: "Speak to them kindly . . . you can't drive them; they won't be driven." (*Gospel Doctrine* [Salt Lake City: Deseret Book Co., 1977], p. 316.)

Part 2
What Makes a Successful Family Home Evening?

5
Successful Family Times

Almost every parent places a high value on having his family feel close and unified. And few of us would argue against the idea that ideal family home evenings provide a splendid opportunity to strengthen our personal relationships with each other. The catch seems to be, "How do I hold a successful home evening?" Rest assured that it can be done, and quite easily, especially if you don't try to do everything yourself or make yourself totally responsible for family home evening success.

To begin learning how to hold more successful family home evenings, read the following experiences of other families who have held successful family times together. As you begin to read these experiences, notice what the families do. They rotate responsibilities, vary structure, change settings, and use many different approaches. Even the size of the families fluctuates. Opportunities abound for improving our family time together, and one way we can learn is by seeing how others are doing it.

Everyone Has a Turn

I guess I will always remember this family home evening because it started out on a down note but ended on an up note. We have a wide span in the ages of the children in our family, and on this particular night our fifteen-year-old was having a fit because our six-year-old had planned our family night. (They each have a turn from time to time.) The six-year-old had decided we were going to play games, namely, spin-the-bottle, button-button, and a new one called sardines. We explained to all the children that this was Lisa's night, and that we were *all* going to have fun!

Spin-the-bottle went about as expected, with older brother doing a lot of cutting up, and button-button was about the same. Next came sardines. None of us had ever played it, so Lisa carefully explained what to do. First we turned off all the lights in the house except those in the room we were in. Then one person went to hide while the rest of us counted to twenty-five. We then turned the light off in our room, leaving the house in total darkness. The object of the game was to find the person who was hiding and to join him in his hiding place, trying to lose the other family members as you searched. One by one people began to disappear until only one person was searching. When the last person found the group and tried to squeeze into the hiding place, there was all kinds of fun. We hid in the bathtub, we crammed into the broom closet, and we squeezed under the bed and other unlikely places. It took a lot of discipline not to snicker or laugh as each person joined the group.

We played until everyone had had a turn to hide. After we finished, we talked about how much fun we had had and about how careful we had had to be to follow the rules to make the game a success. In an informal way we tied it to life, and then we knelt for family prayer, all feeling very warm toward each other.

Spontaneity versus Structure

30

It was the week before school started, and we were having our family home evening. My father conducted, and we first took care of family business and then discussed the week's activities. After this, my little sister led us in singing, "I Am a Child of God," and I accompanied with the flute. Mom said the opening prayer. Instead of the usual lesson format, our parents had arranged for a film, "The First Vision." It really held our attention, and as the film ended we felt a great love for the Prophet Joseph Smith and also for each other. We took turns bearing our testimonies and reaffirming the love that we all share. My father then gave blessings to my older sister and me, as we would be returning to school. Because my father honors and respects his priesthood, he didn't merely pray, but blessed us with the power and authority that come from the influence of the Spirit. When he had finished, we all hugged each other through tears. After some cake and ice cream, we played a game together. I can't think of a time that I felt closer to my family. We all felt that we had something to offer each other and the Lord.

Talking Time

Although our family does not really have family home evening (my parents are not members), I had an experience that made me hopeful about how it could work. My boyfriend (who is also a member) came to visit to meet my parents. He brought with him a large bag of pecans, gathered just a few days before from the tree in his back yard. Together we covered the dining room table with newspapers and then sat down and cracked nuts by ourselves, just talking about nothing in particular. Gradually my parents joined us, and we spent a pleasant evening laughing and learning more about each other. We all shared a special feeling of love that night, and I hoped that good things might come from our example.

The Important Things

31

It was the end of the year, and we were grateful to be in our new house. We had all worked hard together, and now it was nice to just sit back and review the things that had happened. My brother had left for his mission, so as we sat around the warm fire, we really missed him. We had the usual lesson, scripture reading, and prayers, but then, almost as an afterthought, our dad asked each member of the family to tell the three things that were most important to him or her in life. It was really great to have mom and dad tell us how much we meant to them and how much they meant to each other. It's not something that we express often, and as a family we all felt very close.

Home Evening in Sleeping Bags

Early last summer while it was still very cold at night, our two youngest boys begged us to sleep out as a family for our family night. As their mother, I'm known as the worst camper in the world. I love a warm tub and a nice soft bed and am notoriously cold—always! But with much coaxing I relented. We put on the woolen underwear, dragged the sleeping bags out into the back yard, and in the far corner of our lot we set up our "camp." We spent the next hours looking for the Little Dipper and Big Bear and gazing in wonder at the Milky Way. During the night I almost froze and spent most of the time at the bottom of my sleeping bag, but our two boys have never forgotten their home evening under the stars. Those were some of the best hours we ever spent together.

Mountain Picnic

I was home from my mission, and my sister and her new baby were visiting with us for the day. Since it was Monday, we decided to have our family home evening together and enjoy a ride in the mountains. Everyone climbed in the pickup, and we headed for the hills.

The evening was quiet and beautiful. There was

32

such a feeling of peace and serenity as we drove through the hills together. The hot dogs and marshmallows roasted over the crackling campfire tasted great, and we had fun crossing the creek and climbing a nearby hill. I remember the deer and rabbits we saw and the freshness of the mountain air, but most of all I remember how I felt to be with my parents and brothers and sisters amid the beautiful handiwork of God.

Lively Lessons

In one of our home evenings, my dad brought out some quotations that he had printed on different-shaped colored papers—some were like stars, some clouds, squares, and triangles. He put these all around the room without saying anything. Then, after we had our opening song, prayer, and took care of our family problems and upcoming activities, he gathered up all the signs. He held them on his lap and said that he was going to show us each sign, one at a time, and we were to explain what the quotation meant. If we were right, we got a candy kiss. Some of the quotations were:

"Don't let the fact that you can't do all you want to do, keep you from doing what you can do."
—Francois de Salignac

"Keep in mind that even if you're on the right track, you'll get run over if you just sit there."

"Funny how a man generally can do more than he thinks he can, and almost always does less than he thinks he does."
—Kurtis Rowley

33

"An idea not coupled with action will never become any bigger than the brain cell it occupies."
—Arnold H. Glasow

"There is no limit to what can be accomplished if it doesn't matter who gets the credit."

"It is well to think well; it is divine to act well."

—Horace Mann

"One of these days is none of these days."
"Do it!"

—Spencer W. Kimball

We all got involved as he showed us each sign and we shared our ideas about it. Then he asked us what the main subject of the lesson was. We soon figured out that our lesson was intended to motivate us to act on our good ideas and intentions rather than to just think or talk about them. Finally, we each chose and wrote down just one thing we could do that week to put this lesson into action. Dad left the signs up around the house the next day so no one could forget!

Magazine Articles

My wife and I often use articles from the *Ensign* to start our family home evenings. We choose an article from an area that we are trying to improve in. We read it together and discuss it and then try to choose something from it that we can implement in our lives. We find the First Presidency messages and the conference issues usually work the best, although we have also used other excellent articles.

Another thing we do occasionally is to share the lessons we have heard in priesthood or Relief Society meetings. This has given us a very good way to really discuss the gospel with each other and has provided us with some of the best home evenings we've had.

34

Coat of Arms

During one of our family home evenings, each family member made a personal coat of arms. We were each given a piece of paper shaped like a shield. The shield was divided into five sections. Then five questions were asked of us, and we were to draw a picture to represent each of our answers. The questions were: (1) Which word would you choose to best describe you? (Tall, strong, gracious, prayerful.) (2) What is your strongest talent? (3) What is your favorite memory? (4) How do you want others to remember you? (5) If you could have one wish for the whole world, what would it be? We had enough time between questions to draw our picture-answers on the five sections of our shields. When we finished, each one told what the pictures on his coat of arms meant. This was very meaningful to me because I learned what was truly in the hearts of my family members, and my love for each one increased.

The Prophet's Counsel

For this family home evening, we attached a long piece of white paper to the wall with masking tape. On the table we spread many issues of the *Ensign*. Each member of the family picked out an issue and went through it looking for messages from the prophet. When he found an article or a talk, he would quickly skim through it and select statements of specific counsel and then write them on the paper with a felt-tip pen: "Plant a garden," "Don't shop on Sunday," "Fellowship an inactive family," "Paint and clean up barns and yards," and so on. We were amazed as each one added his findings to the paper and our list grew. Each of us came to realize more than ever how practical and inspired the prophet's messages are. After looking over the list, we chose two items that we felt we needed to work on as a family. Then we planned how we could help each other put them into effect during the month.

35

The Element of Surprise

I had just received my mission call to New Zealand. It was late summer, and I was working in Salt Lake City, living with my grandparents and trying to earn and save as much as I could. On the last Monday before I was to return home and make final preparations for my call, my grandmother, "Umie," promised to take me out for a spaghetti dinner. As I began the day's work, I could see that I needed more than eight hours to finish all there was to do, so I phoned Umie to tell her I would be late. She urged me to come as soon as I could, though I really didn't think it mattered what time we got to the restaurant.

When I arrived home, I discovered Umie was gone. Grandfather said she had been called over to my aunt's house for a while. He suggested that we drop over to the park to watch my cousin play football, then come back and go to dinner. I loved football, and my cousin, so I said, "Let's go!"

As we drove into the park, I was stunned to see two girls who looked just like my sisters run by. A quick glance over the park made me realize there were no football games being played. Then I spied my sisters, brother, parents, cousins, uncles, aunts, and Umie all gathered around some picnic tables. I had been fooled—my final spaghetti dinner had turned into a final family home evening.

While I was still very surprised, my grandfather took me by the arm and we joined the group. After a lot of hugs and greetings, I noticed two beautiful home-made cakes on the table—one shaped like the north island of New Zealand and one shaped like a missionary! Umie got everyone organized, and then each relative shared a fact or bit of information about New Zealand—items on the weather, culture, population, and Church membership. We all learned something about the country where I would be serving. Then Umie passed out some cards and each person wrote why he or she thought I would be a good missionary. The simple words on these small cards were an inspiration to me for two years. I received insights into myself and my potential. I felt the need to live up to the expectations of

36

my family and hoped that the people of New Zealand would see the same qualities in me. Whenever I felt disappointed or discouraged, I had the cards with me and could reflect back on this family scene and gather strength to go on. After writing the cards, each relative presented me with a small gift, everything from socks to white shirts. Then we had a picnic of all kinds of good food and some of that beautiful cake. The night ended with a prayer asking especially for blessings for me as I began my mission.

Little Treats

A really exciting part of our family home evening was having surprises at the end of the lesson time. After we had our closing prayer, kneeling, we would squat on the floor and hide our eyes while mom and dad would tiptoe around and put little surprises by our heads—writing tablets, a new pencil, a stick of gum, a small book or toy—and at the signal we could open our eyes and look. This was always exciting and gave us something to look forward to. It also helped us try harder to be good during family home evening. I guess maybe I was a bit of a challenge to my parents sometimes, because one night my dad gave me quite a surprise. When I opened my eyes there was a new baseball bat, something I'd wished for for a long time. That surprise was worth every lesson I had listened to when I was small.

Positive Comments

When I was sixteen I was fostered by a bishop's family. I had come from a hostile environment. The bishop's goal was to make me a part of the family. Three weeks had passed, and I just wasn't getting along with them. The bishop decided to have a family home evening where we could all air our feelings. We started with his fervent prayer for unity, but with what followed I thought it all in vain. Everyone was given the opportu-

37

nity to say what he thought about the other family members. It was like World War III breaking out between me and the bishop's children. After a time, the bishop slipped in a comment: "Don't you think Don has some good points?" There was silence—then finally one comment, slowly another. Soon everyone began talking positively. The tears started to flow. The Spirit of the Lord rested upon us. At that moment there was a bond made. Everyone told everybody else how much they loved each other. I will always remember that home evening, as it changed my relationship from an outsider to a part of the family.

Private Consultations

I remember most a family night when each child had the opportunity to take each of his brothers and sisters, one at a time, into a room, and in a private atmosphere and without fear, to tell the other those things that he didn't like or that he thought could be improved on. Then he was to tell them something he admired in them, and they were to express love for each other. This not only relieved a lot of tension at a time of stress, but it also gave me a chance to get closer to my brothers and sisters by pointing out good things and expressing my love to them. It also gave me an understanding of the things I needed to do and work on.

Sharing Spiritual Experiences

My father had taught the lesson in our home evening that night, and just before closing he said he wanted to share something with us. He told us a very personal spiritual experience he had had a month before. Up to that time, my father had never done this. As he concluded, I felt a bond with him not only as my father but as a friend, another person. That experience changed my image of my father. It helped me realize that my parents were just like others who told of

38

spiritual experiences—they had them too. Sometimes we fail to share these experiences with those that we're closest to.

Mom and Dad Are People Too

We had settled down to have our regular home night when something unusual happened. Dad began telling about an incident that had occurred at work that day. That story prompted one from my mother, who shared an experience from her years of teaching. This had a domino effect, and all of a sudden two hours had passed. I learned more about my parents' thoughts, feelings, and experiences in those two hours than I had in the previous fifteen years. We forgot all about the opening song and prayer. From that time on, my parents began to share more of their feelings in our home evenings and other times, and I shared more of mine with them. I really wanted to hear about them as people.

Extended Family Home Evenings

My brothers, sisters, their families, my parents and grandparents, aunts, uncles, and cousins (approximately thirty people) all meet together in the summer for an extended family home evening. We choose a park that is centrally located between residences. Generally we have a potluck dinner for these occasions, but sometimes we assign each family a part of the meal. A typical menu is sloppy joes, all kinds of salads, and watermelon for dessert. There are usually no planned activities, but the fun is spontaneous. After dinner, while parents and grandparents talk, younger members of the families play tag, keep away, and soccer. After that we have arm wrestling and the telling of favorite stories. All in all, it is really enjoyable, and I think the presence of more than the usual family home evening group has a lot to do with it.

Family Testimonies

When we have our "greater family home evenings" we involve aunts, uncles, cousins, and grandparents. On one of these evenings we had a testimony meeting that was especially tender because every child, grandchild, in-law, and outlaw had an opportunity to express his or her feelings about the gospel. Many tears were shed that night, and many prayers of thanks filled our hearts that each one in the entire family was headed in the same direction and supporting the others as we tried to trek forward. It was a very rewarding night for our grandparents to feel the spirit of each of their posterity.

Dinner, Missionary-style

I am a convert to the Church and served a mission in Italy. After my return home, I began dating a girl whose family were all very active members. A month or so went by, and one day she and her family invited my parents and me to their home to share a family home evening. My parents accepted, and I was very excited for them to have this opportunity. We planned together, and when we met, we all gathered in the kitchen. I explained to them that we were going to cook an Italian dish together, *Spaghetti alla Carabonara*. We gathered the ingredients: an egg for each person who would be eating, two packages of bacon, one chopped onion, and about half a cup of olive oil, pepper, salt, Parmesan cheese, and spaghetti. We then divided up. Some got a large pot of water boiling and added a tablespoon of salt. They cooked the spaghetti about fifteen minutes. Others heated a small amount of olive oil in a frying pan. They then browned chopped bacon and onion. Someone else beat all the eggs together in a bowl. When the spaghetti was done, we quickly drained it, added bacon, onion, and olive oil mixture, and stirred while adding the beaten eggs. Salt, pepper, and Parmesan cheese were

40

added to taste. Everyone was fascinated with the recipe and enjoyed preparing it as well as eating it. After we finished eating, I showed a few slides that I had selected from my mission experiences. It was fun and spiritual, and my parents enjoyed this shared family home evening very much.

Christmas Eve Testimonies

The best family home evening I remember didn't start out as a formal home evening. It was Christmas Eve, and my husband and his parents and I were sitting in the living room in front of the fireplace listening to Christmas carols. My husband suggested that we should bear our testimonies. My first reaction to this was not exactly positive—instant panic! What would I say? How would I express what I felt? My husband started. At the warmth and love of the expression of his feelings, my thoughts of what to say were melted into deep gratitude for our Savior. As I listened and bore my testimony that Christmas Eve, the bond of love between us all was made more secure than it ever had been before.

A United Family

When my older brother was leaving on a mission and my two older sisters were leaving for Brigham Young University, we realized that our family would probably not be together again for a long time. We had all been very close through singing together, playing sports together, and watching and helping each other achieve in school and all aspects of life. During this particular family home evening, my father had us reflect on each member of our family and tell the most special thing about each one. We also bore our testimonies to each other. I recall this experience as if it had just happened—the tears and expressions of joy we felt in having grown together as a family.

41

As you read the personal experiences for this section, we hope you were struck not only with new insights or ideas to try, but with some of the similarities—that some of the experiences shared by these families were also occurring in your own family.

Notice the great variety of things families were doing—from carefully designed times together to cooking spaghetti or simply driving off to a picnic; from meeting around the table to meeting in sleeping bags; from accommodating very personal family needs to extending the group at times to include grandparents, aunts and uncles, cousins or friends. Variety, then, must surely be a basic key to holding successful family home evenings. You may want to ask yourself how long it has been since you have changed the setting of your family meeting. Are the same people conducting and giving the lesson or leading the discussion from week to week? Have you ever considered expanding your family circle occasionally to include relatives or nonmember friends? As you recall the personal experiences of this section, you will also note that none were elaborate or complicated. With just a little forethought, they are all within our reach.

As we gathered these experiences, we asked many families what they remembered about their very best family home evening. Their response was always the same: "The fruits of the Spirit are an outpouring of testimony and love among the family members. Any one such experience seems to become an anchor to each family member to hold to for years to come." What a generous gift from a gracious Father to any of us who are willing to try to gather our families closer together, and thus bring them closer to him!

6

The First Secret: Everyone Participates

Whatsoever ye sow, that shall ye also reap. (D&C 6:33.)

As we travel around the Church and meet with young people, we often ask them how they feel about their family home evenings. Too often the youth have responded, "They're boring." Unwilling to accept such a general answer, we have pursued the matter a little further by asking, "What makes you feel your family home evening is boring?" The common response, especially from the teenage group, is, "Mom and dad preach too much!" With further questioning, some have explained that there is too much lecturing and being read to and not enough discussing and participating. A few young people revealed that they felt mom and dad were sometimes using them as a "captive audience," unloading parental frustrations and gripes rather than using the time together to have an exchange of ideas focusing on a gospel principle.

Experience suggests that families would have many more enjoyable times together if parents emphasized maximum participation by all family members. It *is* boring to have someone read or lecture to a family week

43

after week. It is better to have all family members involved with telling, discussing, reading, and coming to conclusions than to have one parent trying to do everything alone. A family meeting is everybody's meeting, and the wise parent will want to involve everyone. This can be easily accomplished if we obtain a clear view of our family group assets and create a participation agenda.

Family group assets. Families as a group have a number of assets that separate individuals do not have. Considering these family assets will help us realize why we should encourage constant participation and discussion in our family times together. One important asset is that there is more information available in a family collectively than in any of its members individually. The family has a distinct advantage over any individual in solving problems and challenges that require extensive knowledge and information. Even if one member of the family knows much more than anyone else about a particular subject, the unique knowledge of a less-informed family member might fill in some vital gaps of information or experience. For example, dad may know a great deal about chemistry and nutrition relating to the Word of Wisdom, but mom knows a lot about preparing foods, and little Erica knows which foods taste the best to her.

Another family asset is the varied ways available to approach a problem. Individuals get into ruts in their thinking. They are sometimes handicapped because they persist in a particular way to solve a problem or achieve a goal. Even though members of a family may think similarly, at least their individual approaches may be unique. Each can contribute by helping others out of their thinking ruts. If you ask your family for the best way to help your boys raise money for their missions, you may be pleasantly surprised with the variety of approaches suggested. In fact, the family members themselves may be astonished to have their own thinking expanded by someone else's suggestion.

A third asset that comes when we involve each

44

family member in participating in the family group is a willing acceptance of solutions and decisions. When we participate together and influence each other in the discussion of a problem, lesson, or idea, we tend to accept the solution more quickly and easily than when one individual solves everything for us. Most small-group research suggests that when one individual solves a problem, he still has the task of persuading others to accept his solutions. However, when group members have a chance to think, air their views, question, and decide, they generally commit themselves more readily to the decision or solution because it is partly theirs. The greater the number of people contributing to a decision, the greater the number who feel satisfied and responsible for making the decision work. Sometimes it's even better to use a low-quality solution that has a good overall acceptance than a higher-quality solution that lacks acceptance. Mom and dad may much prefer that the TV set be permanently sent out for repair and the whole family become avid readers, but an acceptable beginning may be to limit viewing to specific times and reward the hours spent in reading.

A final asset and final reason why all individual family members should participate openly in family time together is that group decisions are better understood by those involved in making them. Chances for failure are greatly reduced when the family members who are expected to carry out the decisions have participated in making them. When the whole family is involved in talking, thinking, and deciding together, it is much easier for family members to understand the conclusions reached because everyone has seen them develop. All have a full knowledge of the goals, obstacles, alternative possibilities, and the factual information that was presented. It would be difficult for a family member to be closely involved in a decision on dating frequency, for example, and then to say, "I don't understand the decision, and I'm not going to do it."

Participation agenda. Many families prepare a sim-

45

ple agenda or chart to make sure that everyone who meets together has something specific to contribute to the meeting. This kind of preparation is easy to make and insures that everyone feels a part of the family meeting. In order to use the assets of the family and encourage everyone to become involved in a family time together everybody should: (1) be invited to attend and be informed about the date, time, and place (from time to time you might even put a special sign on the refrigerator or bulletin board to announce a particular family event); (2) know in advance what important decisions or items will be discussed, especially if family members need to gather some information before they come; (3) see the agenda or meeting chart and have an opportunity to add something to the agenda if it is urgent; (4) be able to be seated comfortably and hear and see everything that is going on; and (5), perhaps the most important item, understand the meaning and importance of any items discussed. Give your family the opportunity to hear the facts, ask questions, propose points of view, and participate freely in all of the family's decisions, goals, and conclusions.

Family times together are most enjoyable and least boring when all have an opportunity to participate. A family meeting agenda might include one, several, or all of the following items:

1. Song, hymn, recorded hymn, musical solo, scripture, or reading.

2. Prayer.

3. A reminder of why we are holding a family meeting and its benefits to us as individuals.

4. Giving congratulations to each individual for something they achieved during the past week.

5. Discussion of last week's goals, lesson, or delegated business.

6. Discussion of any problems, family work assignments, or rules or policies that are causing difficulty.

7. Correlation of individual activities coming up during the week, and who could help whom with what.

8. Planning the next family night or family activity.
9. Lesson or purposeful family activity.
10. Closing prayer.
11. Short game or activity.
12. Special treat or dessert.

Notice that a whole family hour could be developed out of one agenda item. A family could listen to songs, sing songs, create songs, discuss songs, and record songs. Family members could discuss musical likes and dislikes and varying influences of music. Families could decide how to build a satisfying collection of tapes, records, and sheet music. Possibly a fund-raising project for purchasing a quality stereo system or a musical instrument could be discussed. Any item on the sample agenda could be expanded into a full family meeting discussion. Or, as some families do, you could briefly treat each agenda item weekly in order to more fully organize your family and discover specific ways to help each other. If formal agendas seem undesirable for your family time together, you might want to consider a simple chart like the following:

Family Member's Name	Preparation
Dad	Lead compliments and correlation discussion
Mom	Offer opening prayer
Susan	Find some opening music
Vicki	Give closing prayer; prepare short game
Mark	Prepare a special dessert and record important items in the family notebook
Becky	Involve family in lesson discussion

47

Few people are able to hold a good meeting unless they have been taught how. Few children can participate freely in a family meeting unless they are taught how. A good plan and a few months of practice are absolutely necessary before everyone understands why they are having a family time together, how it helps them succeed as individuals and as a family, and how to participate so that the meeting is fun.

Be patient. Don't enforce your personal ideas about family meetings. Raise questions and let the family participate in discussions, and in time the participation and joy in family get-togethers will increase. Soon your children will understand that they, like Nephi of old, have been "born of goodly parents." (1 Nephi 1:1.)

As everyone participates in family discussions and decisions, they will soon say with Harold B. Lee that "the home is the basis of a righteous life and no other instrumentality can take its place nor fulfill its essential functions." (*Improvement Era*, December 1962, p. 936.)

7
The Second Secret: Everyone Practices Supportive Responses

A soft answer turneth away wrath: but grievous words stir up anger. (Proverbs 15:1.)

Perhaps nothing in the world hurts us deeper or longer than some of the careless things that we say to each other. All of us have had our feelings hurt, our self-image shattered, or our enthusiasm destroyed by someone who spoke unkindly to us. And, ironically, though we would never consider physically injuring someone, we often hurt the ones we love most by making sharp, critical comments about their ideas or behavior.

Before reading further in this chapter, it might be beneficial for you to check up on how you respond in particular situations. To discover your response style, complete the following quiz.

Response Style Quiz

Instructions: Read each of the following statements and

on the basis of what you know or do, place the word *true* or *false* in the appropriate space.

_____ 1. I usually listen to people and then try to analyze their problems and give some advice.

_____ 2. Some people's personalities and the way they talk totally turn me off.

_____ 3. In most conversations, I find myself speaking and listening in about equal amounts.

_____ 4. When someone else is speaking, I interrupt to clarify what they mean.

_____ 5. My comments to members of my family are about half praise and criticism.

_____ 6. Members of my family know that I love them because I tell them so from time to time.

_____ 7. As people grow older they learn how to make more supportive responses to family members.

If you marked all of the above questions *true* you are probably a somewhat average responder. If you had predominantly more false answers than true answers, you are probably wondering how to be a more loving and understanding person. Few things draw us closer to each other than kind, supportive responses. Parents who spend most of their time criticizing their children and condemning their ideas, rather than listening to them and praising them, commit one of the most cruel and hurtful acts in our society. The same is true of children, friends, and spouses when they criticize and disparage each other.

If the quiz caught you a little off guard or you don't understand why *true* answers are not the best answers, reread each question and note the following additional information. For question number one, we answer that most people just want you to listen and show understanding. They do not want you to interpret, evaluate, or judge them. If you marked question number two *true*, you will likely find it quite difficult to be a supportive person. When you have made a negative judgment about a person it is extremely difficult to follow with a positive response. Question number three reminds us that we should spend much more time listening and making supportive responses than adding to the conversation. Question four suggests that most of us spend too much time interrupting each other. (Communication research shows that in conversations between men and women, men cause ninety-six percent of the interruptions, and in parent-child conversations, parents cause eighty-six percent of the interruptions.) Again, question five reemphasizes that a half-and-half mixture of praise and criticism is woefully deficient. Think of what would happen if our response ratio were more like fifty praising comments for every half of a criticism! Question six draws attention to the fact that praise is most effective when it is specific. A generalized response like, "I feel grateful to all of you," is best followed by a specific, "for keeping the house clean and neat while mom and I were on our trip." And unfortunately, as question seven might imply, growing older doesn't necessarily correlate with making more loving and supportive responses. People will make more kind responses because they learn how to do it, not because they grow older.

Our first suggestion about successful family times together was to make sure that everyone participates. But that is not sufficient to create an atmosphere of love and happiness. It is equally important that we respond to everyone's participation with kind words and constant praise. For just as we can cause pain and personal suffering through cruel and unthoughtful words, we can bring joy and happiness through sincere praise.

The book of Proverbs provides us with an abundance of scriptural direction for learning how to make kind responses: "Whoso keepeth his mouth and his tongue keepeth his soul from troubles." (21:23.) "Even a fool, when he holdeth his peace, is counted wise." (17:28.) "Better is a dry morsel, and quietness therewith, than an house full of sacrifices with strife." (17:1.) "The heart of the righteous studieth to answer: but the mouth of the wicked poureth out evil things." (15:28.) "Pleasant

51

words are as an honeycomb, sweet to the soul, and health to the bones." (16:24.)

With the wisdom of the scriptures before us, let us examine the kinds of responses that most family members make to each other. In families we often respond or reply to each other in three typical ways: with a criticizing response, a questioning response, or a praising response. The criticizing response is the most destructive. The questioning response is usually better than being judgmental and critical but is often taken as probing with the intent to find something wrong. For most situations and most people, the praising response is the most useful.

No doubt you have noticed how your relationship with your spouse and your children waxes and wanes. Even in the best of families people sometimes feel quite close to each other and at other times quite distant. One way that we can improve upon our mutual happiness and unity and make our family time together more successful is to become better acquainted with the three types of responses and avoid the careless, hurting ones.

The criticizing response seems obviously a poor response to make when a member of the family has tried to achieve something or thought of a creative idea. All of us would agree that we should avoid sarcastic, embarrassing responses. Certainly we understand also how devastating it would be to ridicule someone's sincere effort to accomplish something good. Yet we often quickly judge each other, give unasked-for advice, and sometimes snicker and laugh at someone else's ideas. Sometimes we speak ill of someone because we think we are wiser. What kind of response would you make if your child said, "What's the use of trying to get along in this family? No one helps me when I need help." Many parents, becoming a little upset, would say, "That's a terrible thing to say. You especially have no reason at all to feel like that. You don't appreciate all that is done for you every single day." That parental response is both a critical and a judgmental response. Rarely does such a

52

response help solve a problem or build a relationship.

Once you become aware of the number of critical responses being made in your home, begin to identify them as they take place. Ask the recipients of criticisms how they feel. Try to encourage all members of the family to avoid that kind of punishing response, especially during family times together.

Let us examine for a moment the second type of response, the questioning response. If a family member has done something that you believe is not right, rather than immediately criticizing and judging him, you could ask questions to get more information about the thing he did or why he did it. Although this sounds like a fairly effective way to respond and is certainly less harsh than the criticizing response, it often is received as a subtle form of criticizing. For example, what if your child made the emphatic declaration that we suggested earlier: "What's the use of trying to get along in this family? No one helps me when I need help." And you responded with, "Why are you so upset? Have you figured out all the things the family is doing for you? Do you think that you should reconsider your statements?" Notice that although you made questioning responses, they sound as if you are judging.

Though sometimes helpful as a response method, questioning must be kept soft and used mainly to keep a conversation going. Journalistic questions such as "When?" "How did you feel?" "Why?" and paraphrasing what the person just said are ways to remain relatively nonthreatening while at the same time soliciting information to further your understanding of a matter.

The praising response is often the very response that is most effective for producing confidence and love among family members, yet in many families it is the least used. We all want and need each other's approval. There is enough difficulty and disappointment in life without compounding it in the home through careless and unkind responses. What kind of praising response could be made to the child who complains: "What's the

53

use of trying to get along in this family? No one helps me when I need help." In this circumstance the child could be sincerely praised for trusting you and sharing his feelings, for thinking about getting along in the family, for helping without expectation of reward, and for thinking about specific times when the child felt he needed help and didn't receive it. The child who receives these praising and understanding responses will tend to continue the conversation, risk more information and feelings, and find the support necessary to solve his problem.

All family members need to consider the following ideas:

1. Try not to say "should" or "shouldn't." These responses are generally judgmental and critical. It is better to bite down hard and figure out something to praise, and then ask a question if you would like to understand more about something. Don't say, "You shouldn't use so much makeup." Praise the person's attention to grooming and style and ask, "What look are you trying to achieve?"

2. Don't say, "You disappoint me." This is a criticism of the other person. Consider saying, "I feel confused. Can you help me understand what is happening?"

3. Avoid phrases like, "You never . . . ," "Why don't you ever . . . ," or "You always . . ." Again, criticism rarely works well.

4. Do say, "You look great in that color." "You do that well." "You certainly accomplished a lot of work today." Give praise. Give compliments. Praise and compliment each family member at least once a day.

Kind, praising, loving responses are the second secret to family success. Sincerely and specifically praise everyone for everything you can each day. Encourage each family member to become a giver of praise and an avoider of criticism. "Therefore, strengthen your brethren in all your conversation, in all your prayers, in all your exhortations, and in all your doings." (D&C 108:7.)

Part 3
Teaching Instead of Preaching

8

Special Teaching Moments

Three parables in the fifteenth chapter of Luke describe a lost sheep, a lost coin, and a lost son. Each loss comes about in a different way. The lost sheep casually wanders off. The coin is oblivious to being lost. The prodigal son chooses to wander away. Young people become lost in similar ways. How can we reach these precious sons and daughters and secure them in the family fold? We must teach and keep in touch with each son and daughter individually, rather than assuming that the task is accomplished by admonishing the whole family once a week. A family is composed of individuals. If a family member is continually taught in the same way as every other family member, he may become lost.

The family experiences that follow illustrate ways of teaching instead of preaching, and emphasize reaching the individual.

Buckets of Love

I love it when my dad gives lessons. He always puts such a novel touch to ideas. One time he brought two buckets into the family room—one filled with water, one empty. Then he had each of us think of something that made us upset or frustrated or discouraged that day. For each thing we named, he took a cup of water out of the full bucket. Then he told us that we are like that bucket, and when things happen during the day that disturb us, a cup of self-esteem is taken out. Gradually we get closer and closer to our breaking point and the bottom. Then he turned to the other bucket. He asked us for suggestions on how we could help a person whose bucket was empty to fill it up again. With each suggestion, he had us step up and dip a cup of water back into the empty bucket. Then dad concluded that home is the place where we come to get our buckets filled, and that we should watch for and be sensitive to others, because we are responsible for helping to fill our brothers' and sisters' needs.

Treasured Choices

It was my turn to give the lesson, and I sent my family on a treasure hunt all over the house. But at each station there were two or three things before them, and they had to decide which one they wanted and write it on their paper. At one place there was a can of Coke and a can of Sprite. At another station there were some popular paperbacks and the scriptures. There was a music station with hard rock, soft rock, and classical music. In the bathroom were a bathroom scale and some candy bars. I gave each family member a paper with clues that would take them on different routes so they wouldn't be going to the same place at the same time. Everyone knows what is right, but when such choices are right before you it's tempting to take what you want instead of what is best. When everyone got back to the living room, we talked about how we felt when we saw the choices, and what helped us decide.

Paper Projects

58

Each of our family members was handed a piece of paper. We were told we could make anything out of the paper we wanted to. It was fun because there was a feeling of friendly competition. Each person tried to make his object as clearly defined as possible. This turned out to be slightly difficult because we were not allowed to use scissors—we had to tear the paper. After everyone had finished his project, we all took turns trying to guess what each other had made. It was quite an experience because we learned how hard it is to work without the proper tools. We were taught how difficult it would be for the Savior to use us to influence others if we were not prepared.

Strange Menu

For our family night we were each handed a menu with some really strange names of food on it. We had just two minutes to make up our minds and give our order. In a few minutes the food was brought to the table. I was one of the lucky ones because I had ordered a "Super Scooper, Atomic Power, Tie Saver, and Staff of Life"! In other words, I received a spoon, a bowl of chili, a napkin, and a piece of bread. Others were not so lucky—some received a stick of celery, a napkin, a piece of margarine, and Jello. We needed to learn that a lot of things that look good in print, or sound really great, in reality may not be satisfying at all.

Pick and Speak

Often in our family home evenings we pass a box of different objects around. Each person has to reach in and pick out one item and then relate it to the gospel. For example, you might pick out an empty candy wrapper and talk about how what is inside is more important than outward appearances. This stimulates the mind and helps a person remember gospel principles and scriptures, and everyone gets to participate.

59

Sharing the Harvest

During the summer we grew a garden as the prophet counseled us to do. In our garden we planted some small pumpkin seeds. By October those small seeds had transformed themselves into an awful lot of large pumpkins. One Monday night, after it got dark, we loaded the pumpkins into the car and went off delivering. We would turn off our lights, sneak up to the door, put down the pumpkin, knock, and then run like the dickens! The most exciting delivery we made was to our stake president's home. Our families are very close, and the next day at school their boys were talking about the pumpkins, and so were a lot of other people. It was a thrill to me to do something for others in secret and to share our generous harvest.

Missionary Shower

Prior to our son's departure for a mission in Denmark, our family decided to give him a "missionary shower." Grandparents, aunts, uncles, and cousins all came together. All brought thoughtful gifts, but the anticipation and excitement of the younger children was almost overwhelming. Little Laura, just turned three, could hardly wait for her gift to be opened. She eagerly sat at the missionary's feet in anticipation. When he finally picked up her little package she couldn't resist helping to tear away the wrapping and exclaiming, "See what I got ya?" She held up a bright red toothbrush. Other anxious little ones followed with their packages—a tiny sewing kit, a ball-point pen, and a comb. This was *their* missionary, and *they* were helping send him on his mission. The children are still talking about this wonderful night when they were able to "help with a missionary."

Recording Personal Histories

60

As I was tucking the children into bed after our home evening, they asked me if I would tell them more about when I was a little girl. I shared some experiences, and we laughed and talked for a while and reemphasized the need for family and personal histories. As I was just getting my six-year-old Jimmy convinced that it really was time for bed, he said to me, "Mom, can just you and I have some private time so I can record my personal history?" It was late, but sensing his deep concern and sincerity, I agreed that it was important and that now would be a good time since all was quiet. Together we got the tape recorder. At first he was a little hesitant, but then he began with: "I'm sitting here in a little part of my front room with my mom, recording *me*." Soon his heart opened up and he related many wonderful ideas and experiences about kindergarten, friends, baptism, life after death, piano lessons, and family experiences. Then he looked toward the ceiling and said, "I'm recording this for my kids—is anybody listening to me?" Though the hour was late, I'm glad we took a moment to record Jim's experiences and feelings for his yet-to-come children.

Remembering Together

We have been working on our personal histories in our family. We take just one assignment each week so no one feels overwhelmed. We all began with "The First Things I Remember." Then we've written about what we know about our grandparents (special experiences and memories with them), a favorite birthday, when we were baptized, special spiritual experiences in our family, and our first Church calling. We try to complete the writing while we are together so we can feel a sense of accomplishment each time.

Missionary Letters

In one of our family home evenings we wrote letters to the missionaries serving from our ward. Each person in the family was given one piece of stationery. (The youngest dictated their messages for an older child to write down.) Each person started a letter and then

61

passed his stationery to the next person until each had added something. We wrote six letters at once! Missionaries love to receive this kind of mail.

Serving Together

During one of our family nights, we all felt the need to perform more service to others. As we discussed this with our children, we decided to contact a widowed neighbor and see if we could come and mow her lawn. She agreed and further consented to sharing supper with our family. On the appointed evening we went over, and while my husband mowed the lawn with the older children helping, this sister and I cooked hamburgers and visited in the kitchen. After the mowing and sharing supper and warm conversation together, our little family went home filled. We all agreed it was one of our simplest but best family times together.

Year's Supply

Mother and dad went through our year's supply of food and made an inventory. Then they prepared a list of things we needed to replenish. When the canned goods sales came on, our whole family went to the store together. We went on "missions" up and down the aisles searching out the items we needed. When we got home, we all helped to unload and bring the things into the house. Together we dated the new stock and then rotated and put things away on the storage shelves. Mom and dad didn't really need our help with this project, but by sharing in it we each felt we were learning about welfare and keeping the prophet's counsel.

Newlywed Goals

62

We were just married, and this was our very first family home evening together. The first thing we felt we needed to do was to set some goals for our new life together. We started by listing individual goals for the coming week. Then we made a few which we would be working on together, such as setting up a bank account, writing thank-you notes, and working on a scrapbook of our courtship. We also planned some long-range goals: checking into and selecting a school where my husband would begin his master's program, planning for some kind of physical exercise that we could participate in together three times a week, and choosing a list of outstanding Church books to add to our library and one to begin reading together. After we had discussed our goals and were satisfied that they were reasonable, we closed by bearing our testimonies to each other. (We posted our goals on the refrigerator to help us keep them in mind.)

Goal-Setting Booklets

After several years of marriage, and as our children were into their teens, it seemed to us that we were all preoccupied with our varying responsibilities and very busy, but somehow we had a sense of drifting that made us feel uneasy. About that time I became acquainted with the personal progress program of the Young Women. I was so impressed with the idea of personal goal-setting that I thought I would like to try it with my family.

With my husband's encouragement, I made up some little booklets and divided them into six areas: Spiritual, Service, Recreation, Cultural and Education, Social, and Home Arts. (I felt it important for boys to know homemaking skills as well as girls.) In each section of the booklet there were places to write the desired goals, steps to accomplishing them, dates they were to be accomplished, names of people to report to on progress, and when the goals were finished.

63

To introduce this idea, we asked the children to think of one thing that they had been wanting to do but had been putting off. They were to write this goal on an index card. Each of us had one week to accomplish our goal and to report our efforts at the next family meeting. One week later the children felt good about what they had done. One daughter had finally baked the cake she had wanted to take to a neighbor; another had practiced the piano every day without being reminded. One son had cleaned out his closet, which he had always meant to do but had never found quite the right moment. The children now understood our message and the real fun began.

Individually and as a family we set our goals. One son chose to do better in math. He set his goal in the Cultural and Education area and recorded the steps to accomplishing it. He chose a time each day to work on that subject. He chose to report to his teacher. One daughter wanted to learn to make bread. After accomplishing that goal, she set a new one to prepare a meal for the family once a week for a month. Another son set a goal in the Service area to help an older neighbor by shoveling his walks when it snowed. It was a very mild winter, and the shoveling wasn't necessary, so he helped him fix his car instead.

As a family, we felt the need to be more diligent in having our evening family prayer, so we chose this as one of our goals. Because of the difficulty in our schedules, we decided that at 10:00 P.M., no matter who was at home, we would kneel together for prayer. Our goal was to try this for one month. It worked, and it has now become a regular part of our family routine.

Another of our family dreams was to go on a vacation to Hawaii. We discussed this with the children and reached the conclusion that if they would each earn and save money toward their airfare, we would try to make this a reality. Each child was given an amount to save according to his age and ability to earn. How exciting it was for all of us to find that each one had his money earned long before the deadline, and some spending money to go with it. We took our long-dreamed-of vacation.

64

We learned a lot as we worked on our goals. First, anything worthwhile takes effort to achieve. Second, goals can easily be forgotten in the rush of things unless we keep them visible. For this reason we used the index cards and then recorded the goals in our booklets after we completed them. As we reported our progress in our weekly family meetings, we would also ask if anyone needed help. We set a general target date for all of us to complete our goals from the various areas; it was the day our vacation began. There were some last-minute efforts to complete some goals, but everyone met the deadline. More important than the vacation was the good feeling the children were beginning to have about themselves. They could see what they were accomplishing. They were setting and finishing short-range goals, and long-range goals were becoming realities. Our family has certainly not arrived, but we feel that we are directing our lives now instead of just drifting.

Weekly Goal-Setting Sessions

Setting goals is now a regular part of our weekly family time together. We keep a notebook of family business and assignments. After a song and prayer and a look over the week's calendar together, each family member in turn tells two or three or more things they want to accomplish that week. The "secretary" records the goals in the notebook. Our dad's goals range from giving a good elders quorum lesson to gaining a new client or increasing his running distance. Mom may set a goal to complete her visiting teaching that week or to help our youngest learn the letters of the alphabet. The children choose goals that include striving for 100 percent on a spelling test, reading alone from the scriptures, reaching a Cub Scout achievement, or building a hut. Our four-year-old sets his own goals: "Be nice to Jimmy; make a fire with Dad; learn to make my bed." When we meet again the following week, we each report orally on our goals. There is always a cheer or applause

65

when we can give an accounting of success (and maybe a treat or "ribbon" when mom and dad want to make a point), or friendly "boos" or hisses or words of encouragement if we haven't quite made it yet. Of course there are more personal goals that we each set as we struggle to refine ourselves spiritually, and we simply report: "This one is a private goal."

Forewarning with "What If ... ?"

My husband designed this teaching situation to give family members practice in making choices before being confronted with actual situations. We created an imaginary situation for each family member that fit his or her daily activities. Then each one was handed a slip of paper with a description of their situation and was asked how he or she would respond. Some of the situations were: Charlotte (16)—"What would you do if you were with a date at a movie, and even though it was rated PG it made you feel like you were watching an R?" Vicki (8)—"What would you do if you were in a store with a girlfriend and she slipped a candy bar into her pocket and walked through the checkstand without paying for it?" Dad—"What would you do if you were in your priesthood meeting and the teacher was teaching some ideas that were false doctrine?" We gave the family members a few minutes to think over their responses. Then they reported their decisions and how they had arrived at them. The family then discussed all of the situations, each person commenting on the way he would have responded to them. Older children who had recently passed through some of the problems given to the younger ones were able to share their experience and strengthen their younger brothers and sisters. The family was very enthused about this evening and in the following days and weeks it almost became a game to make up situations and ask each other, "What if . . . ?" We have repeated this experience whenever we have felt

66

the need to fortify our children before they are placed in difficult and new situations.

Family Scripture Reading

In the last six years, in spite of the fact that we have never had a "perfect" morning at scripture reading, each one of us has been strengthened individually. It all began with our oldest coming home from school in tears one day and declaring that she didn't think she had a testimony. We met as a family to try to solve this problem, and everyone, right down to the three-year-old, had an input. They decided the solution was to study the scriptures. They voted to start with the children's Book of Mormon stories, to have me read to them, and then to move into the "hard stuff"—the Book of Mormon itself. On completion of the children's version, we asked the children how they wanted to read the "hard stuff." There were several suggestions, all the way from listening to tapes and following the text to reading and using workbooks. But they were emphatic about not wanting explanations and discussions—their main objective was to read aloud, each taking three verses, to be able to say they had read the Book of Mormon from cover to cover. The only major fighting that took place during our fifteen-minute reading interval (6:45-7:00 A.M.) was when one child would try to read an extra verse without getting caught! When our daughter reached the fifth grade, she stood up in our fast meeting and bore her testimony: "I know the Book of Mormon is true, at least up to Alma, because that is where we are."

Our three-year-old was too little to read but always repeated a few sentences after me when it was her turn. When she was four (it was during the Christmas rush, and we were all involved in our family business), she came to me and said, "Mom, I don't feel good." I asked her why, and she answered, "Because we aren't reading the scriptures." Though she could not understand what

67

we were reading, she could understand and feel the absence of the Spirit.

One day our six-year-old interrupted a conversation with great excitement, "Mother, mother, you're using Book of Mormon language!" "What did I say?" "You said, 'therefore!' " In months of reading, that one word of scripture—repeated so frequently for emphasis—had made a deep impression on her.

So, amid the curling of hair, the eating of breakfast, a state of semi-lethargy, intermittent dozing or crying, and the wee bit of contention over how many verses are read, we have finished the Book of Mormon, Doctrine and Covenants, and Pearl of Great Price, and we are halfway through the Old Testament. My children set a goal to read the scriptures, and with fulfilling it has come discipline, self-respect, and confidence in the gospel.

Favorite Scriptures

In our family we like to discuss in depth a favorite passage of scripture. At the end of our home evening one person tells what his or her favorite scripture is. During the week that follows, everyone in the family researches that passage of scripture. Then when we meet the next week, everyone gives his insights into that passage. This helps us become well-acquainted with the scriptures and provides many cross-references that support and clarify the doctrine of the Church. It has strengthened our testimonies and given each member of the family a chance to participate in home evening.

Bread of Life

68

While reading the New Testament for our scripture study, we reached the sixth chapter of John. In verses 30–58 the Savior explains that he is the bread of life. Having looked ahead, my wife and I anticipated this opportunity to make the scriptures live for our children. We first explained the background of these verses by discussing the children of Israel in the wilderness and the foreshadowing of the coming of the Savior and his atonement. We then read and discussed the verses in John together. Then my wife took us to the kitchen where she had some bread rising. She divided the dough, and we each received a portion to shape into a loaf. We baked our loaves and ate them for refreshments. We asked our children to remember every time they ate bread that Christ is the living bread of life.

Scripture Clues

My sister and I planned a treasure hunt to spark up our family scripture study. We thought it would be fun to take all of the clues from the scriptures. We wrote the scriptures on pieces of paper and hid them. We gave the family the first scripture and everyone looked it up and tried to figure out where to go. They brought their scriptures along to look up each new clue. We used words like "jewels" (Malachi 3:17), which led to our jewelry box; "vine" (John 15:5), which led us outside the house to the patio; "swaddling clothes" (Luke 2:12), which led to the baby's dresser; "old bottles" (Matthew 9:17), which took us to the cupboards where the empty fruit bottles were; "loaves" (John 6:26), to the breadbox; "candlestick" (3 Nephi 12:15), to the dining room; "herbs" (D&C 89:10), to the spice rack; and "oven" (Malachi 4:1), which brought us to the kitchen, where we found Danish pastries in the oven. We shared the pastries and had some hot chocolate while we laughed about some of the clues. But we had learned about the rich imagery of the scriptures and how the Lord used practical examples to teach the people.

Reader's Theater

Mother decided to take a new approach in teaching our family correct principles. While preparing a Relief

Society lesson on appreciating Shakespeare, she was prompted to instill a love of his work into each of us. So at the age of twelve, along with my younger brothers and sisters (the youngest was three), I began exploring the realms of this great writer.

After her own study, and with a lot of faith, mother presented the idea to us that as a family we could perform a reader's theater presentation of *Othello*. We all agreed, and for the next two months we worked to understand and to memorize the play. I recall staying up late into the night many times reading the lines of Desdemona aloud, trying to get the right pronunciation and emphasis. Shakespeare's language also began to be a part of our everyday vernacular. John, age eight, in a fit of fury told the neighbor boy, "Charm thy tongue!" (In other words, "Shut up.")

The learning process didn't stop with lines and phrases. We realized the destructive power of jealousy through the character of Othello; the damage of deceiving words through Iago, the villain; and the importance of respect and reputation through the goodly Cassio. The play even complemented the teachings of the Word of Wisdom as we learned that wine will "steal away men's brains."

Although we performed the play only twice, once in our family home evening and once in a private school, we were blessed both spiritually and academically for our efforts. Being raised on Shakespeare's literature has been an added advantage for us in our accelerated English programs. As a family, our study continues, and we attend the nearby Shakespeare Festival annually. Our mother and dad continue to help us practice the principle of seeking "out of the best books words of wisdom." (D&C 88:118.)

70

Courtesy Training

We had four small sons, and my husband began to be concerned that a daughter might not come to our family. On this evening, he called his sons around him and made plans with them and instructed them about taking mother out on a date. He was anxious for them to learn proper courtesies concerning the opposite sex. He asked them to bring the newspaper and to select a movie at a local theater. A quick decision was made: "Snow White and the Seven Dwarfs" would be the perfect one to see. He taught all the boys and we practiced. He then gave each one a specific assignment: buy the tickets, select the treats, open doors, help me with my coat. When we went on the date, my sons went into action, and each one followed the instructions given by a loving father. Over the years the dates have become spontaneous. I have had dates to the park for picnics, to musical productions, and even to an art museum. Just before our oldest son left for his mission, he took me on a dinner date. We reminisced together and realized there were many special memories we could both recall during his absence. And now I'm looking forward to our date when he returns.

Modern Application

Our home is situated in the foothills of a large mountain range in Virginia. On one occasion my parents led us on a hike up to a nearby hill overlooking the valley. They wanted us to know and feel the meaning of the Savior's mission. There my mother told us a "modern-day" story of Jesus. She used experiences that we were familiar with and applied them to Christ's life. It wasn't long and drawn-out and preachy—but the impact it left was lasting. Afterward, we built a fire and had something to eat. The feeling was especially calm and peaceful.

71

The personal experiences that you have just read included examples of teaching through discovering analogies, making and doing things, setting goals, role playing, studying together, and providing practical experiences with principles. The responses from the family members varied with their ages, needs, and knowledge. The individual members of the family were not all expected to respond in the same way to the lesson. Most of us want to be noticed for what we do, praised for what we are, and allowed to progress in our own way. Children expect no less. They need the opportunity to grow in some ways that they have decided upon rather than in the exact ways that someone else has decided upon. Parents can help children learn and make decisions in a loving environment.

9

Discussion versus Lectures

*For this shall be a law unto the inhabitants of
Zion. . . . They shall . . . teach their children. (D&C
68:26, 28.)*

Often after having taught a lesson, we find ourselves
asking, "Did that really make a difference? Will anything
happen because of this lesson?" As we go from week to
week in our family home evenings, the same questions
arise, and they are healthy questions if we will try to
answer them. In this section we would like to suggest
ways to move from lecturing to discussing in lesson
times. We will also examine a teaching method that will
assist family members to increase their understanding of
a gospel concept, to see how it can be applied in their
daily lives, and to choose and carry out their own application of the principle for one week.

1. *Identify the concept or principle to be discussed.*
This can be accomplished in a variety of ways that would
involve everyone in the discussion. Suppose you wanted
your family to grow in the principle of personal prayer.
You could use a hymn to launch a discussion: "Ere You
Left Your Room This Morning"; "Prayer Is the Soul's
Sincere Desire"; "There Is an Hour of Peace and Rest."
Sing it together, or read the lines in turn. Ask family
members to look for lines that may express what a

prayer is, why we pray, to whom we pray, who assists our prayers. Another approach might be to involve your family with the concordance or Topical Guide in their scriptures. Examine their understanding of the principle of personal prayer: Why did the Savior teach the people how to pray? Didn't they already know how? (See Luke 11:1-13; 3 Nephi 13:5-15.) What does it mean to pray "with all the energy of heart"? (Moroni 7:48.) Or ask each family member to share his favorite scripture on prayer and tell what he has learned from it that helps him understand prayer better. Or begin with a picture of the Savior at prayer in Gethsemane: What is Jesus doing? Is he talking to someone? Who is he talking to? Why is he talking to him? What would he like to know? Can we ask him things? How does he answer?

A hymn, a scripture, a picture, a personal experience, an object, a story, an excerpt from a conference talk—there are innumerable ways to introduce a discussion on a gospel concept or principle. Once you begin the discussion, be sure to let each person finish what they want to say. Don't interrupt. And once you find out what they think, don't launch into your own point of view. Continue to ask questions and listen to their answers. Try to zero in on their main idea and ask questions about it. Don't make judgments about their ideas. See how long you can keep the family members talking rather than turning the discussion to your own views. Keep in mind that discussion and conversation are the best basis for learning.

As you conclude this part of the discussion, make sure that the concept you are teaching is now clearly identified (if it is the first time they are exposed to it) or that the family members have expanded their knowledge and understanding of it. Your youngest child may be hearing about a concept like fasting or repentance for the first time, while older children are hearing it repeated. Be sure that each benefits from the discussion. Take time to emphasize and point out the outcomes or "fruits" of using this concept or gospel principle: that the

74

family will feel happier; they will be able to improve; they will feel closer to the Spirit. This will help family members to recognize their growth in the principle later on.

2. *Explore a number of ways to apply the concept or principle.* When family members have a knowledge of the concept, the next step is to understand how to apply it. Try to draw on the experiences of the family members. What do they all experience from day to day? If they are enjoying a time of progress and most things are going well for them, is there a relationship between these experiences and the principle of prayer? (See D&C 46:32.) What if they were experiencing discouragement, or if one family member in particular or a friend were having that experience—could they apply the concept to these situations?

You may want to have a family member write the principle "personal prayer" on one side of a large piece of paper or chalkboard, and on the opposite side list the applications as they are discussed.

After exploring some experiences in common, ask the family members to suggest specific applications. If Scott is preparing for a priesthood ordination, how might he apply the principle? If father is seeking new employment, how could he apply the principle? How could the family apply it in his behalf? Could the principle apply to Dawn, who is trying to learn to ride a two-wheeler? How? Can Shauna apply it in goal-setting? Would it have to be a spiritual goal?

3. *Have each family member choose one way that he or she will apply the concept this week.* Having discussed and illustrated the general application of the principle to situations the family members have in common, and then to some more specific situations, each person should now have a good idea of how to use the principle. At this point, invite each family member to choose one way that he will apply the principle personally during the coming week. Perhaps he will choose to apply it to a particular improvement he is trying to make. Perhaps he will try to pray more frequently or consistently. Whatever

the choice, the application should be specific and reflect his personal decision.

This is a crucial moment in any teaching situation. At this point all the effort of the earlier discussion could be lost unless a method of daily practice and follow-up is built into the instruction. If we were to stop here, within minutes the telephone, doorbell, television, homework, and other responsibilities and daily routines would press in to vie for our attention and energy. Our teaching time would become a dimming light in the long sequence of the week's events.

This is the moment to ask family members to devise a creative way to remind themselves to carry out daily their individual application of the principle. In some families children have taped posters or pictures on the ceiling over their beds to remind them on retiring and rising. Others tie a string to their finger, put a rubber band on their wrist, or put a marble in their sit-down pocket. Some put a small decoration on the dinner table that recalls the concept or principle taught, and some make individual cards with a space to mark off progress or performance each day. Whatever the choice, the reminder should keep family members aware of their plans to apply the principle.

Sometimes another person can help keep us on target. Family members may choose to pair up to remind each other of their daily "practice," or they might arrange themselves in other combinations. A close friend or daily associate with whom we can share our plan may help to remind us during the hours of the day while we are away from our homes.

As family members apply this third step of the lesson plan and begin to use the principle or concept on a daily basis, they progress from knowing to doing. This step is central to our growth in the gospel. Without it, we could be filled with knowledge but otherwise empty. With it we grow and, having life within us, we in turn become life-giving.

4. *Have each family member share his experiences*

76

with applying the principle. After choosing one way to apply the principle and practicing it for one week, family members should be invited to report their experiences. Allow each to respond and tell what happened. Be sensitive to each family member. If there is a need to clarify the principle further, use this time to answer questions family members may have. Be sure to give encouragement and recognize all attempts to apply the concept that was taught. You may feel the need to ask questions that will help family members clarify their experience: Did anything unexpected happen? What suggestions would you have for someone trying it for the first time? Do you feel differently about the principle now than you did before? Finally, be sure to emphasize and point out the fruits of using the principle. This will help family members to assess their progress and feel joy in their growth.

As the four lesson steps are applied in our families each week, we should see an increase in our ability to follow a gospel principle more consistently in our lives. Through working on a specific concept repeatedly we become more proficient in its application. We should also feel an upsurge of strength and begin to move off some of our spiritual plateaus. Our children will feel less lectured to and more personally involved as we bring our families in closer harmony with the Lord's counsel: "Ye must *practise* virtue and holiness before me continually." (D&C 46:33, italics added.)

10

Helping Children Experience Gospel Principles

And these words, which I command thee this day, shall be in thine heart:
And thou shalt teach them diligently unto thy children, and shalt talk of them when thou sittest in thine house, and when thou walkest by the way, and when thou liest down, and when thou risest up. (Deuteronomy 6:6-7.)

Almost every hour of the day, parents have opportunities to help children experience gospel principles. In one incident, a nine-year-old boy had just received a generous gift from his best friend—a white mouse. Just as the mother of the family got over the initial shock and was able to adjust to this new pet, the family's blessings were multiplied further: the mouse gave birth to five babies. The babies grew. Luckily the boy's sister shared his enthusiasm for animals, and together they took on the dilemma of what to do with all the mice. They debated and struggled with the possibilities, then came to their mother for help. She sent them to find the scriptures and then asked them to open the Doctrine and Covenants to section 9. Together they explored the principles in verses 7-9. Then the boy and girl left to deliberate together. They knew they could keep only two of the mice, one for each of them. They felt an acceptable solution might be to give some of the mice to the local pet shop. But which ones should they give away, and which ones should they keep? They narrowed things down to two choices: keep the mother and one new baby, or keep two new babies. Together they made a list of the advantages and disadvantages of the two choices.

After studying it out in their minds, they agreed that the boy would keep the mother mouse and together they would share one baby. They then selected one little black-and-white baby from the litter to keep.

That evening the brother and sister prayed together and told the Lord what was happening and what they had decided, and asked for a confirmation of their decision. They felt at peace and comfortable about it, but decided to test their feelings overnight. The next morning they conferred again. Both still felt good about their conclusion. They said a prayer together and then sought out their parents to announce their happy decision.

Opportunities that afford the kind of teaching illustrated in this incident are all around us every day. But often we find ourselves under pressure, and in our haste we make the decisions for our children, we usurp the stewardships we so recently delegated to them, or we overlook their sensitive times and label them a "stage" or "phase"—something to be lived through rather than taught through.

Increasing awareness of daily teaching opportunities. You might begin by inventorying with your spouse each child's activities, involvements, and needs. Pool your unique insights and relationships with the child. Consider the daily work assignments at home, the subjects the child is studying at school, the kind of environment he encounters at school, his social growth, his special interests, his friends, his spirituality. Try to assess exactly where each child is in his development and anticipate the things that are just ahead for him that

79

may present a challenge or problem. You might ask yourself: In what principles does this child need growth and strengthening at this time? If you are aware of his routine activities and personal needs, you can more easily match them to daily teaching opportunities.

One spring day, a mother approached her daughter with routine efficiency to ask what she might like to accomplish when school was out for the summer. Armed with paper and pencil to formulate a list, she did not anticipate her daughter's response, "Oh, not this again." The mother sensed her misstep, quickly generalized the conversation, and in a few moments both left each other for their own individual responsibilities.

The mother went to the sink and rather thoughtfully began cutting up fruit for a salad. In a short time her daughter was back in the kitchen needing someone to listen to the Articles of Faith she was memorizing for Primary graduation. Seeing the beautiful fruit, she offered to help if mom would also listen. She practiced and together they chatted.

The mother began to inquire generally about school and friends and the current activities of the child. They worked and laughed together while gradually the conversation shifted and her daughter began to express some of her deep interests. "Mother, tell me about patriarchal blessings. What exactly are they? How do you qualify for one?" The conversation that followed touched them both. The mother did her best to answer, and then her daughter quickly left the room. In a moment she was back, and this time *she* brought the paper and pencil. At the top she wrote in bold letters: "My Special Goal, to Get My Patriarchal Blessing." Underneath it she wrote: "Beginning now and through the summer, I want to read the Doctrine and Covenants and the Pearl of Great Price, two pages each morning."

Even with the best of intentions, we may make a false start, but if we turn our desires to the interests of the child, we can know and feel what should be taught.

Teaching while working together. In our daily family routines there is always an abundance of work—something that needs cleaning, fixing, maintaining, taking out, or putting away. We should involve the children in these tasks and remember that they would much rather work with someone than work alone. We can use these times fixing the car, painting the house, canning fruit, washing precious figurines, or cleaning the windows to be together and to learn together. What great possibilities for experiencing gospel principles there are in sponges and water, planting time and harvest time (and fighting weeds!), caring for animals and pets, following the pattern precisely when sewing the dress, making old things like new again, repairing tiny parts that can affect the function of a machine many times their size!

And what about our church "work"? Why not involve our children, when appropriate, in experiencing gospel principles by sharing gospel responsibilities? If we have a speaking assignment, is it possible that one of the children could come along—or even participate? Just riding together to and from the assignment may offer great benefits. If we are helping provide a meal for someone who is ill, we could let the children know of the circumstances. Perhaps they could help with the cooking and carry something in when we deliver the meal.

Whatever activity is taking place, we should explain to the children what is happening: Why we are fasting; how that will help the situation or person. Why we are going to tithing settlement; what we are going to do when we meet with the bishop. Why the priesthood leader will put his hands on daddy's head; how we can "help" in the setting apart. Why that young man comes to the door each month to collect fast offerings—and perhaps the children could even help determine how much money should be placed in the envelope, and maybe even put it in.

81

As age and circumstances permit, there are many opportunities for sons to share in exercising the priesthood. Younger brothers and sisters have a memorable experience when an older brother performs their baptism, and so does the older brother.

Soliciting children's ideas for lessons or talks is another great opportunity to share gospel experiences, assess their growth in specific principles, and let them contribute and feel the value of their own personal gospel knowledge.

There are many possibilities for experiencing a gospel principle together in the simple act of delivering a priesthood or Relief Society report. We might explore the stewardship responsibility of the leader for the people enrolled, dependability and accuracy, records kept on earth and in heaven. Whatever Church activities we are responsible for or participating in, we should help the children understand what is taking place and why, and then think of ways they could be involved to experience some aspect of that gospel principle.

Teaching through the environment. We have talked about direct involvement of parents helping their children to experience gospel principles. There is also an indirect but very powerful teaching influence exerted by parents on children in the home. President David O. McKay expressed it in the following incident:

"A father visited his son's new home. The son was proud to show him the various rooms and the new installations in the kitchen. After they were through with their visit, the father said, 'Yes, it is beautiful; but I see no signs of God in your home.' And the son said, 'I went back; and as I looked through the rooms, I noticed I had nothing suggestive of the presence of the Redeemer or the Savior.'" (David O. McKay, *Man May Know for Himself* [Salt Lake City: Deseret Book Co., 1969], p. 110.)

Are we teaching our children the gospel through the physical environment of our homes? It might be of interest to walk through our own homes and then consider the following questions:

1. Are there any pictures or objects that remind us of the Savior's love for us and his place in our lives?

2. Are there other objects or pictures that teach or tell of gospel concepts?

3. Is there any evidence that we appreciate our national and family heritage?

4. Is there a place or places where we can display our efforts at developing our talents?

5. Are there spaces that invite us to become acquainted with "the best books," "the law of the gospel," "things both in heaven and in the earth," "a knowledge ... of countries and kingdoms?" (See D&C 88:77-80, 118.)

6. Does good music have a place in our homes?

7. Is there a general feeling of order and cleanliness as we walk through our homes? (At least once a week?)

8. Are there spaces that we might give special functions to—a place for one person to be alone, for two to converse privately, a "laughing place"?

The questions should give you some idea about the ways we can teach through the physical environment of the home. There are many excellent pictures, maps, charts, and reproductions of art being published in the Church magazines; these could be used as part of the decor of our homes. President Kimball has suggested that a picture of one of the temples be placed in children's rooms to help teach them about the importance of temple marriage. This could be accomplished in the simple purchase of a post card, or if we are near a temple or traveling, we might take a picture of the temple with the child or family standing in the foreground.

Just as we have provided space in our homes for food storage items to meet our physical needs, we can provide space for spiritual food. We need to nourish our children with life-giving books, art, music, and gospel knowledge and experience every day. Then we will be fully prepared, and "they shall not be beaten down by the storm at the last day ... but when the storm cometh they shall be gathered together in their place, that the storm cannot penetrate to them." (Alma 26:6.)

11

Teaching through Example and Testimony

The Son can do nothing of himself, but what he seeth the Father do. (John 5:19.)

Two powerful teaching tools are available to parents independent of their education, their particular talents or abilities, their access to Church programs or materials, or their length of membership. These tools are personal example and testimony. Parents may be prone to overlook the effectiveness and application of these two tools.

The power of personal example. Consciously or unconsciously, we teach daily a pattern of habits, attitudes, and conduct, a mode of dress, a response style, a system of values, and much more to our children. We do it by the model of our own behavior.

Parents have a distinct advantage over their children. They are "in charge," older, bigger, stronger, and more experienced. And because they are all of these things, they are also able to do more than tell the children what behavior is desired of them—they can show them through their own example. In the following three incidents, note how the teaching occurs. Is it done consciously or unconsciously?

84

The worn copy of the *Relief Society Magazine* carried the date 1938. Some of the pages were dog-eared. The cover was "decorated" in red pencil with the exploratory scribblings and "letters" of a three-year-old. Inside the magazine, the same pencil had been applied to underline sentences and paragraphs with wiggly red lines. The three-year-old sat in a child's wicker rocking chair beside her mother, who was underlining her scriptures and magazine in preparation for a Relief Society lesson.

On a Saturday afternoon a busy father, engaged during the week for long hours at his office, now turned his attention to cleaning the family car. Soon after the hose was on and the sponge and cans of polish were out, an older son wheeled out his dirt bike for inspection. He was followed by the four-year-old who pulled up on his Big Wheel bike. Soon both were imitating dad, making minor repairs on their vehicles and all working together at their family car wash.

A little boy came racing into the room exulting, "I did it! I did it!" "What did you do son?" asked the father as he lowered his newspaper. "Dad! See, it's like you do!" and he held up the result of his many days' practice—a paper airplane, folded just "like you do."

In the three examples given, none of the parents were consciously aware that they were teaching. Are you taking full advantage of this powerful teaching tool of personal example? What are some of the behaviors you would like your children to acquire? Would you like them to know and love the scriptures? Would you like them to be truthful, or eager to learn, or kind? Stop for a moment and think about ways you would like your children to behave. Just today, or this week, what have you been asking them to do? Now think of your own behavior today, this week, and see if the things you desire for your children are being taught to them not only by your admonitions, but by your own example.

We may fall short ourselves in the attributes or behaviors we would like our children to develop.

85

Teachers, too, must be continually learning and trying to improve. Whose behavior will we choose to imitate? The scriptures are the revelation of our Heavenly Father to us. Through them we learn who he is, how he lives, and what his life is like. Contemplate any attribute of God and you will have the pattern for the behavior of a wise and loving parent. An exciting exercise is to choose a quality such as justice or mercy and to follow it through the Topical Guide or concordance and see how our Heavenly Father and the Savior show us correct behavior.

As we practice improving our own example as parents, we are counseled that "in patience ye may possess your souls." (D&C 101:38.) Growing, teaching, progressing, and learning are all processes that require great patience—both for us as parents and for our children. How marvelous it would be to grow from A to Z and skip everything in between, because, after all, we already know what Z is like, and we really want to hurry and get there. But a much wiser Father knows a child will neither master nor endure Z without the intermittent steps. So, with patience he proceeds with us, and we with ourselves and with our children, "line upon line" and "grace for grace" as he taught us by example.

The power of personal testimony. In chapter 5, families shared personal experiences in response to the question, "What do you remember about your best family home evenings together?" The answers always included the element of personal testimony. Interestingly, people recalled this kind of experience with their family even after several years had passed. The scriptures give abundant witness to the effectiveness and lasting impression made when personal testimony is used by parents to teach their children. Enos records: "The words which I had often heard my father speak concerning eternal life, and the joy of the saints, sunk deep into my heart." (Enos 1:3.) Alma, in torment at the recognition of his sins, recalls the teachings of his father on the atonement of Jesus Christ. (Alma 36:17.) In the *Lectures on*

86

Faith we read that it is "human testimony" that arouses one to seek a knowledge of God. (Joseph Smith, *Lectures on Faith*, comp. N. B. Lundwall [Salt Lake City: N. B. Lundwall, n. d.], p. 23.)

Parents can share their testimonies with their children in many ways. The most elementary way is to simply tell your children of your own conversion to the gospel. Just how did it happen? Whether the story begins with you as a nonmember, as a child, on a mission, or later, let your children know how you learned of the truth of the gospel and gained your faith in Jesus Christ.

Conversion to the gospel may have its beginning in a single event, but from that time forward a testimony grows and is strengthened through varied experiences. The retelling of spiritual experiences—times when you have had a prayer answered, received a special insight into a problem or subject of study, been prompted to do something or refrain from doing it, were able to magnify a calling, were privileged to exercise a spiritual gift—all of these incidents in their appropriate order and time may be shared with your children.

Sharing testimonies formally and informally. Often during regular Sunday testimony meetings the time is not long enough to accommodate all who would like to bear their testimonies. At such times, some families have returned to their homes after the meeting and have sat together for a time to express their testimonies to each other.

Some families use special occasions to share their testimonies with each other, such as the times when a family member prepares to leave home for school, a mission, or marriage. A child's baptism might be a good time to invite a grandparent or other relative at a family gathering to tell of his or her conversion and baptism. As a son is ordained to the priesthood, some fathers seek out a private moment to express their feelings and personal experiences concerning this power conferred from God. These are not opportunities to lecture or top the experience the child is having; they are moments to

87

rejoice together and share to whatever degree of maturity the child has reached.

The settings mentioned thus far might be considered formal ways of sharing testimonies with children. The opportunities for teaching informally through using testimony are even more numerous. Sharing nature's beauties with a child, from looking for all the different kinds of seeds to sleeping under the stars at night, gives ample opportunity for testimony bearing, and all creation is there as a further witness of God's reality. "Any man who hath seen any or the least of these hath seen God moving in his majesty and power." (D&C 88:47.)

Our task is to recognize the opportunities to draw the attention of our children to heavenly things as they exist in earthly, day-to-day experiences. "And behold, all things have their likeness, and all things are created and made to bear record of me, both things which are temporal, and things which are spiritual; things which are in the heavens above, and things which are on the earth . . . all things bear record of me." (Moses 6:63.) Teach children to see the Lord's influence in the creations around them and in the events of their lives.

Preserving our testimony for our children. We can record our testimonies to benefit our children now and in the future. Nephi describes this process in these words: "And upon these [plates] I write the things of my soul . . . for the learning and the profit of my children." (2 Nephi 4:15.) Your "plates" could be as small as the note written by a father and left for a child who had just experienced a disappointment: "I love the Lord. I know he loves you. Trust in him." That small note may be one of few written communications, a physical reminder for the child of his father's love and testimony. Your testimony may find expression in a letter, or it may lengthen into a journal. The scriptures were such letters and journals and were also passed from father to son.

88

Some families are taking advantage of modern technology to preserve testimonies for their children. Recently a grandmother celebrated her eighty-fourth birthday. With the help of her grandson, she made a film to be shown for this special occasion. Children, grand-children, and great-grandchildren watched her on the film seated in her favorite chair telling of her conversion to the gospel in a foreign land, of her young brother coming to the United States with the missionaries' help, and how he raised and sold calves until there was enough money to send for her and each family member in turn. They listened to her own voice, which still had the trace of an accent, as she told of her helplessness at not being able to speak English. They watched her eyes light up as she told of meeting her future husband. Long after her physical passing, they would learn from this living record of her testimony.

As you use these varying opportunities to share your testimony with your children, teach them of their responsibility to know for themselves. Invite them to try it out, to "experiment" on the Lord's words, to "do the will" of the Father, to "ask God."

In whatever form you may choose, consciously use the power of your example and testimony to teach your children. Be patient in your own growth as you strengthen yourself in order to strengthen them. In the exercise of their own agency there may be times when they will choose not to listen, but if parents consciously apply themselves in meeting their opportunities, one day each child will recall, "he taught me ... in the nur-ture and admonition of the Lord—and blessed be the name of my God for it." (Enos 1:1.)

Part 4
Successful Family Activities

12

Forging Family Bonds

Family activities are usually more enjoyable than non-family activities. Why? Because the members of the family have a special relationship to each other. Children tend to have total confidence in their mothers and fathers. And brothers and sisters, even if they argue among themselves, are quite ready to defend each other against anyone outside of the family who picks on them. This sacred family bond prompts us to want to share many activities together in order to keep abreast of each other's thoughts and feelings.

In the personal experiences that follow, notice how the family members achieve a great feeling of freedom and intimacy as they participate in family activities together. Then, as you read the instructions about how to make family activities successful, see if you are building family traditions and using places, foods, holidays, priesthood programs, and service projects as the basis for your fun.

Sagebrush and Sand

On Saturday morning everybody would work together to get the duties around the house done so we could have plenty of time for our family picnic. We would all jump into the back of my dad's old truck and head out to the desert—the sagebrush and sand that we learned to love. Usually dad had already picked out a spot where he had been previously with the Boy Scouts, and we were always anxious to see where he would take us this year.

When we arrived at our destination, we would play games that got us all dirty and messy—and we loved it! One of the games was called "capture the flag." We divided into teams, and each team had a flag. The object of the game was to capture the other team's flag and not get caught. We would crouch down in the dirt, sometimes even slide along on our stomachs, so the other team wouldn't see us sneaking up on them. The game often involved sacrifice. A typical strategy was for one team member to create a diversion so the enemy team members would chase him. In the meantime, we would capture their flag.

After the games, we would build a fire and roast wieners. The big kids helped the little kids (there were ten of us) and mom supervised. After eating, we would sit around the fire and sing. If we coaxed long enough, we could sometimes get mom and dad to tell us stories about when they were kids growing up in Utah.

These were the desert outings that helped to develop within me a love of nature, a love of music, and a lifetime closeness to my family.

Appreciating Nature

I live in Colorado, the Rocky Mountain state. Our family loves to go to the mountains, so on one day we took a picnic up to our favorite spot near a stream. We hiked all around the area and just looked at all of the beauty around us in the rocks and trees, the water and sky. When we got back to our picnic spot we all asked each other to tell about our favorite creation. We talked about how grateful we were for the beauties of the world and for each other. After dinner, we watched the

94

shadows lengthen and the sun sink into shades of yellow, orange, and red. As we drove home, we sang songs together, and I felt a greater closeness to each family member than I had ever felt before, and a stronger sense that I was part of a family that loved me.

Kite Flying

One of my favorite family activities took place on a Saturday afternoon in March. The planning and preparing took place almost instantly. Mom and the girls packed a lunch (the baked chicken we were going to have for dinner that night and any other goodies we could dig out of the refrigerator and cupboards), and the boys and dad went to the store to get "a couple of surprises." When they got back, we piled into the car with a picnic basket, two blankets, and a mysterious-looking sack that the boys were guarding with their lives. After we played at the park and had our lunch, dad and the boys unveiled their secret—a sack full of kites! Since it was Dawn's first experience with kite flying, dad helped her assemble her kite. My older brothers, nineteen and sixteen, had theirs together in minutes, and when the wind was "just right" and everyone was ready, up went the kites! I'm still not sure who had the most fun, the spectators or the kite flyers. Long after one of the boy's kites got tangled in a tree, and the other's "just wouldn't go up," Dawn's kite was a flying speck of color in the great blue sky. Now whenever the March wind blows, we always remember the day when we dropped everything just to go fly a kite.

Surprise Dinner

It's always a challenge to serve a meal to a large family and have every child pleased with mother's menu. On one day we all went to the store together. Each child was allowed to buy a favorite food that he wanted for supper. Each one was to keep his purchase a

95

secret from the others so the meal would be a surprise. (The only real problem was that they were doing such a great job of being secretive the store manager thought they were stealing!) After we arrived home, we all helped prepare the food. It wasn't a very well-balanced meal, but we sure had a lot of fun.

Annual Camp-out

Delta, Canada was a quiet place. My father used to go there when he was a boy, and this quiet setting offered our family several summers of fun. The annual family camping trip became our family bond-maker. At camp there were no doors to separate us, no television to distract us. In the middle of nowhere, we became the source of our own entertainment. We learned to appreciate each other.

Because we were out on the lake a lot of the time, we learned to watch out for each other with a much greater intensity than was needed at home. On one occasion, five of us were caught out on the lake in a terrific thunderstorm. We were in a rowboat, and in those anxious moments we each took our turn at the oars pulling with all our might, working together to get off that lake. Through this experience and many others, we learned to care for each other and that we could rely on each other.

Eighth Birthday

A family in our ward holds a very special activity at each child's eighth birthday. One family member reviews a little personal history of the child and each family member tells something special about this brother or sister. The comments are written down and kept for his personal history. The child can choose his favorite meal for this day. The gifts are always a journal and his own set of scriptures. It's kind of a celebration of his being accountable, and it really helps to build the self-esteem of the child.

96

Engagement Party

Just before I married, my family honored my fiance and me on a special evening together. We started with a song and prayer, and then some small cards were passed out to each person. The family members were asked to write why they thought my fiance would make a good husband and why I would make a good wife. When the writing was finished and the cards gathered back in, David read my good qualities aloud to the group, and then I read his. This was fun, and we learned some new things about each other and were challenged by our families' expectations. They then presented us with some gifts. Each gift had a scripture attached to it, and we had to read the scripture and try to guess what was inside. These were all very practical gifts like sugar, toothpaste, and salt. For dessert my sister-in-law had baked a scripture cake. Here is the recipe. It really works!

ROMANS 4:3 — 1 SAMUEL 30:12

4½ cups 1 Kings 4:22	(4½ cups flour)
1½ cups Psalms 55:21	(1½ cups butter)
2 cups Jeremiah 6:20	(2 cups sugar)
2 cups 2 Samuel 16:1	(2 cups raisins)
2 cups Song of Solomon 2:13	(2 cups figs, chopped)
2 cups Numbers 17:8	(2 cups almonds, slivered or chopped)
2 tablespoons Judges 14:18	(2 tablespoons honey)
1 pinch Luke 14:34	(1 pinch salt)
6 Isaiah 10:14	(6 eggs)
½ cup Judges 4:19	(½ cup milk)
2 tsp. 1 Corinthians 5:6	(2 tsp. baking powder)
8½ tsp. 2 Chronicles 9:9	(½ tsp. nutmeg, 2 tsp. allspice, 4 tsp. cinnamon, 2 tsp. cloves)

Follow instructions in Proverbs 23:14

Cream butter and sugar; beat in eggs one at a time. Add flour (sifted before measuring), baking powder, and salt alternately with milk. Stir in honey. Add spices. Blend well, then add raisins, chopped figs, and almonds (slivered or chopped). Pour into well-greased loaf pans and bake 50 minutes at 325° F. Cool and slice. Keeps well in refrigerator or freezer. May be baked in large tube pan.

Cool and slice after a few John 11:9

97

Camping Reunion

A week-long camping reunion is the big event of the year in my mother's family. I especially remember the trip we made to the Red Fish Lake area. What a great sight to see six separate families in their campers, with tents, canoes, and fishing rods! What a wagon train!

After arriving and finding enough sites close together, the family spent the day setting up camp. I always loved the hustle and bustle as my aunts called to each other, and the steady sounds as my uncles cut and chopped wood. The kids would try to get their chores done as quickly as possible so they could run among the trees and go exploring.

The big event of that year was the canoe race. The competitors were divided into age groups. I don't remember much about the race I was in, but no one in the family will ever forget the adult race. Uncle Gordon, my dad, and Uncle Leo were competing. Uncle Gordon thought he would be smart and win the race by sitting in the very front of his canoe (which made the back end stick up out of the water). When the whistle blew, my dad and Uncle Leo streamed gracefully across the water while Uncle Gordon found himself paddling in a circle. We laughed and laughed and wished for all the world we had a motion picture camera. Uncle Gordon still hasn't lived down his great race.

Evenings were the best part of camp. Uncle Leo would get out his guitar (though he could only play a few chords), and we youngsters would try to learn the songs our parents knew, such as "Down by the Old Mill Stream" and "K-k-k-katie." My dad, not to be left out, would always bring up "Mairsy Doats." We'd roast marshmallows and nearly get sick on s'mores. Then mom would call out in her clear voice, "It's time to get ready for bed." I always wanted the campfire activities to last longer and the talk to go on forever. Who remembers what we talked about? What I do remember from that young age is how important I felt just to be sitting with my mother, my aunts, and my grandmother. Such experiences drew and held me close to them.

Gospel Game

We play a family game that is fun and helps us learn how to explain a principle of the gospel. We sit in a group and one person is "it." He chooses a word like *tithing* or *repentance* and tells the word to the group. We then explain this principle by each person giving one word and trying to build sentences that tell about the principle. You can also use incidents from Church history or the life of Christ, or other gospel subjects.

Family Olympics

During an Olympic year, our family had its own Olympics. Our mom and dad gathered us into the kitchen where we all popped popcorn and made popcorn balls. Next they arranged a whole series of "Olympic" games—jumping, running, shot-put with cotton balls, javelin throwing with soda straws. My parents modified the games so that each child could win in at least one event. The prize was a popcorn ball and kisses from mom and dad.

Game Night

We have a game night once a month in our family. Some of our favorites are Rook, Monopoly, Clue, and Uno. Recently the boys have also enjoyed Dungeons and Dragons. We always buy one good game for Christmas and feel this has been a good family investment.

Spinning Yarns

99

We have a game we like to play in our family whenever we get together in a large group. We make a ball of yarn with many colors tied together in varying lengths.

The ball is passed around a circle to each family member, and depending on the length of the piece he unwinds, he tells about what he has been doing, or shares an experience from his summer, the past year, or whatever length of time it has been since the family last met together. If his piece of yarn happens to have a knot tied in it, then he also has to tell something funny or embarrassing that happened.

Teotihuacan Triangle

One of the most exciting family activities we have is playing a game called Teotihuacan triangle. To play you need at least five people. One person makes up the categories and keeps track of the score time. The other four players work in teams of two. Six subjects are used in each game. These six subjects each have a list of seven words attached. For example:

Noah
1. Flood
2. Forty days
3. Animals
4. Two by Two
5. Ark
6. Gopher wood
7. Family

One player on each team of two people gives the clues and the second player must guess the word. Example: "What made the ark rise?" "The flood." One subject is covered in each round. Adjust the time limit of each round to meet the ability of the group playing. Award a point for each word guessed in the list of seven; the winner is the team with the most points. The opportunities for learning and fun are tremendous.

100

Music for Everyone

One evening everyone in our family chose two pieces of favorite music, one spiritual and one that could be any style. It didn't matter if it was a record or sheet music. We took turns playing or listening to our pieces, and after each piece we told why it was one of our favorites and what we liked about it. We not only enjoyed the music and got to know each other's favorites, but we had several spiritual messages. Every reason given for each piece that was shared was unique and interesting.

Sing and Learn

While in Primary our children learned the Articles of Faith by singing them. The idea worked so well that we adapted it as a family and have learned many scriptures by singing them to simple melodies we made up. The children enjoy this very much, and we have even composed some little songs for family events, like "The Bedtime Parade," and for times when we work together or have special feelings to share.

Christmas Eve Activities

We always get together as a family on Christmas Eve. On one such occasion we began with our usual custom of singing hymns. There was a lot of excitement in the air as the children were brought together to perform the story of Christ's birth. Each child was dressed or draped in shirts, scarves, and sheets to meet the requirements of his role. As each one came "on stage" for his part, a kind of gradual transformation seemed to be taking place right before us. These were no longer noisy, overexcited kids eagerly awaiting the arrival of Santa in the morning. A quiet reverence settled over us as we watched and listened. As custom dictated, we continued by presenting some personal talent in turn. Grandpa Barrus is always saved for last to sing, but even burly grandpa shed tears on this night. The unity we experienced made us feel in harmony and in tune with each other. Never before had the music we all loved

101

so well taken on such a special meaning as it did that Christmas Eve.

Three Christmas Traditions

At Christmastime, we bake pies for our adult friends and cookies for the children's teachers at school and at church. One night is set aside for baking. The kitchen is always in an uproar, and mom is flustered with so many little helping hands, but it's fun and warm and sweet-smelling. Then we all go out and deliver the goodies hot from the oven. The surprise and delight we encounter is worth all the work.

On Christmas Eve, we give homemade gifts. We set aside a night to make the gifts. Everyone is assigned a certain room in which to create. The fun comes in running back and forth between rooms to borrow materials and in hiding creations in progress.

Finally, Christmas Eve is a tradition in itself. That night, either mom or dad tells the Christmas story by candlelight. After the story we all give a verbal gift to Jesus—one child promising to set a better example for the other children, another child promising to try harder to help mom, and so forth. Then we exchange our homemade gifts while we enjoy traditional goodies.

Gifts for the Savior

Last year at Christmas, we had family members prepare short talks about different aspects of the Savior's life. We then shared some special feeling or experience we had had about the Savior during the past year. We wrote down gifts we wanted to give to the Savior during that year, something that would show our love for him. The papers were sealed in envelopes and put away to be opened next year on Christmas morning. Everyone then brought a monetary gift according to his ability, and the money was placed in a tithing envelope to be turned over to the bishop as a donation to the new

102

temple being built in our area. After this we opened our presents and visited with each other.

New Year's Eve Quiz

On New Year's Eve, we enjoy being together as a family. One of the highlights of the evening is a game we play. Each family member makes up questions for a quiz about what happened in our family during the year. (We often consult our journals to refresh our memories.) Some of our questions might be: How many inches did Richard grow this year? What did we give mom for Mother's Day? What did Cindy wear to the prom? What grew best in our garden this year? Who was the safest driver in the family? What was the score at Mark's winning game? What was our greatest family accomplishment this year? We keep score and give funny prizes for each family member. Mom and dad have some pictures of the things we did, and together we add them to our family scrapbook. We end with pizza, and each of us helps choose what things to put on it. It's always a great night together.

Thanksgiving Blessings

On Thanksgiving Day, just before we begin a sumptuous turkey dinner, we like to put three or four kernels of dried corn on each plate. When we gather around the table, we remind the children of the Pilgrims and recall how the Indians helped them to plant their corn. We then take turns removing one kernel at a time from our plates and naming something for which we are thankful.

Family History

One Sunday afternoon as we were sitting together, our parents shared some experiences of their early life. They included their courtship and marriage, which was rather exciting to hear about. Then they told just a little about our grandparents, who are not members of the Church, and I got very interested in finding out about their early life. We decided on that day to begin a family history. We also picked out another nonmember relative and decided to get our pictures of her copied and to make a scrapbook to give to her. We hope to build a closer relationship with her in this way.

Memory Night

Every so often we like to have a "memory night" in our family. I have mementos, school papers, souvenirs, and pictures for each child. I just date them, put the child's name on them, and put them into a folder as the events occur. On memory night I get out the folders, and each child puts his own in order, dividing the material up into smaller segments. It's lots of fun as we sit around the table with the materials and the memories. After enough material has accumulated, we make a lovely scrapbook for each family member.

Nostalgia Night

We held a "nostalgia night" recently in our family. We included the married children and the grandparents. We asked each member or couple or family to come prepared to share a favorite family memory. (If they wanted to illustrate it with a few slides or photographs, they were encouraged to do so.) Some brought journals and scrapbooks to help them tell their favorite memory. As each person talked, we tape-recorded his part. It was a great night, and naturally we gathered a lot of information for histories and genealogy. As we concluded the evening, we announced that we were going to transcribe the tape and would furnish everyone with a copy—that this was the beginning of our family history, and we hoped everyone would help us in the coming months to complete this information together.

Reading As We Go

We have always enjoyed reading together as we travel. If we know there will be some uninteresting miles along the route, we try to choose the book together before we leave. We take turns reading while the younger ones just enjoy listening. We have especially enjoyed *The Story of the Trapp Family Singers,* Maria A. Trapp; *A Wrinkle in Time,* Madeleine L'Engle; *The Wind in the Willows,* Kenneth Grahame; *Rascal,* Sterling North; *The Chronicles of Narnia,* C. S. Lewis; *The Black Stallion,* Walter Farley; and *Charlotte's Web,* E. B. White.

Other Countries

We have had some wonderful times together learning about our brothers and sisters in other countries of the world. We assign each family member a topic about a chosen country to research and report. Some of the subjects include geographical and physical features, customs and culture, history, religion, government, and the activity of the Church in that land. We prepare a food of that country for our meal that day and try to have something on the table that comes from or represents the country. If we can, we often have some kind of music played or sung that is typical of that culture. When we studied Mexico, we put together our own mariachi band with the children playing musical instruments and a conglomeration of other things such as pie plates, sticks, and pans.

Beethoven and the Family

One day as our son was routinely practicing for his piano lesson, I asked if he had looked to see who had written the piece he was playing. With nine-year-old exuberance, he had learned the piece but hadn't been concerned about the extras. We began a little discussion about Ludwig van Beethoven and about the source of the simple theme our son had learned to play from the Ninth Symphony. One thing led to another, and I asked if he would like to hear how this melody sounded when played by a symphony orchestra. Enthusiastically he turned on the stereo, and we sat on the floor together listening to the last movement.

Soon the music drew the attention of the other children and each came and found a spot to sit down. A few minutes later, when their father came through the door from work, he was greeted by the whole family sitting on the floor in front of the stereo with "Freude, Freude" echoing off the walls! Since this was dad's favorite symphony, he joined in, and things really began to develop. As a family we decided to learn more about Beethoven and his music. In the next few weeks, we saved to purchase another of his symphonies, the children learned several more Beethoven pieces for the piano, and we found that the symphony season coordinated with our needs. Properly prepared, we attended as a family a performance of Beethoven's Ninth Symphony. For each of us it was a memorable and truly joyous occasion.

After reading this quick overview of various activities families are doing together, we hope you will want to gather your family around you and try some of them. Some activities need a little preparation; others can occur spontaneously. We should try to have some of each. It's always fun to simply drop everything to go fly a kite, make homemade ice cream, take a ride in the rain, walk along the beach, or just look at cloud shapes together. Each family needs these momentary breaks. Did you notice also that in many of the preceding personal experiences the families temporarily took themselves away from the interruptions and temptations of the world? Regular family activities can provide a welcome haven for families to regroup and strengthen each other.

13
Building Family Traditions

And he shall turn the heart of the fathers to the children, and the heart of the children to their fathers, lest I come and smite the earth with a curse. (Malachi 4:6.)

Family cohesiveness, love, and unity don't just happen. Close-knit families are not born, they are made. One way to succeed in building family unity is to create and strengthen family traditions. Traditions are the practices, beliefs, customs, and knowledge handed down from one generation to another. They are things that we repeat in our daily, weekly, and yearly schedules. All of us feel a greater degree of security when we can depend on a daily supper, a weekly Sunday meeting, or a yearly vacation. Sometimes a physical setting or place, like the home of our grandparents, becomes a permanent monument to which we can return often and feel secure. Most family members experience the need for some structuring and ordering of their lives. Events, activities, and ceremonies that are pleasant and repeat themselves provide that order and security.

There are three basic kinds of traditions found in a Latter-day Saint home. One set of traditions stems from the gospel and consists of such repeated activities as attending church on Sunday, paying tithing, holding family prayer, and fasting. Another group of traditions consists of the customs that a family has developed on its own. These vary from family to family and may focus on such repeated activities as a family Sunday dinner, an annual camping trip, or nightly bedtime stories.

A third set of traditions has to do with traditions that our forefathers have handed down to us. For example, we pass on family names to our children. We hold family reunions highlighting special traits of a prominent forefather that we want to emulate in our lives, and we decorate our homes with memorabilia from our heritage.

Realizing that we can strengthen our family by building family traditions, let us first consider how to develop gospel-centered traditions.

The book of Proverbs teaches us to "Train up a child in the way he should go: and when he is old, he will not depart from it." (Proverbs 22:6.) The Book of Mormon bears witness of a remarkable account of gospel-centered tradition in Alma 56:47: "Now they never had fought, yet they did not fear death; and they did think more upon the liberty of their fathers than they did upon their lives; yea, they had been taught by their mothers, that is they did not doubt, God would deliver them." Do you think that these two thousand young men had only one or two lessons on overcoming doubt by substituting faith, or do you think that such teaching had to be repeated over long periods of time in order to become so effective? Probably that kind of personal growth came through repeated instruction and learning experiences—in other words, by establishing a tradition of belief.

Holding a family home evening can become a gospel-centered family tradition. In homes where family time is scheduled for each Monday evening, a tradition is established which all family members know they can depend on. With that recurring dependability, it becomes easier for a busy father to say to his business associates, "I'm sorry, but I have a previous appointment for Monday evening. Perhaps we could meet at another time." Children will ask for family home evening and help secure this special time if it is being held each week. In one family, if the phone rings during this special time together, the children answer by saying, "I'm sorry, we are holding family home evening. Could you call back later?" When family home evening becomes a tradition, it provides an opportunity to relax, to be undisturbed, and to enjoy each other as family members. It is the family's island in a swirling stream of weekly events.

Consider the following checklist of gospel-centered traditions. Which ones would your family want to initiate or strengthen?

1. We pay tithing each month.
2. We have family prayer each day.
3. We hold a weekly family home evening.
4. We plan how to keep each Sabbath day holy.
5. We fast regularly.
6. We attend Church meetings weekly.
7. We magnify our Church callings.
8. We engage in reading the scriptures consistently.
9. We contribute regularly to missionary work.
10. We respond to calls for welfare assignments.
11. We have a tradition of giving priesthood blessings in our home.
12. Temple marriage is the tradition in our family.
13. We serve on missions.
14. Our family eating habits exclude items not in harmony with the Word of Wisdom.
15. We consistently read good literature, select beneficial television programs, listen to uplifting music, and attend worthwhile cultural events.

Observe which activities are practiced consistently in your family. Now consider which traditions you would like to strengthen. Look back over the list and the activities your family regularly engages in, and see if the members of the family know that those are traditions

109

which have become established in their lives. Finally, ask yourself how recently family members were praised for doing so well. It is easy to take things for granted and to forget to thank each other for being faithful to gospel principles. For example, how many times has anyone expressed appreciation for belonging to a family in which everyone attends church meetings on Sunday without making a fuss about it? Or when have family members shown appreciation for everyone trying to fast when there was a special need to give their love and support?

If certain gospel-centered traditions need to be improved, then discuss with family members which traditions they think Heavenly Father would like the family to strengthen. With the family, plan an activity that could become a tradition. After trying out the tradition, assess the degree of its success, modify it a little if necessary, and observe whether it helped to unify the family members.

What special traditions are unique to your family? Perhaps you have a favorite story describing how dad proposed to mom. Or is it traditional to have pizza and root beer at a time when the family watches television together? Do you have a tradition of singing certain songs as you travel long distances in the car? What about special ways that you celebrate birthdays or baptism? Do you hug or kiss each other after daily family prayer? Is there a traditional Sunday dinner in your home? What is different about it? Do you eat in the dining room or use special dishes? Are special guests invited or special manners observed? Do you have special family traditions related to the celebration of Christmas, Easter, Mother's Day, Father's Day, Valentine's Day, Halloween, New Year's Eve, Independence Day, and Thanksgiving?

Children love special family traditions. They depend on the security of repeated activities. Even adults need some structure and pattern in their daily activities. Encourage your family to recognize and maintain its useful family traditions. Many ideas will not become traditions, but with a little work and planning the best will endure, and each tradition will help to strengthen your family.

Other traditions that appear in many Latter-day Saint families are those derived from our ancestral heritage. Observing the traditions of our forefathers gives us another opportunity to see whether we are fostering and carrying forward the great heritage that has been passed along to us. The most common areas for locating interesting traditions from our forefathers are: (1) discovering the origin and meanings of their (and our) surnames and given names; (2) examining their facial features and physical characteristics; (3) locating and studying the geographical area where they were born and raised; (4) determining their character traits; and (5) collecting and reading interesting stories about their lives.

We often fail to realize or value the heritage that our forefathers have given us; we inherit their names, traits, appearances, and a birthplace with little choice on our part. However, by recalling some of their distinguishing characteristics and strengthening the best ones, we can continue to unify our own families.

The origin and meaning of names. It is interesting to discover the origin and meanings of the given names and surnames of our ancestors. Many surnames were originally chosen because of a person's place of residence, his occupation, or a personal characteristic. Almost all of our first names and middle names were selected for a meaningful reason. Do we and our children know why our names had special significance to the parents who named us? Are we aware of the hopes, aspirations, and directions that those names provide us?

Physical characteristics of our ancestors. Our parents, grandparents, and great-grandparents had physical features that have been passed on to us. By obtaining all the available pictures of our ancestors and examining them carefully, we can discover new qualities about ourselves. We may also discover different features associated with each of our several family branches.

The geographical area where an ancestor was born or raised. We can learn much about how our ancestors lived by studying the history, customs, and geography of the area where they lived. For example, knowing that a certain grandfather was raised in a small farming community in Germany during the last of the 1800s can reveal much about his daily activities if we read a book about that community, country, and time period.

Character traits of ancestors. Personality characteristics of ancestors are best discovered when they repeat themselves throughout a variety of different experiences. When, for instance, an ancestor was confronted with problems or challenges at work, home, and church, did he seem to continually despair, or did he appear optimistic? The search for our ancestor's character traits becomes exciting when we find out how they were able to handle life's challenges, and then try to find those same sterling qualities in ourselves and our children.

Stories about our ancestors. Collecting and telling stories about our forefathers is a good way to strengthen family traditions. Stories about the sacrifices that ancestors made to join the Church and assist their families make deep impressions upon all of us. Experiences that contributed to the strong testimony of our forefathers need to be repeated.

Family traditions provide security as we go through life. We can return again and again to our traditions and find emotional and spiritual strength.

14

Five Kinds of Family Activities

In the beginning God created . . . (Genesis 1:1.)

Family vacations, dinners, celebrations, welfare projects, and service activities provide great opportunities for creating successful family times together. Why? Because each activity is fun in and of itself, and each one is something that everyone can participate in. Everyone enjoys the idea of vacationing, eating, celebrating, and helping. So all we have to do is see how creative we can be in each of these fun areas of family activity. You may even be surprised at how easy it is to create a series of family activities for the whole year that are more meaningful and satisfying than nonfamily activities.

Let us consider five areas in which exciting family activities can be created. As we examine each area and read examples of what successful families are doing, you may want to make some mental notes about how to use these ideas in your own family.

1. Family vacations. We take vacations to get out of old ruts, see and experience something new, rest, gain a new point of view, invigorate our bodies, do something we don't have to, back away from routine responsibilities, relieve stress and tension, explore new opportunities, free ourselves from other people's problems, and become closer to our families.

Everyone in the family should have an opportunity to suggest vacation ideas. Initially, when gathering family members' ideas, record them all. Don't worry if they exceed the family budget or the vacation time available. If you place all kinds of preliminary restrictions on the planning, family members will not share the ideas that are the most attractive to them. A greater production of possibilities will occur if limitations are not mentioned first. Granted, the range of ideas may vary from a trip to the local zoo to a vacation in Paris, but at least if you listen carefully, you will hear the real desires of everyone's heart. Some members of the family will be interested in seeing things, others in doing things. Some will express desires that will reflect very personal and individual needs, while others will want to keep up with "the crowd."

Don't be concerned about the range of ideas contributed by each member of the family, and be sure mom and dad express their personal preferences. It's more fun to list every idea and then figure out how to combine ideas and still stay within the family time and financial limitations. One family was able to do the impossible by combining a vacation with one of dad's business trips. Another family decided to do a little fund-raising before their vacation. A third family used a stay-at-home vacation to engage in several day-long activities from which they returned home each evening.

Two of the greatest enjoyments associated with family vacations are the anticipation and enjoyment of planning and the traveling to and from the destination. Too often we miss the excitement and stimulation that is readily available in our families because we don't allow enough time beforehand for the various members of the family to think and plan together. Half the fun of a vacation can take place before the actual vacation ever starts. Children, especially, love to dream about a trip, discuss it over and over again, and tell all of their friends about it. It's also fun to learn about the vacation by reading books, looking at maps, checking pamphlets,

114

and quizzing friends. And then, of course, it's an absolute delight (and much easier on mother) when everyone picks out his own traveling clothes and the toys, papers, and books he wants to take along, and sees to it that arrangements have been made for pets, responsibilities, and items that must be left behind. And don't overlook the excitement of everyone knowing about the starting time and the frequent travel breaks that will be taken during the trip.

The actual traveling together can be one of the most enjoyable parts of the vacation if properly planned. See that every member of the family makes suggestions about rotating seating arrangements; snacks; toys to play with; games that can be played in the car (puzzles, tic-tac-toe, each choosing a favorite number and counting how many times it can be seen on license plates); pads and pencils for writing and drawing; books, magazines, and newspapers to read; songs to sing; diaries and simple school assignments to be caught up; a pillow to be shared; litter bags; Handiwipes; and so on! When thoughtfully planned, the trip to and from a vacation spot can be an extremely useful time for families to play together and draw closer together.

2. *Special meals and foods.* Remember to include in this kind of activity the fun of preparing the special food, of eating it, and then of enjoying the after-meal socializing. Ways to use this kind of activity are virtually unlimited and can be repeated many times during the year. (Mainly because we all seem to spend a lot of time eating!) Here are some food-centered ideas that families have found successful and that may stimulate other ideas for your family.

The diet dinner. Several members of a family were interested in dieting, so they planned a diet dinner to see if they could persuade the rest of the family to support their weight-loss program. They found a diet plan that they wanted to try and prepared one of the sample dinners listed in the plan. Interestingly, not only was the dinner nutritious, but the members of the family

115

also agreed that they would do without high-calorie desserts and drinks if they could have such a nice variety of good-tasting food for their meals.

The wheat breakfast. A father and mother who were impressed with the idea that "all grain is good for the food of man ... nevertheless, wheat for man ..." (D&C 89:16-17), decided that they would plan and serve a wheat breakfast. They found some excellent recipes for whole wheat pancakes, hot wheat cereal, and wheat muffins. With the agreement of the whole family, they prepared a "wheat for man" breakfast using some of the recipes they had found, combined with other nutritious menu items. The children gave their suggestions to make everything even more tasty for them, and now the family enjoys a few more wheat items in their regular menus than they did previously.

The special Sunday dinner. During a family home evening, a family discussed their knowledge of dinner table manners, table decorations, placement of dishes and silverware, and general comfort when eating out in a nice restaurant. The consensus was that everyone had a lot to learn and indeed did not feel as informed as necessary, especially when escorting someone to dinner. Plans were made to go to the library and find some instruction on these matters. Then the family divided into teams of two members each. Each team was to plan and serve a Sunday dinner using the nicest dishes and linens. The team was also to explain why they set the table as they did and how to properly eat the foods that were prepared. This whole series of dinners became a happy family activity in which everyone participated and learned. In fact, that dinner activity grew into a tradition that has now been expanded to include friends and relatives.

116

A hobo supper. Children seem to delight in breaking with daily routines, and that includes the routine of eating from dishes and drinking from cups and glasses. In one family a child thought it would be just great if everyone ate from a pot or pan, vase, or something else unusual—and had to eat everything with a large spoon. When it came time for dessert, everyone had to feed someone else! Other members of the family suggested that it might be fun to wear old clothes. Thus the hobo supper was born. Everyone loved it, had a great meal, and even figured out a few appropriate games to play after the supper. One was a relay to see which team could send each member to a chair to thread a needle, take a stitch, unthread the needle for the next team member, and do it faster than the opposing team. In another game, a sack filled with appropriate hobo items was passed under the table, and everyone tried to identify the items by feeling them rather than seeing them.

Creative foods and eating places. Quite a number of families are letting family members plan creative Jello salads, strange-looking cookies, and wild-shaped sandwiches. Any of these can be done with just some odd-shaped containers, cookie cutters, and the sparkle in a child's eyes! We can also be imaginative with the places where we eat. Eating outside the house in the yard or at the park can be fun. Canyons, beaches, lakes, streams, deserts, and mountains provide interesting places to eat. And don't overlook the possibilities of eating in a child's room, on the stairs, in a hallway, on the driveway, under the table, on the family room carpet, or in a closet. The more inventive everyone is in planning, eating, and enjoying each other's company, the more fun everyone will have.

3. Holidays. A third area to consider when planning successful family activities is special holidays. Celebrations and traditions associated with occasions such as Christmas, Easter, Independence Day, or Halloween suggest all kinds of family involvement. For example, most families think about Christmas as a time to work together on such things as selecting a Christmas tree, decorating the tree and the home, making Christmas gifts, visiting community Christmas displays, helping someone by giving a needed present, making special Christmas treats, planning a Christmas Eve activity, re-

117

membering the Christmas story, and expressing love to friends and family. You can think of many more activities for your family that will give everyone an opportunity to work and plan together. If your family activities are successful and repeated each year, you will have established strong traditions that will help secure and unify your family.

Easter as well as Christmas serves to remind us of the Savior and our love for each other. The Easter celebration gives us several more opportunities to engage in successful family activities. Together, families plan Easter baskets, treats, or meals to make the day a special one. Many families plan to share knowledge and testimonies of the resurrection of Jesus Christ. And, as we mentioned earlier, Independence Day, Halloween, indeed every holiday listed on the calendar provides us with a reason to plan family activities. Imagine the fun that could be created in the family on April Fool's Day!

4. Priesthood programs. The genealogy, welfare, and missionary programs of the Church give some families additional ideas for family activities. Several families have organized themselves so that one person is chiefly responsible for promoting genealogy work in the family, another for helping everyone to enjoy some welfare activity each month, and a third person to stimulate some kind of missionary effort. This organization is similar to the elder, seventy, and high priest division of responsibilities. Usually some family members still need to collect a brief personal history, a duplicate pedigree chart, a book of remembrance cover, pictures of immediate relatives, or life stories or testimonies of parents or grandparents. Each acquisition can be a family project and add to the fulfilling of the priesthood genealogy program of the Church and family.

118

In one family, instructions were handed out for an easy way to start a personal history. Each member of the family was asked to imagine that he or she was going to die tomorrow, and was asked: "What would be the single most important thing you would like to tell your family and friends?" Each family member was then instructed to write that down on a piece of paper or in a notebook. The next time the family met together, they were told to write the second most important idea that they would like to leave for their family and friends to read. Once the personal history was underway, they were asked to develop a loose, chronologically arranged list of important events in their lives and write about those. The members of this particular family used part of a family home evening, about twenty minutes, to begin their personal histories. Most commented that if they had known it was this easy, they would have started years ago!

Welfare activities are natural for all members of the family. Working together at the Church farm or canning factory and then fixing a treat afterward is always fun for family members. Planning a food-storage program for each individual is an exciting personal activity. Understanding fasting, testimony bearing, and contributing of fast offerings as well as planning and paying tithing together adds considerable unity to families. Even families with young children are able to participate in welfare activities because most of the involvement is tangible, and almost everyone likes to handle things and do things.

Staying active in the missionary program of the Church and following the admonition "every member a missionary" has suggested many family home evening discussion topics and activities. Quite a number of families, after careful planning and discussion, have assisted missionary work by making financial contributions, writing letters of encouragement to missionaries presently serving on missions, sharing their testimonies of the gospel with carefully selected nonmember neighbors, sending copies of the Book of Mormon and family testimonies to nonmember friends, studying the missionary approach and discussions, and volunteering to serve as missionaries and tourist guides for the Church. Some are even studying a new language in their families or keeping fluent in one they already know.

Happily, it seems quite possible to be fully active in genealogy, welfare, and missionary activities each month if families organize, plan together, and are consistent.

5. *Service projects.* The Lord himself said, "Verily I say unto you, Inasmuch as ye have done it unto one of the least of these my brethren, ye have done it unto me." (Matthew 25:40.) There are people all around us who need something cleaned up or fixed up and who would appreciate help; people who are sick and would enjoy a visit; people who are lonely or discouraged; people who are elderly, crippled, or shut-in; and people who are our neighbors but whom we hardly see. These people all give us an opportunity for serving them. If you have not become aware of your neighbor's needs, consider asking your children or consulting with your bishop.

Again, the real secret to enjoyable and useful family activities in this area of special service projects comes in planning together as a family and participating together in carrying out the plans. After you have selected a person to help and a service that would be helpful, make some decisions about who will contact the person to be served; what tools, gifts, or refreshments need to be taken; what special preparation each member of the family needs to make; and how your service will be done so that it will be easily accepted by the person you are trying to help. Even if you just plan a short visit with someone, have each family member prepare to contribute something to the conversation.

Service projects need not be large and time-consuming. It is better to do smaller and more frequent projects of love than to become bogged down in attempting something too large and too complicated. Consider also that it is not always necessary to leave your home. Sometimes the shy, elderly neighbor or the lonely friend would be helped more by being brought into your own home. The new atmosphere of your home, the friendly family relationship, and the comfort of an unhurried meal may be the most useful help your family could render.

120

Remembering to use places, foods, holidays, priesthood programs, and service projects to stimulate family activity will provide opportunities for the family members to work together each month of the year. Even the smallest of children can participate in some way. "To every thing there is a season, and a time to every purpose under the heaven: ... A time to weep, and a time to laugh; a time to mourn, and a time to dance. (Ecclesiastes 3:1, 4.)

Appendix A
100 Things Happy Families Are Doing

Here is a brief summary of 100 things that happy families are doing. (Just in case you decided to start at the end of the book and read forward!) We were amazed at the variety of activities and immediately started checking each item to see if our families could use the suggestions. We also found the list to be a useful springboard to generate ideas for variations of the activities. Maybe your family is already doing what other families are doing, and you can add ten new activities to the end of the list.

1. Raising pumpkins and secretly sharing them at Halloween time.
2. Holding a "missionary shower" to help prepare a missionary.
3. Using a cassette recorder at bedtime to record a child's personal history.
4. Using signs and posters for presenting ideas in family home evening and then leaving them up for a week as reminders.
5. Writing a family letter to distant relatives, friends, and missionaries.
7. Analyzing their year's supply of food on the basis of individual needs.
8. Using the first family home evening of the year to plan financial, educational, physical fitness, social, and spiritual goals.

9. Pairing up with another family member to check on goal progress.
10. Keeping a notebook of family business and assignments.
11. Reading scriptures before dinner.
12. Bearing testimonies to each other in family meetings.
13. Making things out of paper, without using scissors or other tools, to encourage inventiveness and cooperation.
14. Selecting, memorizing, and explaining to the family favorite passages of scripture.
15. Holding goal-setting interviews with each family member.
16. Reading scriptural stories to children at bedtime.
17. Having a free-agency treasure hunt to pick between good and bad drinks, music lyrics, and clothing styles.
18. Sharing supper with a lonely neighbor.
19. Starting personal histories by writing about "the first things I remember."
20. Creating a special-shaped gelatin dessert for a family home evening.
21. Receiving priesthood blessings in connection with beginning a year of school.
22. Planning a library of Church books for the home.
23. Planning a music collection for the home.
24. Learning a language together and practicing at mealtimes.
25. Practicing praising each member of the family each day.
26. Using treasure hunts to spark up scripture study.
27. Taking mother out on a date.
28. Holding a lesson on a nearby hill overlooking a beautiful valley.
29. Going to a familiar part of the desert for picnics.
30. Hiking and observing and then telling about a favorite creation in nature.

31. Secretly buying a sack of kites to assemble at a family picnic.
32. Planning activities to enjoy in the car while driving on a vacation.
33. Each child buying one secret food item at the store for part of supper. (Maybe not a well-balanced meal, but fun!)
34. Camping away together so there will be no interruptions from other people.
35. Giving a journal or scriptures and having a favorite meal when a child is baptized.
36. Renting a chalet for a few days for the family to enjoy each other or celebrate a special occasion.
37. Holding family "Olympic games" complete with prizes.
38. Selecting and playing or listening to everyone's favorite piece of music.
39. Developing a picture genealogy for each member of the family.
40. Holding a game night once a month.
41. Giving a verbal gift to the Savior at Christmas by promising to do something better.
42. Making up a quiz from the past year's events in the family and giving prizes to see who can answer the most questions.
43. Working on home beautification projects.
44. Fellowshipping nonmember neighborhood friends.
45. Holding a "memory night" to share past experiences.
46. Studying the scriptures.
47. Opening savings accounts for a specific percentage of each person's income.
48. Participating in a family physical fitness program.
49. Learning a new recreational activity together.
50. Rotating among family members the planning of family home evening.
51. Watching general conference on television together and writing down one item each General Authority asks Church members to do.

52. Discussing personal dress, grooming habits, and manners that enhance our appearance and represent us well as Mormons.
53. Making a tradition of family times together by planning to be together each week for purposeful activities.
54. Analyzing together the kind of movies, television, magazines, books, and music that enter the home.
55. Attending the temple regularly and discussing the importance of temple work.
56. Developing a pedigree chart and family group sheets.
57. Learning basic safety and first-aid skills together.
58. Helping each other find suitable jobs and career opportunities.
59. Providing help with schoolwork when necessary.
60. Having a child work with dad or mom when either is engaged in performing an employment task or household task that can be instructive to the child.
61. Practicing the skills of growing, canning, freezing, and drying foods.
62. Teaching the children how to save for missions.
63. Building Sabbath-day traditions.
64. Learning how to resist harmful influences through forewarning.
65. Practicing effective listening skills.
66. Inviting returned or active missionaries to Sunday dinner.
67. Learning how to brainstorm ideas for cooperative decision-making.
68. Posting a chart to show who is doing what during the next family home evening.
69. Learning how to pray about specific family needs.
70. Discovering through questions the favorite color, breakfast, books, scripture, hobby, game, and season of each family member.
71. Systematically studying the counsel of the General Authorities from conference reports and planning with the family how to follow it.
72. Sleeping under the stars together in the backyard.

73. Using *Ensign, New Era,* or *Friend* articles to start family home evening discussions.
74. Making up a list of great qualities of each family member and posting it for a week in a conspicuous place in the house.
75. Converting the garage for a family theater production to share with the neighborhood.
76. Visiting a business, factory, airport, or other place of interest together to give children ideas for employment or careers.
77. Setting aside some time in a family home evening to praise each family member for something accomplished during the past week.
78. Finding ways to pray together more often.
79. Inviting people who have achieved success in music, art, leadership, or other fields to family home evening to share their experiences.
80. Giving trophies and certificates to family members to recognize their achievements.
81. Having enjoyable evenings by planning for restful activities such as reading, sharing a bedtime story, listening to music, or enjoying a snack.
82. Teaching the advantages of comparative shopping.
83. Using faith, prayer, effort, and shared experiences to overcome the habits of faultfinding and criticizing.
84. Learning about Church duties and callings through asking leaders and family members and by reading books of instruction.
85. Praying about decisions to determine if they are right.
86. Deciding through family discussions what Sabbath activities are restful, cause us to think of the Lord, and would be done by the Savior.
87. Kissing and hugging each other after family prayer.
88. Writing notes of appreciation to each other and leaving them in surprising places.
89. Preparing a place in the home equipped with pencils, paper and scissors, and other items for doing schoolwork.

90. Coping with anger by pausing for a few seconds and thinking of the Savior.
91. Taking upon themselves the name of Christ, remembering him, and keeping his commandments in order to have his Spirit.
92. Parents asking each child, "What is the most important thing I can do for you today?"
93. Having older children teach younger ones and vice versa.
94. Sharing household chores.
95. Helping someone who is discouraged by visiting and sharing encouraging stories and a special dessert.
96. Sometimes splitting the family in half by age and having dad meet with and teach one part and mom the other.
97. Giving each family member a book of remembrance or journal to start his own record-keeping.
98. Making a "fix-it chart" for all the little things in and out of the house that need repairing, and working on them together.
99. Conducting a talent search in the family and finding instruction to strengthen each individual's talent.
100. Providing small surprises for each other—a note, an unexpected phone call, a tiny gift—for no special occasion.

Your additions:

101.
102.
103.
104.
105.
106.
107.
108.
109.
110.

Appendix B
Family Check-up Quiz

This quiz will give you a quick profile of your family and help you pinpoint areas that may need improvement as well as areas of success. To begin, circle the answer that is closest to the way your family is functioning now. *F* means frequently, *O* means occasionally, and *UN* means usually not. When you have completed the quiz, summarize the scores according to the instructions.

1. We vary the type of family home evening activities and the setting or place of our family home evening. F O UN
2. Our children share in planning, preparing, and participating in lessons and activities. F O UN
3. Our children go to their father for blessings. F O UN
4. My spouse and I spend uninterrupted time each day listening to each other's concerns. F O UN
5. We have interviews and private time with each child. F O UN
6. My daily conversation with my family is filled with many more comments of praise than criticism. F O UN
7. Our family teaching is done mostly by discussion, not lectures. F O UN

8. Our children think family home evening and family time together are useful and interesting.   F   O   UN

9. I think the way we hold family home evenings and family activities in our home is useful and interesting to me.   F   O   UN

10. We select family activities that meet a family member's problems or interests.   F   O   UN

11. We follow up on family lessons and assignments during the next family home evening.   F   O   UN

12. Our family prays together.   F   O   UN

13. We have family home evening each week.   F   O   UN

14. Our family fasts, pays tithing, and attends Church meetings.   F   O   UN

15. We place the stewardship of our family above recreational interests, hobbies, and partying.   F   O   UN

16. Our whole family counsels together on matters that concern the family.   F   O   UN

17. Our home is permeated with uplifting pictures, music, books, conversation, and entertainment.   F   O   UN

18. Our house is clean and tidy.   F   O   UN

19. Family members hug and kiss each other.   F   O   UN

20. I am very honest when taking check-up quizzes!   F   O   UN

Give each circled *F* score 3 points. *O* scores are worth 2 points, and each circled *UN* score is worth 1 point. Now total the scores.

A score in the 20-30 range suggests the family is infrequently participating in the kinds of activities that build greater family strength. Regardless of the reasons for the score, recognize and give yourself credit for what *is* being accomplished and press on. If the score falls into the 31-45 range, the family is on the right track and understands what to do, but perhaps just doesn't do it often enough. Scores in the 46-60 range indicate that the family is making a strong effort to become united and support each other.

Whatever your total score, it may be helpful for you to review the entire quiz and pick out a "usually not" or an "occasionally" that your family would like to turn into a "frequently." Plan together for your family's growth, remembering that changes are usually best made one step at a time. Praise progress and recognize and reward any effort toward improvement.

Family home evenings, family teaching, and family activities should not be seen as brief moments squeezed into our busy time schedules, but as a total way of life. Check up constantly to find out what your family is doing and what other happy families are doing.

Index

Activities: make happy, 14-15; areas of, 113; list of, 123-28
Agenda, 45-47
Ancestors: name origins of, 111; physical characteristics of, 111; geographical areas of, 112; character traits of, 112; stories of, 112
Assets, family, 44-45

Beethoven, 105-6
Beliefs, tie together, 19-20
Bread of life, 68-69
Brigham Young University, 6
Buckets of love, 57-58

Camping, 96, 98-99
Canoe race, 98
Capture the flag, 94
Character traits of ancestors, 112
Children: teaching parents, 10; be kind to, 26
Christmas, 101-3
Coat of arms, 34-35
Comments, positive, 6, 37-38, 41
Communication, 22
Counsel, following, 7
Countries, other, 105
Courtesy training, 70-71
Criticism, avoid negative, 14-15

Decisions, 44-45
Defense, stimulating, 18-19, 66-67
Differences, 23
Dinners, 40-41, 115-16
Discussion: identify concept, 73-75; explore ways to apply concept, 75; choose way to apply concept, 75-76; relate experiences applying concept, 76-77
Divorce rate, 4

Eating places, creative, 117
Eighth birthday, 96
Emotional connections, 23
Engagement party, 97

Family: can be forever, 4; non-traditional, 11; unity, 12-13; group assets, 44-45; solving problems as, 44-45; making decisions as, 44-45; agenda, 45-47; olympics, 99; history, 103-4; check-up quiz, 129-31
Family home evening: introduced, 3; of Filipino family, 4-5; for two, 5-6; at BYU, 6; in orphanage, 7; of mother and son, 7; scripture reading,

132

Brilliant
IDIOT

Brilliant
IDIOT

An Autobiography of a Dyslexic

Dr. Abraham Schmitt
as told to
Mary Lou Hartzler Clemens

Good Books
Intercourse, PA 17534

Design by Dawn J. Ranck

BRILLIANT IDIOT: AN AUTOBIOGRAPHY OF A DYSLEXIC
Copyright © 1992 by Good Books, Intercourse, PA 17534
International Standard Book Number: 1-56148-058-4
Library of Congress Catalog Card Number: 92-4593

Library of Congress Cataloging-in-Publication Data

Schmitt, Abraham.
    Brilliant idiot : an autobiography of a dyslexic / by Abraham
Schmitt as told to Mary Lou Hartzler Clemens.
        p. cm.
    ISBN 1-56148-058-4 (hard) : $16.95
    1. Schmitt, Abraham. 2. Dyslexics—Canada—Biography.
    I. Clemens, Mary Lou Hartzler. II. Title.
    RC394.W6S36 1992
    362.1'968553'0092—dc20
    [B]   92-4593
                                      CIP

Printed on recycled paper stock.

To my first grandchild, Jacob, born on the eve of this book's publication, with the hope that his future academic world will be ready to teach him the way he needs to be taught, should he inherit my family's disability.

Table of Contents

Preface

What is dyslexia? Almost everyone who hears the term believes it means seeing words wrong, with their letters reversed or somehow distorted, out of order, or in some other ways twisted. Dyslexics, it is thought, make mistakes when they try to read, write or spell. But this widespread, everyday view of dyslexia is superficial and simplistic, even naive. Dyslexia is a highly complex, extremely puzzling set of shifting and varying conditions that may (but not always) include the letter and word reversals that everybody knows about.

Brilliant Idiot makes a substantial contribution to our understanding of the dyslexic condition. Abe Schmitt's towering portrayal is rich, meaningful and poignant. It is a book of searing honesty in which the author portrays in unstinting detail the lifelong torments he has endured and overcome.

Who is Abe Schmitt? He tells us he is a "brilliant idiot," but what does that mean? Can any one individual incorporate these contradictory attributes? This utterly convincing—story gets to the heart of the perplexity that assails most dyslexic individuals through their lifespans. Their lives are filled with uncertainty and contradiction. It is painfully, unbearably difficult for dyslexics to reconcile the discrepant elements of their makeups: areas of high competence, even brilliance and genius, coexisting in some uneasy alliance with grave and humiliating evidences of profound inadequacy.

In this revelatory book, Schmitt makes a clean breast of his painful and cruel life history, shows us how he has come to an understanding of his condition, has struggled to find ways of coping with it, of reconciling the disparate attributes into a unified, gifted and highly productive life and career. In the process, he has at last attained tranquility and wisdom. He shows us how the gift of dyslexia has enriched and ennobled him. In offering his life story, Schmitt makes us a gift of compassion and understanding that is immeasurably rewarding.

Schmitt was born into circumstances and a lifestyle that is, for most of us, exotic. His family was part of a primitive and pre-literate peasant village, the "Old Colony" Mennonites in the remote, harsh prairies of Saskatchewan. Into this family came Abe, from the beginning a bewildered and confused child, the family "schladontz" (dunce), a hopelessly inept child who could not even tie his shoes or close his fly.

Schmitt learns through intense self-searching that the global, diffuse—but creative—thinking that characterizes a predominately right-brained person like himself is sharply at variance with his confused, bumbling, left-brained mental processes, so that he is unable to handle the linear thought requirements, the organizational skills, and the verbal fluency which the conventional academic system and traditional teaching methods require. His treatment of some of the characteristic dyslexic attributes is lucid and meaningful.

An important contribution in this book is Schmitt's exposition of various possible and likely predisposing factors related to dyslexia: medical, developmental and sociocultural. He arrives at a surmise, which is nonetheless convincing, about his origins as an Old Colony Mennonite. It may very well be that a common genetic factor within the tightly knit male community is a deeply imbedded proclivity towards language learning deficit and consequent academic inaptitude or incompetence. Perhaps dyslexic preponderance is a major element in creating the homogeneous but migrant culture that moved always to a remote region in a far-off land to shun education, while the outward explanation rationalized this characteristic as the means of protecting their pure and holy religion and lifestyle from the worldly evils of the larger literate civilization.

This book is a testament to the triumphant human spirit and a worthy—indeed indispensable—contribution to our understanding of the broader aspects of dyslexia.

Milton Brutten, Ph.D.
—Council of Advisors, The Orton Dyslexia Society
—Founder, Crossroads School for Dyslexic Children

Introduction

Sören Kierkegaard has said, "Life must be lived forwards, but can only be understood backward." That is what this book is about. I want to tell my dyslexic life story as I *experienced* it, living forward but not understanding it at all: then tell it again, understanding it "backward."

The critical point between the forward and backward directions came when I was in my early fifties. The word "dyslexia" crossed my path and I experienced a sudden "ah ha!" as I felt the meaning of the word and its implications in my life.

During the incubation period of my new self-understanding I was ambivalent. Self-doubt caused me to question the validity of my diagnosis: Am I really dyslexic? Since there is no final diagnosis, dyslexia is a difficult condition to clearly identify. No two dyslexics are alike; each one has an individual cluster of symptoms. There are no methods of certifying one as an "official" dyslexic. Even though I researched the literature and found it enlightening, I could not find any agreement on the diagnosis.

Yet the more I read about dyslexia and attended conventions and talked with other dyslexics, the more certain I became that I had found the missing piece to the puzzle of my life. Now the extreme duality of my academic life came into focus: seventeen horrendously difficult years followed by more than seventeen equally successful years. Only a specific learning disability could account for such a paradox. I have no doubt that the pain of my former years provided me the determination to overcome the obstacles of the latter.

This pattern has operated over and over again in my life. Every crisis, every failure, every setback I have tried to use as an opportunity to win another round and, often, the more dreadful the defeat, the more clear the victory. It is this component that has given me the final push to write this book.

Not only for myself, but for anyone who struggles with a handicap, I want to show that victory is possible. The handicap will never go away, but it is possible to discover the opposite side to the error, and discover it as a gift.

Once propelled into the actual work of writing this book, I was confronted by the very handicap that necessitated the telling of my story. While writing requires a great deal of right-hemispherical, creative thinking, all of that is of little value if it cannot be transposed into left-hemispherical orderliness, as the printed page requires.

I was able to find someone who needed to produce this book for her own growth as I needed to tell it for mine. Telling my story enabled the birth of another author: Mary Lou Hartzler Clemens.

This arrangement permitted me to gather my ten years of journal entries on dyslexia and hand them to her, then add a continual flow of dictated material and have readable literature come out of it.

Having solved my need to find a writer, I still had to summon fortitude to go through with the project. Persons who shared classrooms with me likely experienced the same events differently than I did and may find my account hard to believe. Yet I tell the events as my pictorial memory recalls them and I share with my readers the inner events that accompanied them.

When the manuscript was nearly completed, I took one more risk and made an appointment to have a skillful testing psychologist administer the Wechsler Adult Intelligence Scale to me. I needed to know if I could justifiably use the word "brilliant" to describe myself. My fear was that only the idiot part of me would be revealed. Then what would I do with this manuscript? Or what if the test itself depended on language proficiency? Would it be valid in my case? If not, I decided, I would just discard the results and define myself as untestable.

In spite of my doubts, I proceeded and the results put to death all my fears (See Appendix A). Scoring within the top one percent of the population, I validated the "brilliant" part of the book's title. Yet wherever the test measured tasks such as the organizing or sequencing of data, I scored extremely low, justifying the dichotomy of the title as well. I am, in fact, a brilliant idiot.

In analyzing my performance the psychologist repeatedly used the word "compensation" as a way of accounting for the huge discrepancy between, what I call, my deficient left-hemispherical brain functioning and my highly developed and efficient right-hemispherical brain functioning. He credited this to a lifelong struggle to overcome specific left-sided handicaps.

Not long ago I talked with one of my elementary school teachers. He listened with distant interest as I tried to explain my dyslexia, and then he responded, somewhat regretfully, "When I taught in that school I looked at you and the rest of the Schmitt kids as dull, that your entire family had only marginal intellect, and that is how I treated you."

My need to believe in myself is still uppermost. Self-doubt preys upon me. Consequently, I have applied for and been accepted into the Mensa association, an organization that has as its only criterion for membership that an individual submit test scores verifying an intelligence in the upper two percent of the population.

I grant that may be an exercise in arrogance, but I need to contradict that teacher who thought I was of marginal intellect.

Why did I have to go to such an extreme to validate my claim? Surely the account of my life will be sufficient to answer this question. Self-doubt so ingrained still shows, even at this date so late in life.

—Abraham Schmitt

1.

My Roots

M y birth certificate verifies that I was born August 7, 1927 on Section 17, Township 12, Range 13 and west of the Third Meridian in Saskatchewan, Canada. The maternity room was a farmhouse in the village of Blumenort, which was not legally incorporated and so could not be identified specifically in any other way.

I come from a Mennonite peasant village on the tree-less, windblown western Canadian prairie with no legal name. Here in southwestern Saskatchewan a primitive community of peasants had recreated a culture that they kept intact for centuries against all odds. When I was born in 1927 I was welcomed into a system that had changed very little in over 400 years.

During the early part of the sixteenth century a reformation was triggered within the Reformation. Herein lie my roots. My ancestors insisted on calling themselves neither Protestant nor Catholic, but rather Anabaptists and, later, Mennonites. Because they would not identify with either wing of the spiritual and social upheaval, they found themselves at odds with both and, thus, victims and martyrs on both sides.

The Anabaptists from northern Europe found refuge from persecution in and near Danzig in what was then called Prussia, now Poland. There they found a home where they could live what they defined as the totally committed Christian life. Their efforts to put their faith into practice made them cautious about participating in general society. Their belief in nonresistant love meant they could not serve in any capacity in the military, nor be part of the political system.

They would not swear an oath, nor participate in the educational system of their host country. They reinforced their community and their separateness by retaining the Low German language. "Low" refers to the dialect's historic origins in medieval times in the German lowlands. The language was never written, only spoken.

My ancestors came from Friesland in The Netherlands—an area whose people even today are considered conservative, questioning all change as unnecessary or threatening. This group selected the remotest swamplands in Prussia as their home. They drained the land and prospered, and remained relatively untouched by the world for 200 years.

When acculturation began to threaten, the community immigrated to the Ukraine in Russia at the invitation of Catherine the Great, who was looking for good farmers. Here, too, they chose the remote hinterlands that stood the least chance of outside interference. Since they were the first of many groups of Mennonites to settle in Russia, they became known as Old Colony Mennonites. Descendants of that group still carry the label today, along with qualities that have come to be identified with them: the most old-fashioned, primitive, peasant, conservative and ignorant of all Mennonites. Later-arriving groups of Mennonites to Prussia, Russia and North America accepted more industrialized locations that gave them greater educational and cultural advantages, but my ancestors did the exact opposite—the farther they were from civilization, the better.

Again it was my people who first saw the impending effect of Communism, and by 1874 fled to North America, selecting the unsettled Canadian West rather than the United States' Midwest where their more progressive relatives settled in places like Newton, Kansas, and Mountain Lake, Minnesota.

Just five years before my birth the established church of the Swift Current Reserve, as it had come to be known, packed to move again. Compulsory English education and worldly culture began making inroads and, as before, the community fled. With no further options in Canada, they chose Mexico as their next refuge.

The Swift Current Reserve in Saskatchewan had been purchased by the Old Colony church at the turn of the century and resold to its members. This area of rich farmland covered an area approximately twenty-five miles by fifteen miles. It consisted of twenty villages built on a plan that was developed in Prussia, repeated in Russia, and recreated in western Canada. Even the village names were repeated. My native village was Blumenort, a name that can still be found wherever Old Colony Mennonites have settled, in Prussia, Russia, Manitoba, Mexico and Paraguay.

Each village was laid out like all the others with a mile-long street down the middle and ten farmyards on either side. At the center of the village were the church building and the school yard.

The people who populated Blumenort when I was born were the "unfaithful," those who had chosen not to go on to the next "Promised Land." My father was the only one of his family of eleven brothers and sisters, and his parents, who did not move to Mexico. He, at nineteen years of age, had fallen in love with Maria Friesen and chose her over his entire family. I believe that it is by this one thin thread that I escaped being born in a Mennonite village in Mexico and avoided being as illiterate as most of my 100 cousins there now.

Scattered throughout our villages were recent immigrants who had newly escaped Russia. In Russia they had established a more elaborate educational system and over the centuries had scoffed at the near-illiterate, peasant Old Colony. Now they not only had to live alongside these Old Colony peasants, but they were living in the houses they had built and left behind.

What the people of Blumenort remember about the night I was born was not the arrival of identical twin boys into the Schmitt family, but a killing frost that destroyed all the farm crops and garden vegetables. On that night every family lost their entire income for one year.

The birth of a new baby was not especially newsworthy.

Babies were born almost annually in every farmhouse in the village. This time the village gossip had more than the usual fodder. It was reported that the twins born the previous night had weighed only two pounds each, that one had already died and the other was not likely to survive. Neither my brother Pete nor I ever found out which of us was the one who supposedly died.

We were two of seven children born to my parents in a nine-year period, and the first of two sets of twins. The house we lived in was the smallest in the village. Only eighteen feet wide and thirty feet long, it was divided into two equal-sized rooms. Our living room by day accommodated my parents' bed and sleeping space for my three sisters at night. The girls' beds were collapsible, transforming into seats for daytime use. The other room was the kitchen, which at night held home-made wooden, expandable beds ("schlopbenkj") for the four boys. One of our first tasks each morning was to fold the straw mattresses and bedding, collapse the drawer-like section, and then close the heavy wooden lid so that the room could function as a kitchen again.

The kitchen stove had to be fired up with dried manure and coal dust. Cold winter nights left a layer of ice on the pail of drinking water near the stove, and I can still see my mother coaxing the fire and making breakfast while we all stayed in bed until the worst chill was out of the air.

Attached directly to the house was the barn. This style of homestead originated in Europe in the sixteenth century, and my ancestors took it with them to Poland, then to Russia and on to western Canada.

Having all the farm animals as well as the family under the same roof felt comfortingly cozy. During severe snowstorms no one had to venture out. The animals, crowded into the small barn, kept it warm and even provided some warmth for the house. Our parents were never far away with Dad doing the chores on the other side of the kitchen door and Mother working where needed most. The barn gave us extra space in which to play or, later on, do carpentry work.

Ever-present manure spoke loudly and clearly of our peasant life. We could see it; we could smell it. Animal droppings
covered the entire farmyard surrounding the house. Cows
and chickens roamed freely everywhere. While the barn attached to the house provided not only warmth and coziness,
it also brought animal debris to within feet of the kitchen.

Everybody in Blumenort lived under similar circumstances. The only language we knew was the peasant dialect
that had never been put into writing. Except for the little High
German that my parents read and wrote poorly, they were
illiterate. Many of the villagers could read nor write nothing
at all. No one had electricity, telephone or indoor plumbing.
Everyone used the same kind of bedding—a large bag of straw
whose prototype likely dated to the Middle Ages. Almost all
food was produced on the farms, preserved by pre-refrigera-
tion methods and prepared according to the taste of our
ancestors.

Growing up in this ethnic colony life, I knew with absolute
certainty that I belonged to these 2000 kinfolk and that they
belonged to me. This sense of kinship included anyone who
lived within the prescribed village boundaries and spoke Low
German. They were called "us," and all those beyond these
limits were "them."

The colony was an isolated, self-contained system which
was a world all its own—safe, secure and totally embracing.
The boundaries were clear in our minds and we risked crossing them only later in life. We lived with a definite sense of
being inferior to those on the outside, and shame prevailed
over the entire colony. The fact that we spoke a primitive
language reminded us clearly and continually that we were
illiterate. Outsiders knew a common English language that
we believed was the key to worldly knowledge and wisdom.
Canada belonged to the world, but we did not.

As children we had total freedom within the boundaries of
the colony. We could navigate within or between villages and
no one asked questions. Our parents did not monitor our
movements or our conduct. The system had its own checks

and balances for behavior and it took care of all of us. Morality was understood, so it was enforced implicitly.

As I grew older I realized that our family was one of the most impoverished in our village. It was humiliating, embarrassing and frightening. I worried about our future welfare. My father was one of the poorest farmers in the village. He owned only an eighth of a section of land, which was far less than he needed to provide for a family the size of ours. Contrary to the families around us, none of us would receive land to farm as we grew up.

Dad's personal discouragement overshadowed our cottage all the days of my childhood. Somehow it seemed as if he just could not hold his own and succeed as a farmer. His entire family had left for Mexico while he alone chose to stay. Maybe he was so distraught or disoriented that he could not put his life together without them.

It was a comfort to have my mother's parents living across the street and all her brothers and sisters throughout the villages. That they were able to succeed was a sign of hope for us. My grandfather, especially, was a role model with whom we could identify. He was one of the first to buy a car, a tractor and a truck. He also drove to the city of Swift Current where he learned enough English to converse and read the language.

For some reason Granddad took a special interest in my twin brother Pete and me. He taught us carpentry. When he loaned us an expensive combination plane to take home and use as we pleased, we felt we had been knighted by the most renowned person we knew.

2.

The Idiot Is Born

*U*nquestionably, I was the family "schladontz." (The word literally means "tramp," but is also a counterpart to the English word "dunce.") It became clear to all when I failed to be able to tie my shoes, far beyond the age when all my siblings could.

When I visited my parents recently, my eighty-seven-year-old father looked down at the loafers I was wearing and commented, "That makes sense. You never could tie your shoes." Then he went on, "I remember you walking around with your shoes so loose that you could put them on or take them off without ever having to untie them. And you were always walking through puddles. I'd see your shoes under the stove at night and I knew they'd never be dry by morning."

As a child I was always being told that my fly needed closing or my suspenders were knotted or my shirt was wrongly buttoned or my cap was on crooked.

"Why can't this child learn to take care of himself?" my dad would cry.

A neighbor remembered me as "the most pathetic kid of the Schmitt litter. You looked bewildered and confused; your nose needed wiping and your pants were wet." Then he added, "I cannot for the life of me imagine how you could have become a doctor and a professor." That is the mystery I am now unraveling.

The attitude in Old Colony villages toward education was basically negative, with the exception of the few recent immigrants from Russia. Almost everyone else had close relatives who went to Mexico to escape the encroachment of public education. Many families moved from village to village, always seeking a community that did not have a school.

By January of 1926 the provincial government had succeeded in building a new schoolhouse in the center of Blumenort, and classes began. The five years from 1926 to 1931 saw seven different teachers at the school. Most of them stayed less than a year. Although five were Mennonites from other parts of Canada, each with high school education plus some normal school training, they likely left because of their frustration in attempting to teach English in a hostile environment.

An adult evening school was also offered. The students were mostly recent immigrants, but among them were all of my mother's siblings, one other Old Colony Mennonite, and my father. Each was charged fifteen cents; the ledger notes that several people who could not afford the fee brought a dressed chicken instead. My dad remembers that he was the only one who was completely unable to learn English. On top of that he suffered a futher stigma—that of having even attempted to learn it.

Some of the academic crises had subsided in our village by 1934 when I entered first grade. An outstanding teacher, H.J. Bestvater, had arrived the year before and was trying to bring a measure of quality education to the village. With a classroom of sixty-eight students in grades one through eight, we sixteen first-graders felt quite overlooked. He could do little more than allow us to quietly draw pictures or spend hours playing in the school basement. The following year a second teacher arrived and the first three grades were moved to the basement.

At Christmastime I suddenly became violently ill. I lost consciousness and had convulsions. Someone summoned the teacher, because he owned a car, to take me to the Swift Current Hospital. One week later I awoke after kidney surgery to a completely baffling world. It was beyond my ability to comprehend; I certainly couldn't communicate with it. The cause of my illness was a vitamin deficiency, and my parents felt endless guilt, grief and self-blame for it.

After three months I returned to school, only to discover that I was being put back into first grade. My parents were told that, even though I had been in school for a year and a half, that at eight and a half years of age I had learned nothing so far. I remember vividly the exact moment of being told that I was to move my book from the Grade Two rows to the Grade One rows. From then on I would always be a grade behind my twin brother. My entire world collapsed at that moment. There was no other measure of a person's worth or intelligence than success in school. Here I was singled out in front of everyone and discarded.

For weeks afterwards I would not join the children at recess but hid under the shrubbery to nurse my wound and hide my embarrassment. I spent much of my time either crying or fantasizing a better world. This latter skill I perfected to such a degree that I became able to transform any difficult situation into whatever I wanted it to be. It was an ability that frequently rescued me in later years as I struggled futilely with education.

School meant learning to speak, read and write the English language correctly. What became apparent to me, to the teachers and to my schoolmates was that I could not learn as others did. Other students could take the daily list of five words, learn to pronounce them, read them and then write them correctly as spelling words. But I simply could not do any of that.

I remember one technique that did work better than any other for me. On each of our desks the teacher would write a letter of the alphabet, about ten inches high, in chalk. Then we were each given a full-sized piece of chalk, told to hold it like a pencil and slowly trace over the letter, silently saying its name. This process continued for hours a day, mainly because the teacher was busy with the other two grades in the room. Later he added letters to make syllables and, finally, complete words. This method felt good to me, and it did help me to retain some of what I was supposed to learn.

While the other students were capable of moving on, there was no place for a slow learner like me. Gradually conflict emerged between my teachers and me, and it continued throughout my elementary and high school years.

Learning to spell was almost impossible for me, and it became the source of my great humiliation. On Friday afternoons, if the week had gone well, the teacher would announce a spelling bee. He appointed two of the best spellers to be team captains. They, in turn, would select for their teams the best students from all the grades. I was always the last one chosen, even after the students in all the lower grades had been picked.

There I stood with the youngest and smallest children, totally out of place. Then the contest would begin with the lowest grades' words first. The pressure, the excitement, the anxiety were too much. I stumbled and sputtered over the simplest words and was always the first one out of the contest. I had given the perfect performance for the idiot. Later, on the playground, someone would run past me taunting, "Abe, spell 'rat'!"

I could spend just as much time as my classmates studying the lesson, but when I was expected to remember the words I could not. As a result I spent my recess periods writing the words hundreds of times. Then I was tested again, but the result was little better than before. So I stayed after school to write the same words over and over again. The teacher became suspicious that I was not concentrating adequately and ordered me to work at the blackboard, even during class time, while the other students were doing more pleasurable things.

I spent years at my assigned spot at the blackboard writing words. The teacher kept a constant eye on me, often reminding me to write more legibly and to keep my words horizontal, a task that was extremely difficult for me to do. Any word that was not up to his standard of legibility he ordered erased and rewritten.

Although I was eventually promoted out of this teacher's

classroom, my subsequent teachers adopted the same methods, and I was always assigned to the blackboard to write my
spelling words. It finally ended when I was fifteen years old,
but I was still a pitifully poor speller.

In reading I fared only slightly better. The teaching method
was for students to silently read a section in the reader until
they achieved fluency. I could not read the assignment. The
words were mostly unfamiliar, the letters reversed themselves making the words unreadable, and words switched
themselves around in the wrong order. I remember gripping
my cheeks with my fingers in order to hold my head in place.
I dug my fingernails into my skin until it hurt to keep myself
from drifting off into space. The printed page seemed to float
away, the letters became fluid and only with extreme effort
could I keep them in place long enough to read.

At times my eyes would follow the lines carefully but I read
nothing. My brain had departed. I envisioned myself literally
grabbing my brain to keep it functioning and my eyes focusing
on each word. I refused to let my mind drift again and with
great determination was able to read several paragraphs
before I slipped off again. This sliding away happened as
naturally as falling asleep.

My sister remembers that I always sat near the front, while
she, who was a grade behind me, sat one row over and in the
back. My place in the classroom was determined by the
teacher who decided I was so troublesome that he needed to
keep a constant eye on me.

I had already been involved in an incident, and he had
warned me. Now he was glaring at me. Instead of studying
I was staring at the wall, totally lost in space, gone in a
daydream. Suddenly a piece of chalk came flying through the
air and hit me on the side of my head. I leaped like a prairie
jackrabbit, shocked and confused. I tried desperately to concentrate on the assignment, but within ten minutes I was
drifting off again. Mary saw what was happening and asked
the teacher for permission to leave the classroom to use the
outhouse. Making a loop around the room she stopped by my

desk to tell me to stop daydreaming, that the teacher was enraged already and that the next step would be another spanking. This she could not tolerate.

It was customary for each class to line up across the front of the room and, in turn, read the entire lesson. The tension was so great for me that I stumbled and sputtered my way through the text. I had to be stopped over and over again to correct words I had flipped around or simply guessed at. If I spent sufficient time reading and rereading every page, eventually I had it nearly memorized. Then as the material blurred together before my eyes I could rather successfully half-read and half-recite the assignment.

The patience of my teacher wore thinner and thinner as each year went by. He was confused, since in certain areas I seemed capable, with normal intelligence. In fact I was out-standing at doing projects and handicrafts, arithmetic and material that was verbally taught. The conflict between what he thought I could do and what I actually did became too much for him to bear. He concluded that I was refusing to learn deliberately just to defy him, and that it was a struggle of his will against mine. He became absolutely determined to win.

I knew this was not a struggle of wills. I wanted to learn to read and spell even more than he wanted me to. But I knew I could not. Something inside me simply prevented it, and no amount of effort made any difference. I wondered if some-where in my head something had gone wrong, if part of my brain had been destroyed while I was in that coma.

What made matters worse was that I was so easily and extremely distracted. I heard everything that went on in the classroom where several other classes were being taught simultaneously. Try as I might I could not tune them out, and when anything exciting occurred anywhere in the room, I automatically looked over. Any noise of any kind anywhere and I had to look. I had no choice; it was obligatory.

If the teacher could only have known the power of this distractibility; instead he felt as if his authority was being challenged, as if war was declared between an adult who needed complete control and a child who had none.

Suddenly my name would be blared out in rage from some unsuspected corner. No matter that I had been warned a few minutes earlier to concentrate on my work, I already had forgotten.

"Sit up straight, feet on the floor next to each other, hands on the desk, face forwards!" he bellowed.

He paced back and forth, eyeing me like a hawk. My head turned as a bird landed in a tree just outside the window, and he was prepared for it.

"Abram!!"

How vividly I remember his rage, his face flushed as he screamed, "Get into the cloak room!" and with a few giant strides he headed for his desk and yanked open the drawer (the second from the top on the left-hand side). The whole classroom fell into a deadly silence. He wildly flung out the dreaded strap, terrifying the entire class. I was a ten-year-old emaciated urchin in a state of total shock. I made my way without thinking to what had become, for me, the torture chamber. He broke into the room, grabbed the ends of my fingers and bent them back to expose my palm fully. With a full swing of his arm he lashed my hand. First one hand, then after the command, "Next!" I handed him the other. The number of blows was determined by his anger rather than the degree of my violation.

The pain so exceeded my endurance that I felt only the first few lashes in each hand before they became numb.

I was ordered to go back to my seat, to get down to work, to stop looking around, to concentrate and to learn my reading and spelling. I returned to the room, crying convulsively and feeling humiliated. I decided I was fundamentally defective, that the beatings must be necessary to correct some unknown error in my personality. All of my classmates observed the entire drama and could not understand why I would not comply with the teacher's wishes and avoid a catastrophe that devastated not only me, but the entire classroom. But no one understood the mystery of my failure no matter how often the scene was replayed.

Repeated trips to the cloakroom, beating after beating—as I got more upset I became more distracted. Suddenly I would make the switch to a state of complete self-absorption and vanish into space, totally oblivious to the outside world. And then bursting into my consciousness again came the roar, "Abram!!!"

This open warfare went on day after day. The teacher could reach no other conclusion than that I was defying him. Surely if he ordered me to keep on reading, at least I would keep my eyes focused on the paper. But I did not.

The teacher concluded that I was not only defiant, but also clever—going through the motions of learning on the outside, while inside refusing to learn, withstanding every threat, act or beating on his part.

Within myself I knew that I only wanted to obey the teacher. I was shy, I felt inadequate, and I wanted to please everybody so I might win some approval. I was the very opposite of defiant; I simply could not understand this part of me.

Emotionally I crumbled at every failure. Trying to read in front of the class was excruciatingly embarrassing. Being sent to the blackboard to write out my words was a death experience. What sense of worth I had, or any respect from my schoolmates, was destroyed over and over again. I stood out in the classroom as the isolated and designated idiot. By the time I got the beatings and had returned to the classroom all cried out, my mind simply switched off. There was no power in my thought processes that could comprehend why this humiliation was done, what it was to accomplish, or what I was to do to prevent it from happening again.

My parents' reactions to my devastating school experiences varied. My mother wept every time I came home and reported another beating. She had no explanation and knew that I was not so bullheaded as to deliberately provoke such brutal beatings. She examined my swollen hands and then raged at the injustice that was done. But if she had wanted to confront the teacher she could not, for she spoke no English and the

teacher did not know Low German.   Besides, she was a
woman, and it was not her role to approach a teacher at all.
She spoke about it to her father, who was the chairman of the
school board, but that accomplished nothing.   The village
mentality generally assumed that spankings were necessary
periodically and could do no harm.   The Old Testament admonition, "Spare the rod and spoil the child," was known and
observed.

My father, too, believed the spankings were necessary and
that eventually I would get the message that I was to learn.
But he also had the honor of being a card-playing buddy of the
teacher, a privileged status he did not want to jeopardize.

3.

Adolescence and the Secret Idiot

*B*y mid-adolescence my twin brother and I realized that if we were to survive financially in this world, we would have to do it without the help of our father. Unable to carry his own weight, let alone provide for his large family, he had become completely apathetic. We decided that if he couldn't show us the way, we would show him.

Pete and I were fifteen years old when we approached Dad about the possibility of his purchasing the abandoned farmyard next door. We explained how we would renovate the house, which had four rooms, as opposed to our present house with only two. The barn, we said, could be made to hold at least seven cows, two horses, one stall for heifers and another for calves. We also explained how we could dismantle our present farm building board by board and use the materials to build a new chicken house and pig barn.

The owner of the neighboring property was eager to dispose of it and was willing to deal on a loan basis. Dad could have the entire property for only $1000 and none of it had to be paid at the time we took possession. All our father had to do was trust that we, at fifteen years of age, could provide the facility by which he could make a living. He dreaded what, for him, was such a huge risk; we had to prove beyond all doubt that we could do it.

Repeatedly we walked him around the property, showing him explicitly how we would do it, what materials we would use, until finally he yielded.

A year later we had produced a model farmyard for that humble village. Along with that, Pete and I had established ourselves as builders. The villagers were amazed at the way we mixed our own concrete and poured it according to designs we saw pictured in farm journals. They watched carefully as we recreated the farmyard and marveled at our ingenuity, our youth and our determination to make our father, who had long ago established himself as a ne'er-do-well, succeed.

In spite of Dad the family made a living. The several hundred chicks that Mom raised filled the chicken house with equally as many laying hens. The eggs sold at a good price, and before he knew it Dad had real money in his wallet.

Instead of raising only a few pigs for the family's food he could now raise them by the score and, a year later, sell them at a handsome profit. The same was true with the row of milk cows in the renovated barn. Dad even gained enough confidence to risk purchasing our first motorized vehicle—a second-hand Chevrolet pick-up truck. He was shocked when I gave it a new coat of paint using borrowed spray-painting equipment.

After buying the truck, Dad purchased his first quarter-section of farm land and the implements to raise field crops.

I may have experienced some success as a builder, but I continued to be humiliated in the classroom. The teacher was not qualified to teach ninth grade lesson content so my studies were prepared and sent out by the Provincial government. I sat in the classroom only to work on my assignments, which were then mailed to the Department of Education in Regina for correcting and grading.

Of the five high school students, three in my ninth grade class and two in tenth grade, I was the only one who was strapped. The first incident occurred in the second week of the fall term during the singing of the national anthem. Since I believed I could not sing a note, I hid behind the fluffy headed girl in front of me. Suddenly the teacher stopped the singing.

"Hold it, class," he demanded. "Abe, were you singing?"

I answered that I was moving my lips.

"I saw that," he snapped, "but were you singing?"

Resuming the song he walked to the back of the room and, cupping his hand behind his ear, he leaned to within inches of me. Obviously he heard nothing since I was convinced that I could not make a sound that had any musical quality to it. Thus came about the first strapping of the year in that school.

Years later he admitted to me that as a new teacher he felt he needed to begin his career with authority. I became his scapegoat.

Another incident occurred at Christmastime that year. I had refused to participate in the Christmas concert, knowing that I could not memorize my part. I would have faltered, failed and blushed with embarrassment and humiliation. The teacher then insisted that I stay away from the event completely. My temptation to outwit the teacher was great, and I sneaked into the rear of the classroom to watch my classmates perform. The teacher spotted me and I ducked out of the building.

Stepping out the door he called after me, "Abe, is that you?" but no answer came; I had vanished into the darkness.

On the following Monday morning, we had no sooner completed singing "God Save the King" when the teacher came marching back to my desk, stared me in the face and bellowed, "Abe, were you here watching the Christmas concert?" I knew he had seen me and was trying to force me into a lie to make the punishment all the worse.

I admitted that I had been there. Now the issue at stake became who would lose face. He had warned me in front of all the students not to attend, I had defied him, and everyone knew it. He marched me to the front of the room and, before all the students (not in the cloakroom this time), he battered my hands with all his might.

But I, too, would not lose face this time. My hands had been beaten so often for so many years that no matter how great the pain I would not blink my eyes. I stared him directly in the face with all the defiance I could communicate. I was seventeen years of age and full grown, and I would not shed a tear. As I returned to my seat I winked at the class. The uproar caused him to go into another rage, but no one revealed the reason for the laughter.

What the teacher did not know was how I really felt. The secret idiot was always present with me. No matter how defiant I became, something deep inside told me that I was a defective human being. For some reason I was so different from everyone else that I could not fit into any expected role. Every beating I received was, somehow, deserved. I convinced myself that it was really the secret idiot that had betrayed me again, and that it, if not I, deserved a beating. It was this idiot, which I discovered the year I flunked grade two, that was the reason for the atrocious behavior of my teachers. I simply assumed that they, who knew how to speak English, who had an education, must know something that no one else in the village or in the classroom or, least of all, I could understand. These learned people must have understood the idiot and probably were right in believing that repeated beatings would batter the idiot into submission.

The most profound effect that this had on me was my resolution to get more education, no matter how terrifying even the thought of it was. Then I would some day be on the other side of this ignorance barrier. Then I, too, would understand the idiot. It was only in the educational process that I was confronted by the idiot, but that was where I knew I must find the answer.

A huge gap stood between me and everyone else in the classroom. They could not span this gap and meet or understand me on the other side. Feeling so totally separated from everyone, I increasingly cared little what they thought of me or what they were doing with their lives. All that really mattered was what I did with mine.

Outside of school I was coming into my own in the social life of the village. For an adolescent, life in the villages was exciting and enjoyable. Every village had a group of a dozen or more adolescents, all primed for fun. We could venture to any of the twenty other villages and find a comparable group of young people, ready to do whatever we were doing. We spent a lot of time together, telling stories, joking and pulling pranks on each other or the adults in the village. Since most evenings were cool we often built a bonfire beside the village street and then spent hours relating yarns, either real or imaginary, solely to entertain each other. The one who could be the biggest clown was the hero for the night. Here I was the star, holding the group's attention with my wit. I was thrilled by their laughter; I could withstand their ridicule even when my performance flopped.

We all spoke Low German, making no effort to speak English. An earthy, primitive speech, the language permitted us to invent words or twist them into any form that fit the occasion. The humor it provided could only be appreciated by those of us who lived and spoke the language.

These events were where we fully lived. Education and the English language were considered necessary evils that we all had to endure. So for it to be known that I was beaten at school, more than any other student, had little effect on the group gathered around the bonfire at night. It might even be used as inspiration for a key drama in which we acted out the entire event, ridiculing the teacher for hours on end. We invented outlandish names for him, names that if muttered in school the next day caused an instant explosion of laughter. The teacher's attempts to find out the cause only produced more laughter and his attempts to bring the riot under control required all the threats and rage that he could muster.

On some days episodes like this so unnerved the teacher that he would walk out on the class and retreat to his home a hundred feet away to steel himself sufficiently to face the class again. As the instigator of some of these scenes I occasionally got caught, and I deserved the spanking I received. But the favor I won with the group mattered more to me than bearing the brunt of the teacher's rage.

Experiences such as these with my peer group softened some of the pain I felt, but other scars have taken decades to heal.

During these years I struggled between my need to be left alone with my inner silence and my desire to participate with my peers. If I had too much interaction or stimuli I ended up in mental confusion that could lead to uncontrollable rage. I vividly remember my first such experience—a special Sunday when it was my turn to have the one bicycle that our entire family shared. I had waited three extremely long weeks for this day and it had finally arrived.

Mother always rose early to milk the cows. That morning it was my signal to get up. The sun was bright and the wind was still.

"What a perfect day for me to get the bicycle," I thought to myself as I watched my three brothers still sleeping.

Mother returned to the kitchen to make the breakfast porridge and said, "What's wrong, Abram, that you are getting up so early? It's Sunday. Usually we can't get you out of bed. Now that you could stay in bed, you get up."

My mind heard the words far away and I made no attempt to answer. Early mornings I preferred to be left alone and I usually talked only when absolutely necessary. I was deep in the contemplation of my day and did not want to be disturbed.

When the porridge was cooked I took a large helping. Again from far away came a comment, "You had better eat all you took," and that I let pass, too, without a response. I resented the intrusion and did not want my day spoiled by anyone or anything.

I left the house, jumped on the bicycle and rode around the farmyard. Then I explored the village street. I slowly rode to one end of the village, turned and rode to the opposite end, then back again. All the farmyards were quiet; no one else was on the street. It was just my bicycle and I, and that was the way I wanted it.

With a deep sense of tranquility I left the village and rode out into the miles and miles of roads through the prairie. Since the land was so level, and all the roads ran exactly north and south or east and west, it made little difference which roads I took.

I was free and my mind could ramble as the bicycle did. When I realized that there was not a single human sound in my world I stopped riding and stood motionless, drinking in the pure beauty of that silence. I inhaled all that I possibly could of the moment, knowing that the next week, as I sat in the classroom, I could experience it all again in my imagination. I would need this when I felt I could not sit still for one more second, when everything in me was crying out for escape from the bedlam. If I could allow this silence to fill me now, I could later fly into fantasy, drawing upon every sensation which now was real.

The sun's position told me it was dinner time and I did not want to miss the roasted chicken we had every Sunday. I raced home, only to find that dinner was over with just the leftovers saved for me. When Dad wanted to know where I had been and what I had been doing, I could not explain. I simply told him it was my turn to have the bicycle and I wanted to get as much mileage out of it as possible. No one could understand my need to be alone. I had heard about loneliness, but I had never experienced it. With such a productive fantasy life I was never lonely. For me, being alone with my fantasy was far better than being with people who kept interrupting it.

After dinner I noticed crowds of my peers gathering. Several groups from other villages had arrived and were milling around, arguing and vying for attention. I stood on the perimeter of all this, torn between wanting to be a part of it, to be popular, but also fearing that I was too much of a freak to be one of them. Maybe I should just ride away on my bike and recreate plot after plot in which I was the hero.

Suddenly I was the center of the crowd's attention. They began tormenting me, expecting that I would either protect myself or turn the taunts back on the tormentors. I couldn't think fast enough; the jokes were so well aimed that I became bewildered. I began to crumble but I could not escape. Even my fantasy world could not help me now.

A tough guy stepped out from the crowd of tormentors,

ready to fight. My classmates and siblings urged me to defend
the honor of our village. I knew I was no match for this guy;
I had never been strong and I avoided fights. But amidst the
jeers, taunts and terror I succumbed to rage. I lost all awareness; my world became the size of my body, and my opponent
became everyone and everything that had ever tried to de-
stroy me.

With super-human power I attacked—hitting and kicking
with my fists and feet in such rapid succession that my
opponent did not even have time to make the first move. As
he doubled over and dropped to the ground I continued my
assault. With no regard for him as a human being I leaped
on him, trampling his body and face without mercy.

I was subdued swiftly by a group of friends and led away.
My adversary and his accomplices drove off in humiliation.
For that evening I was afforded a respect I felt I did not
deserve. Neither I nor anyone else could understand how this
frail underdog had suddenly flipped into a frenzied beast.

After awhile I found my bicycle and went for a long quiet
ride in the country again. I was surrounded by a new and
strange tranquility. I could see that guy with his nose bleed-
ing. I could still feel the thud of my foot against his body. I
felt no guilt; instead I had a sense of detachment. This was
not me. I always wanted to be gentle and kind in hopes of
receiving the same in return. What had happened? I recalled
the enormous fear I felt at first, then the torments, and finally
the confusion. My brain no longer decoded anything, my
tolerance switch had snapped, and something else had taken
over. I had become a mindless emotion, a separate being.
Whatever happened was not done by me, but by *it*. Whatever
admiration was earned did not belong to me; it belonged to
the idiot enraged.

In adolescence the romantic urge awoke in me like it did in
my peers, but the secret idiot was there also, undermining and
sabotaging what should have been a natural stage of development.

The derogatory label, "schladontz," followed me into the

dating game. I was still the runt of the litter at home, still the clumsiest, the poorest student, the least athletic. My older brother and twin brother were already succeeding in courtship, but my attempts were generally met with rejection. The girl was insulted that I presumed to be in the same league with her and mortified that I should want to sit on the same bench with her.

Although I was not completely dateless, I never succeeded in the way I wanted to. While my twin was able to charm the most attractive, most desirable girls, I ended up with dates out of sheer desperation, not mutual attraction or compatibility. As a result I cut each one off and fled into my fantasies, nursing my wounds.

In the village, courtship preoccupied every person from age fourteen until they reached adulthood and, ultimately, marriage. Their lives centered around pairing up, dreaming of one another and plotting ways to be together. I, too, dreamed, but it was of a great courtship in some distant future, when, even beyond my imagining, this huge life mystery would be unraveled and I could join the human race.

I did not know how it would happen, but I had already found the inner strength to survive untold humiliation. That inner strength would help me survive whatever lay ahead. I would rise above this existence in some unconventional way and I would endure. I felt as if I had gone through the fires of hell and come out the other side. I decided to survive, just as I had survived the cloakroom experiences when the pain drove me into shock and I could not imagine living through another blow. I could not now lay aside my search for myself in order to find a wife.

4.

Driver's License

When I completed Grade Ten, my education in the village school was finished. With my dad's insistence, both Jake, my older brother, and Pete, my twin, had already left for boarding school to complete their high school education. Dad knew there was no future for us in the village. He did not have enough land to start us off on farms; furthermore, he was absolutely sure that none of his children should follow in his footsteps. He believed that education was the only ladder to the world outside the village.

Because village life had been so traumatic for me, especially my school experiences, I was ready to take the first opportunity to flee it. What I realized, ironically, was that education was my escape route, not only from the village, but also from my idiot self and the unanswered questions that haunted me. I was determined to complete the eleventh and twelfth grades. So I followed my brothers to Rosthern Junior College, a Mennonite school for grades nine through twelve, 250 miles from home.

This step brought me trauma in a new setting. The school advocated academic excellence, and I quickly realized how inadequately prepared I was. My ninth and tenth grade correspondence courses had required no spoken words, and I could not carry on a normal conversation in English when I arrived for the eleventh grade. I entered every class in terror of failure, of being publicly humiliated.

My most painful awakening, though, came when I was suddenly subjected to the caste system established by the Mennonites from Russia. In Russia this system had devel-

oped according to the progressiveness of the various Mennonite groups. The most advanced, and thus the highest caste,
built schools, hospitals and other institutions that even served
as models for the surrounding Russian community. My ancestors were the ones who had settled in the hinterlands to
escape such progress and therefore were assigned to the
lowest caste.

By the time of immigration to western Canada, each group
had acquired a sort of symbol of its status. The Old Colony
group developed the village system, which became its identifying symbol. Thus, whenever I had to reveal that I came from
the village of Blumenort, I immediately felt branded as one
from the lowest caste. I can still hear some of my classmates
sneering in Low German, "Here comes a flat-footed Old Colony
Mennonite." Other times they simply called me, "Darpa,"
which means "a peasant who comes from a village." I felt the
sting intensely.

Every student at Rosthern Junior College was required to
audition for singing. Since singing was such an important
part of the Mennonite community, and Rosthern Junior College was considered the center for the teaching of singing,
everybody there sang. I had never sung. I was convinced I
could not sing. Even in the village where we, like other Old
Colony Mennonites, retained the medieval chant instead of
singing melody or harmony, I did not sing. But the day came
for my singing audition. I remember waiting in the hall
outside the classroom for my turn. I might as well have been
on death row awaiting my execution. On the other side of the
door was a piano and the singing instructor who snarled as I
walked in, "Now let's see what this villager can do."

I stood beside the piano shivering in fright. He tapped one
of the piano keys and ordered me with one word, "Sing."

I was voiceless, petrified, incapable of making a sound.

He tapped the key again and said, "Abram, now sing!"

I said, "I can't."

"You can, too," he said. "Why can't you sing? Just sing that
note," and he tapped the key again, harder this time, and more

insistently.

I said to him, "I've never done it; I've never heard my voice. I don't know what it does."

"I've never heard of such a thing," he said in disgust. "You are defying me. You are just as stubborn as your brothers. Are all the Schmitts the same—bull-headed 'darpa?'"

Then he struck the key as hard as he could and yelled, "Sing!" his voice quivering with rage.

I could do nothing else but open my mouth and utter a grotesque mixture of sounds.

"You're mocking me," he sneered. Again he hit the key as hard as he could and screamed, "Now do it right!"

All I could get out was another squeak. With that he ordered me out of the room, telling me I was a dumb fool who should have stayed on the farm and never tried to get a high school education.

I fled the room in horrifying shame. His definition of me must be correct, I concluded, for I had nothing by which to disprove it. I had lived my whole life in the isolation of the Reserve, which now seemed to be the most humiliating of origins. What else could I expect?

I found my way back to my room and went into a trance. In my fantasy I returned home to the safety and security I had known there. Yet I knew there was nothing for me in that place except a house full of children, more lost than I was, and a barn full of manure waiting to be hauled out.

My brother Pete was my roommate, and when he came we talked about what had happened. He had gone through the same experience and had found a way of picking up the pieces and moving on. I would too.

Academically, my first year at Rosthern was also very difficult. My learning difficulties showed up in several of the subjects I took, especially chemistry. This course was taught in rote fashion, utilizing memorizing techniques, by the same instructor who taught singing. He snarled rather than talked. All these factors triggered the worst of my learning handicaps. I struggled through, but with much belittling and humiliation from the instructor.

At the end of the spring marking period every student's grades were posted in the hall for all to see. I was at the bottom of the class in three subjects and scored an absolute zero in German grammar. In three other subjects I was either in the middle or above. In algebra I was near the top.

As I entered the twelfth grade I discovered that I had a brain that *could* work for me. The principal of the school, K.G. Toews, also taught physics, biology, algebra, geometry and trigonometry. K.G., as he was affectionately called, taught with such a keen sense of the inner essence of each subject that my brain immediately connected with it. Each week he would build on existing knowledge, and I understood.

Very often, after presenting the theory to the class, he would ask, "Now that you know this, how would it hold true if...?" and he would set up a situation.

I remember one brain teaser that he threw at the class during the study of light. He paused, and then asked, "Exactly how big a mirror is needed in order to see one's entire reflection?"

Just as quickly, I exclaimed, "One-half the person's size."

Fifty-nine faces turned to me with incredulous expressions.

"Okay, Abe, come to the blackboard and prove it," K.G. said.

I found it simple to illustrate the fact. With his characteristic glow of "Well done," he affirmed that I was exactly right. My classmates were amazed since they experienced me as an idiot under so many other conditions.

I could learn under this kind of teaching, and, as a result, I had nearly perfect grades in all K.G.'s subjects. I can still feel what it was like to sit in his classes and be able to comprehend everything he was saying. It was as if my brain had been switched on for the first time and was functioning at full capacity.

Biology fascinated me. One Saturday morning in the spring of the year I caught a frog on campus. Dissection was part of our study of anatomy, and I wondered about the possibility of using a live specimen. K.G. walked with me to the chemistry lab to obtain the ether, then instructed me on the proper method of anesthetizing the frog and opening the body cavity without damaging any of the organs. He asked to see the results as soon as I was finished.

I proudly showed him the frog with its heart beating outside its body and the other organs exposed and functioning. K.G. was so impressed that he called the rest of the class together for a special Saturday session.

The following Monday morning K.G. conducted the school assembly program. He spoke on the subject of excellence as the key to success and used my frog episode as his primary example. Excellence, he said, was going to the top, not thinking of duty or grades or norms, but doing the best possible only for the joy of doing it. This, he said, is what I had done on Saturday. His words thrilled me, not because of what I had done, but because of the personhood he gave me that day.

My greatest victory at Rosthern Junior College occurred as I was nearing the end of my senior year. I received a notice from K.G. to come to his office. He had a project which had to be completed by the end of the school year, three weeks hence. He had collected photographs of each graduation class since the founding of the school and wanted them mounted in identical frames with the names of the graduating members of each class inscribed below. The finished portraits were to be displayed in a new section of hallway for the upcoming graduation ceremonies. I assumed he had asked me to help because I enjoyed art and calligraphy.

As honored as I was to be asked, I turned down his request. With the provincial final examination approaching I knew I had to spend every minute I had studying.

He kept insisting that I did not need to, while I protested that I did. Finally he said, "I guess I must tell you something confidential that will settle this."

He proceeded to explain the governmental system whereby students in the top twenty-fifth percentile in each subject throughout the province were exempt from writing the uniform exams. The names of those students had already been forwarded to the provincial government and confirmation of their status had been received by the school. My name was on the list in all but two subjects—German and English composition. And with these, he reminded me, there was little I could do in the way of studying.

"If you haven't understood them by now, cramming these last few weeks will not help much." He encouraged me to study those two subjects while I worked on his project and not worry about any of the others.

My heart did a flip and, before I could recover, K.G. added, "Now, you know that you should be going on to university."

I certainly did not know that, nor did I believe it. Never before had someone whom I regarded so highly pronounced such a blessing on me.

Was K.G. really meaning to say that I, the academic moron, was an academic success? Did he mean that I had the brains to go on to college? He offered to write a personal letter of reference for me if I decided to apply to a university.

This man had just provided my driver's license to living. Now I could continue my journey. I told him that I wanted to apply to normal school, the teacher training school in the province.

For the first time my future career began to take shape. K.G. believed in me. Because of his educational stature in the province, anyone he recommended was accepted.

5.

Too Great a Leap

I sometimes wonder if my move into normal school was too great a leap. I can still experience the frightening and painful feelings that accompanied this time in my life.

My twin brother Pete successfully completed one eight-week accelerated summer course designed by the government to meet the post-war teacher shortage. From there he went to a prairie school for his first teaching position, carrying off each step with a sense of confidence which I lacked. I was desperately determined to go to normal school at any price because that would give me one toehold in my escape from the peasant ignorance of the village.

My old buddies gave a hero's welcome when I returned to the village after high school. With them life was simple, safe and fun. I had received no acceptance letter from normal school, so I took that as a cue to find my place among all the other youth of the villages. Dad gave me a job helping him mow the ditches along the public highways. Pay was minimal but I needed almost nothing for my living.

I distinctly remember that one day I became deeply depressed. I had spent hours picking up beer bottles and tin cans ahead of Dad on the mower. I was overwhelmed that my educational venture—despite the many hurdles I had overcome—was for nothing. The only advancement I could see now was a promotion to the seat of the mower. I passionately hated the thought of being condemned to peasantry. "I must escape; there must be a way," I cried to myself.

Just then my sister came riding up on the family bicycle, bringing us our lunch, and she handed me a telegram. I remember the exact spot where I stood that Friday afternoon as I tore it open.

"From the Department of Education of the Province of Saskatchewan . . . Due to the fact of late cancellations you are now eligible to be admitted to Normal School at Moose Jaw. Please report to the Registrar's Office in Moose Jaw if you accept. Stop."

I turned to Dad and his response was instantaneous. "By all means, go! This life is not fit for a mule. Get out while you can."

By Monday morning I was in Moose Jaw, Saskatchewan, leaving my dad to the life that he also despised, the life he always told us not to follow.

I was now alone in a totally unfamiliar world. For the first time I was outside the Mennonite community. High school had been traumatic, but I was still among Russian Mennonites who spoke Low German. Now I was in a setting whe.re there were only four Russian Mennonite students. I quickly attached myself to them and hung on for dear life in a sea of 250 normal school students, newly graduated from high school.

All normal school students were in the top percentile of their high school classes. But I was now part of an even more select group: a few of us who showed promise were chosen for a special accelerated summer program. At the end of this eight-week course we would be qualified to teach. If we took two more similar summer programs between teaching terms, we would receive temporary teaching certificates.

In spite of the equal footing I had been given with everyone else, I was completely intimidated. I knew about the idiot within me, and I was sure there was no way I could hide or disguise it. I deeply dreaded being caught with the idiot exposed.

Normal school set exceptionally high expectations for study. The pace was accelerated and peak performance was demanded. We were considered the cream of the crop of high school graduates, and we were to produce work that matched that standard.

Everything was done in English without exception. I found
it difficult to talk when called upon in class, for I was self-conscious about my obvious German accent. There was no stigma
attached to this, however, because at that time Saskatchewan
was made up of many ethnic groups all speaking their native
languages. People in my class spoke with French accents,
Norwegian accents and Ukrainian accents.

My fear of being discovered was most pronounced in my
educational psychology class. I knew little about psychology,
yet I suddenly had the morbid fear that whatever was wrong
with me, whatever this error in my personality was, it would
be found out in this class. I developed a phobic reaction to the
class which resulted in my blushing.

I had blushed ever since elementary school when I was so
terrified of the teacher that I would turn crimson red whenever anyone in the class was blamed for anything. As a result
I was often identified as the guilty one even if I had been
completely innocent.

My psychology instructor noticed that whenever she taught
on any subject related to any kind of defect or abnormality, I
would start blushing. She kept me after nearly every class to
talk to me and reassure me that the subject she was talking
about had nothing to do with me. It was merely information
to be studied and not personal knowledge about me. She then
asked if she could do anything to help me. I asked to be put
at the very back of the classroom where there would be no one
behind me. Then, if I did start blushing, my embarrassment
would not be compounded by the fear of being seen doing it.

She quickly agreed, but continued to talk with me after
classes. This was the first time I came anywhere close to a
counseling experience. I remember it warmly as being very
consoling, that I was being guided through a particular crisis.
This was the most I had experienced anyone caring for me.

I passed all my subjects, but the experience had exhausted
me emotionally. With great pride I received my certificate at
the end of the eight weeks and was told I was prepared to

accept a one-room school, teaching eight grades in all subject areas. I was twenty years old, eight weeks out of high school and certified to teach in the Saskatchewan Public Schools.

6.

The Idiot Attempts to Teach

I began teaching at Montford School, located in the Swift Current Mennonite Reserve, only weeks after completing my first summer session of normal school. The area had not fully developed into a village, although all the students were Mennonite and spoke Low German. Their English was halting, broken and fragmented, and mine was not that much better. I discovered, however, that while teaching this class to speak English, I was learning it myself. After several months of systematically thinking through each sentence before speaking, I realized that I no longer thought in Low German and then translated that to English. Now I was actually thinking in English and then speaking it. It was a great personal victory to speak English continuously for the first time in my life.

I had nineteen students in grades one through eight. Each day I prepared sixty-four lesson plans—eight subjects for each of the eight grades. From dismissal time until dark I prepared lessons, putting as much as I could on the blackboards to instruct the students and direct them in their textbook and workbook assignments. After supper in my teacherage I returned to my books.

Without a vehicle, with the nearest neighbor a half mile away and no town within four miles, I spent my days and nights alone except for the time I was with the students in class. It was a bleak, isolated existence.

Learning to speak adequate English continued to be difficult for me; in addition I was persistently haunted by my inability to spell. So I wrote everything on the blackboard either before the students arrived or after they left. I copied all words from a dictionary or textbook to make sure that I had spelled every word correctly.

If I had to use the blackboard while teaching I was always fearful that I was not spelling properly. So I refused to write words. I drew diagrams as illustrations rather than write out facts. I sometimes wrote the first letter of the word on the board and had the students fill in the correct letters. I used every way I could imagine to avoid being caught with my inability to spell.

Remembering the students' names was another dilemma for me. Again I had to devise a gimmick to keep from being discovered. On my desk I kept a seating chart. When I was ready to begin teaching the next grade I simply walked to my desk, read the names to myself and looked at each child. That was usually sufficient to get me through the lesson. If I became uncertain I casually made a trip to my desk and checked the chart again.

To compound my problems in this school I discovered that the previous teacher had been a choral director and music teacher. He had taught these rural school students to sing like a choir. Apparently he had spent much of every day in music instruction and practice, which he enjoyed, rather than in academic subjects which he did not enjoy. Almost all the students had learned to play one or more musical instruments, as well as sing in beautiful harmony.

I came without any ability to sing or lead music, intimidated by the mere thought of it. Because I could offer nothing in the way of music direction I turned over the task of leading the singing to one of the eighth-grade girls who was particularly talented in music. What resulted was a major loss of face for me throughout the district.

Whatever happened in the classroom quickly spread around the community. Anything I did, any error I made, became news that travelled to other villages as well, so that whenever I went home to visit my parents I got a regular update of the gossip circuit's news about this twenty-year-old, baby-faced, first-time teacher. And much of it was negative. My deficits were widely known: my blushing (which happened there, too), my inability to sing or direct music, my spelling mistakes, and my terrible problem with remembering the students' names, especially when I met them outside the classroom.

As much as these items were talked about I knew that the community's primary expectations of the teacher were concerned with maintaining discipline, keeping the students in class the prescribed number of hours and teaching them basic reading, writing and arithmetic skills.

Since I was especially strong in mathematics the students progressed much farther in this area than they ever had before. And though I avoided oral reading myself I had received excellent training in the instruction of reading and felt able to teach it.

Student performance, however, was poor. Many of the students, especially the boys, could hardly read, were poor spellers and seemed confused and bewildered in the classroom. I recognized the similarity to my own elementary school performance, but I assumed it was all part of the Old Colony package. We were of another culture and another language, peasant communities trying to grapple with the English language. I treated the students kindly, in a low-keyed manner. In fact the community felt that I did not maintain a strict enough discipline. But my own emotional scars kept me from being the austere, power-wielding schoolmaster they expected.

There was one exception, however. Three students, who had obviously been strapped by previous teachers, continually tormented and defied me, testing my strength and credibility as a teacher. Finally, when they had challenged me to the limits of my tolerance, I snapped. Within seconds those three boys were down in the basement, receiving the strappings which they, and the community, had been asking for. I won a lot of affirmation for this action and it was quickly fed into the pipeline that I had finally used the approved treatment for classroom control. The behavior of those three boys immediately improved. In fact the atmosphere and attitude of the whole class grew markedly better, for I had finally shown that I could be an "authentic" teacher.

The local school board, made up of fathers of some of the students, met several times in special sessions that year to try to reconcile what they heard from their children about the classroom with their expectations of me, and with their obligation to the district school unit. No one ever talked to me directly about these meetings and I was never sure of their content, but I got some clues from the students whose fathers were members.

Twice during that year the District Superintendent visited my school. Prompted by complaints from the community he arrived unannounced and silently slipped into the back of the classroom. Each time he sat and observed for several hours, then walked out without saying a word.

Those visits were extremely intimidating for me. I was dumbfounded and almost speechless in his presence. Sputtering with a thick tongue in my mouth I tried to present myself as a competent English-speaking teacher. The expression on his face told me my performance was poor.

As the school year drew to a close I received a letter from the Swift Current School Unit informing me that my tenure at the Montford School had been terminated. When I read the letter I did not know what the word "terminated" meant. I needed a dictionary to tell me that I was fired. To this day I still wince whenever I see that word.

7.

The Idiot Gets Caught

*M*y first attempt at being a schoolteacher had ended in failure. I was devastated but, at the same time, believed it was the penalty I had to pay for my peasant background and the tremendous odds I faced in breaking into an English academic system.

I returned to normal school for my second summer session and tackled the teacher-training courses, receiving affirmations for my performance.

Peter found a new teaching assignment in a four-classroom school in Hague, just north of Saskatoon. He had already made a name for himself as an innovative teacher in a nearby town. Being his identical twin, a Mennonite and a graduate of Rosthern Junior College with high honors, I was hired without an interview, sight unseen.

This was the year my language disabilities and my attempts to disguise them publicly collided. Hague was one of the most literate small communities in Saskatchewan. It was a community that represented class. It had been a Mennonite village at one time, but now had a railway station, grain elevators, a grocery store, hardware store and even a physician; it had moved beyond its humble origins. The community demanded quality education from its school system and received it.

This was the place where my experiment at being normal failed miserably. I spent the entire year in a relentless program of disguising my handicaps, living in dread of being exposed. I feared that the idiot would be revealed, that possibly I was mentally ill. I was afraid that my Old Colony Mennonite background would be uncovered and I would be shamed by these higher-class people.

The outskirts of Hague were encircled by huts filled with families from nearby Old Colony villages who had been unable to buy land and now served as menial laborers for the people in town. Favorite jokes began with something like, "Did you hear the one about Henry Wiens from the village of Gnadenfeld who. . ." Uproarious laughter always followed, for everyone knew all the subtle implications that made the story so funny. But I sat quietly listening, fully aware that Henry Wiens could be my fifth cousin.

The shame I already felt about my inadequate spelling, my inability to sing, my poor speech and my blushing created internal terrors that paralyzed me. I knew I did not belong in that town or in that classroom. The students spoke better English than I did and I had nothing to teach them. Who was I anyway, pretending I could be a teacher?

In the classroom I utilized all my gimmicks. The record player led the singing of "God Save the King" while I mouthed the words. I continued to put written work on the blackboard when the students were gone, using my ever-present dictionary to correct every word. A sympathetic student sitting near the front of the class often quietly and unobtrusively corrected my poor speech, which was hard to hide.

I found no comfort in my rented room when the school day was over. Located above a cafe, it was shabby, furnished with a sagging couch that also served as the bed, a kitchen chair and a tiny desk. I hung my clothes on nails in the wall or kept them in my suitcase on the floor.

The cafe was the only eating place in the little town, and the blaring juke box was drowned out only by the loud voices and laughter that often filled the room. Shouts of "Come and get it, your hamburger is done!" and the rank, greasy odors creeping up the stairway just outside my door were constant reminders of my dismal situation. Often I stood at the one

window, staring out onto the main street, wondering why I
was there.

After several months I had a growing sensation that the
prison-like cell above the smelly cafe and the emotional incar-
ceration of the classroom were going to engulf me. I was sure
that all my terror and desperation would soon culminate in
one grand disaster, a psychotic break. Then I, and everyone
else, would be convinced that I never should have left the
village. I would be doomed to the life of an illiterate peasant
and resign myself to a farmyard of my own in some village and
a quarter-section of land.

I had flung myself against life's barricades over and over
again. Somehow they had all given in, but I was never sure
that the next time *I* would not crumble. If I returned home I
would have to face the sneers of my friends. After all, I had
had the audacity to assume I was better than they and could
make it by getting an education.

Lying on my couch I remembered isolated teaching experiences that had worked, when I knew I was a good teacher. I
could conceptualize scientific, historical or literary events and
hold the students spellbound; I could diagram and illustrate
things to amaze them. There had always been older girls in
the class who supported me wholeheartedly and came to my
rescue when I fumbled. Sometimes Agnes, the principal's
daughter, got quietly out of her seat and sneaked to the board
to change the spelling of words before the others noticed.
Sylvia, whose father was chairman of the school board, joined
her at recess in examining the blackboard and fixing any
errors.

Many times, though, I got caught with one of my excruciatingly embarrassing errors. At moments like that I experienced life as a perfect dichotomy. Inwardly, I was a person
who had to hide from everyone else. Outwardly I presented
myself with confidence. The farther I moved ahead academically, the greater the gap between the two. The closer I
returned to the village, the more the two parts became one.
Only in the village, lost in the street crowd, speaking my

native language, was I totally together again.

Lying in the darkness, with only the dull light from the
street coming in my window, I could slip into my fantasy and
escape the day and the noise and smells from below. I hated
to go to sleep at night, for then I lost my only peace. Daytime
came too quickly with the never-ending danger of being discovered.

"Why am I doing this?" I asked myself continually. "Why
do I punish myself like this? Why do I assume there's an
answer somewhere up ahead?"

I knew the wondrous pleasure of leaping into new worlds of
awareness, even if they came only with pain. I had known
enough of these worlds to believe that they would come again
and again, even if I did not know when and how.

On my wall hung evidence of just such an experience. When
I felt most hopeless I would sit and stare at it until it carried
me in a victorious leap forward. Only a few months before in
a creative art class at Saskatoon Normal School I had given
expression to this mixture of feelings. The art teacher was a
young vivacious woman who believed that every person was
an artist. In her enthusiasm she convinced students to come
out of hiding and express themselves artistically.

Our final assignment for the course was to take a three-by-
six-foot sheet of paper and, using abstract shapes, designs and
any type of media and textures we desired, to communicate
our life.

I knew I had artistic abilities but I had never expressed
myself like this before. I abandoned myself to the project.
Huge, black, grotesque shapes appeared in the foreground,
gnarled together, twisting and turning in bitter combat. Farther back the shapes were less tangled until, in the far center
background, were colors of gold and red, pure flames flickering
peacefully.

As my work evolved the instructor often asked me about it.
Although I could not explain it, she smiled as if I were proof
of all she was trying to teach.

When the finished product was presented to the class for

analysis, the teacher and the students commented that they were both deeply distressed and overwhelmed by the contrast of the grotesque, evil objects intertwined in unresolved combat with the distant scenes portraying peace, rest and perfection. The picture hung in the hallway for the remainder of the summer and I observed clusters of students gathering around it, debating its meaning and wondering who its creator, "A. Schmitt," was. I wondered, too, who he was, where he was going.

Now, as I stared at it on the wall of my dingy room, I became certain I would find an answer to life somewhere, sometime, no matter what was happening to me now. But would the solution come too late? Would the present stress be too great?

Maybe this is what happened to the parents of those poor, tattered, torn Old Colony children in my classroom. They had left the villages to find another life but had gotten only as far as the shanties on the edge of town. There they crumbled because they had gone beyond the horizon of the world they could conquer.

I felt a secret affinity with these children. We had a common heritage; some were even my distant relatives. The Old Colony grapevine had already identified me as the grandson of Bernhard Schmitt, a founding settler and teacher in the German school in the village of Aberdeen, only a few miles away. Generally I hated to have this known in town, but one day a small, emaciated, almost illiterate child whose parents had recently moved to town came to me secretly after school. She had something important to tell me, she said. Then she whispered that her parents had told her she was related to me. She named my great-aunts and -uncles who still lived in Aberdeen. She was obviously delighted and probably saw this as a thin thread of hope to which she could hold; maybe she could even learn enough to pass her grade. I knew that the little she had learned was in spite of her parents' opposition to education. I was supposed to rescue her and her peers from the penalty they were paying for their illiteracy.

On the other side was Abraham Derksen, a sixteen-year-old

sixth grader. He had failed as often as was legally permitted and had just been promoted out of the lower classroom to end his disruption there. Now he was assigned to mine.

He, too, knew my origin and muttered slurs to me about my background. Then, to add insult to injury, he murmured them in Low German which he and, thanks to him, everyone else knew I understood perfectly. His size, almost six feet tall and overweight, gave him another edge on me, and his assaults got worse and worse. Finally I was forced to admit my defeat before all the children by seeking help from the principal in the classroom across the hall.

Abraham was permanently dismissed from school, which was probably what he and his parents wanted anyway. Even though it was good for the classroom the experience was too personally defeating for me to feel any relief. I knew how painful it was to be at the bottom of the social ladder, to be the constant butt of jokes. I had heard derogatory laughter, fun being made of the outdated, primitive lifestyles of us peasants. I had to choose between joining with the laughter and denying my own culture, or honestly identifying with the victim of the moment and betraying my disguise.

I believe Abraham knew my dilemma and was secretly pleading with me to discard my front and face who I was courageously. I think then he would have stopped acting out. He would even have thrown his weight on my side to help with classroom discipline. But since he perceived me to be a fake he believed he had the right to ridicule me unmercifully. In the end I had to have him removed so that I could save face.

Reports of this incident reached the ears of the school board at the same time that they were meeting to consider my status as a teacher. They discussed the incident at great length and saw it as failure on my part to maintain classroom discipline, one of the strongest attributes of a good teacher in the prairie school system. I also found out that my conspicuous handicaps were discussed in detail. They knew them all since their children were in my classroom. The facts must have been reported with great amusement around the family supper tables. "Imagine a teacher who can't spell! When he writes on the blackboard he makes so many mistakes that the students have to correct him. And then he blushes beet red! And imagine. . .he's an 'Alkalenier'! How could anyone from a village get a teaching license! And why didn't anyone know this before he was hired?"

The chairman of the school board spoke for them all when he announced, "It is impossible for us to carry on with this teacher when our children know more than he does."

They felt betrayed, shortchanged. "How could we have been so taken in? How could we have missed it?" they asked themselves, baffled. They had a responsibility as school directors. This was too close a call with ignorance and I symbolized that ignorance.

They placed a call to K.G. Toews, my high school principal, to see if I had really graduated and, if so, how he could explain my poor performance. Mr. Toews remembered me well, described to them my achievements and acknowledged that he had written a letter of recommendation. But he, too, was totally baffled by my performance as a teacher as it was described to him.

I received a letter from the secretary of the school board terminating my services. I had done my very best, but in the end I was exposed and I was undone. Fired again.

Many years after my graduation from Rosthern Junior College I was invited to come back and deliver the commencement address. I was thrilled to accept the invitation. I saw it as my chance to make peace with my Rosthern experience, my time of feeling so bitterly inferior. I was returning with five college and graduate degrees and six published books. Because of speaking widely, I had become a sort of public figure, at least within the Mennonite media world. I felt ready to meet many of the people in my graduating class.

I entitled my speech, "Life Can Begin Again, and Again." Basing it on the subject of the transformation of the human personality, I spoke about my belief that every human being has the built-in capacity to make enormous leaps forward. I told my story, knowing that this belief was central to explaining what had happened to the inadequate, defective person who had attended that school and was now returning as the honored commencement speaker.

After the speech I was mobbed by classmates and others, including a group from nearby Hague who were incensed at the action of the school board in firing someone who went on to get a doctorate and write six books. I told them about my learning disability and why the board had to do what it did.

I knew that two of my fellow teachers from that year at Hague were still living and I decided to visit each of them. One was Lillian Dueck who taught grades three, four and five, while I taught grades six, seven and eight. She remembered the students' comments concerning all my spelling errors, mixed-up words and incorrect grammar. She told me how much she had pitied me.

"You couldn't spell the simplest words," she said. "At times I didn't know what to do about it, it was so awful. I could not talk to you about it because I didn't want to hurt you. I simply felt sorry for you. I often wondered how it was possible for you to write a book. Are you the same person that the students made fun of because you knew less than they did?"

She told me how she had tried to tell the students not to mock me, but to help me in whatever way they could. I credit Agnes' and Sylvia's helpfulness to Lillian's coaching.

Rudy Penner, the principal and teacher of grades nine, ten and eleven, had another vivid memory from that year. Rudy and I had agreed that he would teach music to my class while I taught agriculture to his. I do not know why I assumed I could teach a course in agriculture, except that I had taken it myself in grades eleven and twelve and I could read the textbook. I did know that I could not teach music!

One day at the end of agriculture class I wrote seven questions on the board as the assignment for the next time. Since I had not prepared ahead I did it from memory. The class was watching so I could not check my spelling or my grammar.

After class we switched rooms, and Rudy immediately noticed the written work on the blackboard. His eye caught all my errors—misspellings, words out of order, letter reversals, incorrect grammar. He marched to the front of the class, took a piece of colored chalk and, with the entire class watching, dramatically and emphatically marked every error and corrected each mistake.

Then he turned and glared at the class. "Who of you did this?" he demanded.

There was no response. All the students were perfectly silent. He asked again, insisting that the person responsible for such inferior work be identified. In the eerie silence that followed Rudy realized that none of the students had done it. By the pain hanging in the room he knew that it had been done by me.

Rudy was overcome by such intense pity that he nearly cried. He silently picked up a brush and slowly and deliberately erased everything from the board until he had regained his composure. Then he proceeded immediately into the next lesson without any comment.

No student ever talked to him about it, nor did he ever discuss it with anyone else until he told me thirty-three years later.

8.

The Idiot as Sinner

As my life seemed to be crumbling around me at Hague, I began to define my problem as spiritual. My life in the village had been nonreligious. Our identification as Mennonites had no spiritual or religious connotation. When the official church hierarchy and its devout followers had moved to Mexico two years before my birth, the remnant who remained and occupied most of the homesteads practiced no religion. During the eighteen years I lived at home I never saw the inside of a church.

On a few occasions Bible-toting evangelists arrived and attempted to "save sinners" like me. I held their words at a distance, thinking they might have some answer to my problem out there somewhere, but I saw no connection. A few of the villagers had salvation experiences, and they became ever-present reminders of the path one ought to follow. My Uncle Bill, only five years older than I and someone whom I admired greatly, was one of these.

Being a Mennonite school, Rosthern Junior College conducted chapel services, taught Bible and church history, and required Sunday worship attendance. All this had only a negative impact on me because it aggravated my painful rejection by the village caste system. When I compared the dramatic change that the "new birth" experience had made in Uncle Bill's life, I concluded that it obviously had not happened to anyone at Rosthern. Although I enjoyed the Bible and church history courses I saw nothing life-changing about religion.

It was not until my world was disintegrating at Hague that

I began considering otherwise. There had to be answers to my bewildering questions.

Two months after my arrival in town I received an invitation to Sunday dinner at the home of the Peter Schellenberg family. I felt highly honored for they owned the only hardware store in town and lived in one of the finest houses. No doubt they ranked high on the social ladder; the central location of their property conveyed such a message.

Shortly into our visit they asked me about my living accommodations and the quality of food at the greasy spoon. It was almost unbearable, I confessed, which they had already concluded. Then they extended an invitation that would change the rest of my life.

Mrs. Schellenberg, with deep and sincere concern, asked if I would like to move into their house. They had an extra bedroom, she offered, I could eat with the family, and she would do my laundry for the price I now paid for my present hole in the wall. Her generosity and hospitality simply overwhelmed me, and I gratefully accepted.

Mrs. Schellenberg and I talked intensively. I learned that she, too, had come from a peasant background identical to mine. She believed that no matter how well one was educated or married or succeeded, one never lost the stigma of those origins. She had never escaped that shame.

In the months that followed, Mrs. Schellenberg became my sounding board as I talked aloud about my daily struggles at school. She helped carry those difficulties with me, representing love to me in the purest, most unselfish form I had every known. In addition I would discover that the holes in my socks had been darned and missing buttons had been sewn on my shirts in the clean laundry pile on my bed. I began to see that the source of her unconditional love came from her deep commitment to God. Her freedom to love came from her certainty of God's love for her.

Before long I followed the Schellenbergs to church. I was curious to know where such selflessness had its origin. Sunday after Sunday I heard the message of faith proclaimed, and six days in between I received the fruit of that message from Mrs. Schellenberg.

When I opened a conversation with her about it she was quite willing to share her faith in a simple way. As far as she was concerned the "new birth" she had experienced made her equal, in Christ, to anyone. Any stigmatizing she had received, even from a fellow church member, had no effect on her. It only meant that the gospel message had not been understood by those who assigned higher stations to themselves.

This unadulterated Christianity was too attractive for me to reject. I had to pursue it further. Until then I had always seen Christianity tainted by personal ambition, social status and prejudice. The hypocrisy that declared me as the sinner to be saved, yet rejected me from the lives of those proclaiming the message, was far more powerful than the invitation to accept this faith understanding.

When on one Sunday an announcement was made that a catechism class was forming for people seeking membership, I felt a deep pull on my heart. Several days later I sat on a kitchen stool watching Mrs. Schellenberg iron my shirts. She had a peaceful smile on her face, completely at ease that she was doing this work for the glory of God. I asked her about the class. She assured me that I would be welcome and would find it rewarding, but she urged me no further.

The first class began the following Sunday night and I was there. Catechism had been a tradition among Mennonites for hundreds of years. Membership in the church required instruction in the basic beliefs, and tradition required memorizing the answers to 218 questions asked in the catechism, all in the High German language. True to form, I could not memorize; therefore I could not learn even the first lesson.

The pastor provided me with an English translation but it helped very little. I spent hours at night and on weekends with Mrs. Schellenberg asking me questions, but I could not retain the answers.

To add insult to injury I was in a class with several girls

from Old Colony backgrounds, all of whom had dropped out
of school before completing the elementary grades. They, with
so little education, memorized the entire catechism in the
German language, while I, the schoolteacher, could not master the first lesson.

In spite of this disgrace I found myself, for the first time,
studying the scriptures with a desperate hunger for an answer
to my problems with life. After just one lesson taught by Rev.
Henry Klassen I asked to see him alone. In a very simple
ritual in a small cloakroom he led me through a faith commitment ceremony. That moment made an indelible mark on my
life that has never gone away. For ever after I have gone back
to that scene as the birthplace of my spiritual self. Just prior
to that I was completely overwhelmed by my lost condition.
Immediately afterwards I was absolutely sure I had met my
God, Savior and Lord whom I would never betray and who
would never abandon me. This was a lifelong contract, never
to be broken. It remains so today. Although my spiritual
journey has taken many turns in the road I have never really
doubted its beginning and its authenticity.

I defined my "new birth" experience in absolute terms. The
first day back in my classroom I gave my testimony to my
sixth-, seventh- and eighth-graders. It made no difference to
me whether this was appropriate or not for a public school
classroom. Tears streamed down my face as I told of my
newfound faith in Christ. The classroom was dumbstruck.

One week later I was fired. I knew it was because of my
poor teaching and not due to the religious nuisance I had made
of myself in the classroom. I considered it the Lord's leading
and decided quickly that I needed to follow a new calling.

In order to devote full time to biblical studies I enrolled at
Canadian Mennonite Bible College in Winnipeg, Manitoba.
This was a total faith venture since I did not have the money
to pay my way. That did not matter, for I was now in God's
hands.

9.

In His Steps, But Ashamed

Now that I committed my life to Jesus Christ I was ready to follow, no matter the way or price asked. I had been freed from a burden of spiritual guilt only a few months before and my obligation was now to repay it in gratitude and service for Christ.

I read, with total absorption, the old novel, *In His Steps,* and was just as eager as the members of that fictional congregation to follow in Jesus' steps, whatever that required. Unfortunately I had no idea what it meant.

To begin my journey I went to the Canadian Mennonite Bible College (CMBC) on Wellington Crescent, a prestigious location in Winnipeg, Manitoba. Immediately I discovered dramatic class distinctions at their worst.

I had expected everyone to be as perfect a Christian as the novel described; every person would be walking "in his steps" and I would simply fall in step with them. After all, they had been members of this mystical body of Christ for a long time so they must know the way. I, as a babe recently born into it, expected them to nurture me. Very quickly, though, I was engulfed with the sense that I did not fit. I was ashamed of myself. My self-identity as an ignorant farm boy from an Old Colony village reemerged to torment me again. The barriers that Christ was supposed to have broken down were still in place, even between me and my fellow believers.

This fact bewildered me throughout that year. How could these people, the students and faculty of this small Bible

college, proclaim the message of faith and prepare themselves
to be more effective witnesses of this great salvation and
freedom, while I, as a brand new member, felt so alienated?

Just weeks before being fired at Hague the chairman of the
school board had sold me my first Bible. It was large and cost
more than I earned in one month of teaching. But it was
precious to me. From the very first day at CMBC I carried it
with me from class to class. The thumbnail index helped me
find the scripture references which the instructors tossed so
rapidly to the class. It still took me quite a while to locate the
correct tab, then to proceed to the right chapter and verse.

To make my biblical ignorance less obvious I sat in the back
of the room whenever I could. One day, while waiting for class
to begin, a fellow student leaned back and, taking my Bible
from me, began exclaiming loudly about the enormity of it.
Soon a large circle of students got into the act. Someone
concluded that the only place he had ever seen one like it was
permanently set on a pulpit. Another commented that I must
be rather confident of getting a pulpit to have already purchased a pulpit Bible. With the snickering laughter that
followed I was shattered.

Suddenly in my mind I went back to the village that I never
should have left. My skill at escaping a painful situation stood
ready to serve me again. But now I was at a Bible school. I
had come here to be liberated from my bondage to the past.
My "born again" experience was to have set me free. Yet here
were other "born again," liberated people laughing at me and
my Bible, the symbol of my victory.

My old self-condemnations were ready to erupt, but now I
had developed a new skill. I took Jesus with me into my shell
and simply talked to him. I believed he understood me, no
matter what went on around me. With him I was safe.

During this year I developed severe headaches. I found
relief only in sleeping. Since the dormitory was in the same
building as the classrooms I could easily slip into bed at any
time. I would take my Bible with me and curl up under the
covers, head and all. I could fall asleep instantly no matter

how bad the headache. I fantasized that, in my conversation with Jesus, he was calling me home to be with him. I died each time I fell asleep.

Looking back I am sure that my headaches were due to the irreconcilable tension between my wanting the world to be perfect and not finding it so. In my attempts to escape my horrible self-image, my acute self-consciousness and my entire shameful past, I took several trips to heaven every day.

One night several months into the semester I was drifting around the center city area and came upon a building with a sign identifying it as the Winnipeg School of Art. The lights were on so I went in. A friendly receptionist eagerly showed me around. She took me into the studios where classes of all types and levels were being taught. I was impressed with the way the instructors moved from one student to another, giving encouragement and individualized instruction. I was warmly greeted and invited to enroll. The school offered evening classes, reasonable tuition and had an immediate opening, so I quickly signed up.

I felt at home from the beginning. I loved experimenting in the whole variety of media—charcoal, oils and water colors— and I eagerly tried my hand at sketching scenery, portraits and figures. I was in my glory. The students were all absorbed in their own projects, so little social interaction was expected of me. The instructors were competent, self-assured and superb teachers. Classes were small, so I received a lot of attention and instruction.

Here there was no battle for me to fight. There were no class distinctions, and I had no preconceived notions or expectations regarding other people's behavior or responses to me. My self-imposed crises at CMBC had made it necessary for me to escape to a secular setting where I felt unconditionally accepted.

Yet even here I felt compelled to have my religiosity show. In a portrait class I sketched the model but adapted the clothing and the background so that it became a portrait of Christ. When I finished the piece I brought it back to CMBC where it eventually was hung on the wall of the chapel. Soon afterwards I was asked to teach a Saturday morning art class at CMBC which was attended by students, faculty and members of the community. Before long I was invited to design the logo for the school, which is still being used, as well as to do the design and layout for the yearbook.

I spent my days preparing for my art classes as well as pursuing my regular studies.

From that point on, I knew there was an artist within me. That new self-image began to legitimize my acute sense of feeling different. Artists were expected to be different—introverted, self-absorbed and misunderstood. That described who I was.

As good as this experience was, it proved to be merely a side trip. I still had to deal with the much more practical issue of how I, as a uniquely different person, would find a place in the world, support myself and conquer the idiot. Art gave me momentary comfort but no long-range solution.

At CMBC I finally found a person whom I trusted. Rev. Beno Toews had an office just off the main reading room of the library and there I found a safe refuge. When entering or exiting the office, though, one was always in full view of the other students in the library. I am sure my vivid memory of that fact is due to the embarrassment I felt at being seen there so often. But inside the office Beno Toews spent time with me that I still recall with a warm glow. We read scripture and prayed together, and I know he was concerned about my welfare. I do not know if I told him of my past or of my present struggles, but he must have known I needed a haven and he created one. I often wonder if his caring for me directed me to a vocation of caring.

At that time my only reason for being at this Bible college was to learn to know the Bible. For many others it was a stepping-stone to the best pulpits in the Mennonite churches of Canada. I had no such goal, but study the Bible I did. As a total beginner I was not even sure of the difference between the Old and New Testaments. The introductory course guided me into the scriptures, where time and again I read with amazement the accounts that all my classmates had known from childhood. I followed the footsteps of Jesus through the gospels and drew detailed charts to illustrate them. Likewise I followed the Apostle Paul on his missionary journeys, drawing maps which showed where his epistles had been written and the churches to which they were sent. All this gave me not only great satisfaction, but good grades as well.

I had not known that the Bible could even be understood, yet by the end of the year I could open to any part and have some sense of what it was about. While I did not know how to deal with the emotions that continuously assaulted me, I knew how to study. I may have been a thoroughly distressed human being, but I was determined not to be an ignorant Christian.

As in the past my inability to sing was a source of humiliation for me at CMBC. Here, every single student was a member of the choir except me, and they rehearsed in the same building we all occupied. During choir practice I often wandered aimlessly through the hall, listening to the beautiful voices blending in harmony. Here I learned to appreciate choral singing of hymns, chorales and the great oratorios, especially Handel's *Messiah*. Every glorious note of that music rang clearly in my head and found expression somewhere deep inside me.

Not only was CMBC known for its music, it was also a mecca for matchmaking. Had it been created as a place for future pastors to find well informed Christian wives? Everyone seemed to find a partner here.

Not to be left out I gathered all the courage I had one evening and escorted a young lady home from a skating party. There was nothing special about her except that she was alone on the ice as couples began departing. At the end of the walk I suggested that I could meet her again at the next all-school skating event.

To this she abruptly responded, "I prefer that you not. I do not wish to be identified with you."

I returned to the skating rink on occasion, but for the remainder of the year I skated solo, around and around the rink, ashamed and alone. The haunting feeling that I was a defective human being kept coming back over and over again. I spent a lot of time talking to God as I skated. I was absolutely sure that I belonged to him. His fascinating story made such perfect sense and his effective redemption was so real that those mortals around me could not take away my peace with God. I had no problem with God; it was with people that things kept going wrong.

My most brutal experience occurred near the end of the school year. Intended, I am sure, as a simple prank, it proved to be ghastly for me. Instead of pajamas I wore a long, old-fashioned nightshirt to bed. Mrs. Schellenberg had made it for me while I was living in Hague and had convinced me that it was far better than any other form of nightwear. Made of thick flannel it was as long as a floor-length dress. I loved the elderly Mrs. Schellenberg and this gown represented all the love and caring she had shown me the previous year, the year of my great conversion.

As usual I had gone to bed early that night, maybe because of a headache or maybe just to avoid the social contact of the dormitory. Suddenly a group of guys burst into my room, yanked the covers back, pulled my gown off over my head and dashed out. Hearing the uproar up and down the hall I knew someone was wearing it and a mock wedding ceremony was being performed. No doubt my nightgown was the bridal gown and the fellows in striped pajamas were the groom and the preacher. Gales of laughter reached my ears but I lay curled up under the bedcovers sobbing uncontrollably.

"Is this how a one-year-old babe in Christ is treated by his brothers?" I kept asking God who, I knew, was still there with me.

One beautiful spring night I walked all the way from Wellington Crescent, across the bridge into center city and back again. It was a long way, but I wanted to settle in my head exactly what this year had meant to me. Why had I was excruciatingly lonely and horribly ashamed of myself. I could still speak only the Low German of the peasants, not the High German language that was used here. I had been excused from the choir, the pride of this school, because I was an outsider who came from a background so simple that his people chanted instead of singing in four-part harmony. It was obvious that I had accidently strayed into the wrong school. But where should I go? I wanted so much to live my life for Christ, but how was I to find my way when I was continually buffeted about by my mentors?

Halfway back, along a winding, tree-lined street, I was so engulfed by a sensation that I stopped in frozen posture. I felt God all around me and Jesus Christ there too, so close I could speak directly to them both.

I broke into tears and began pleading, "Take me home, Lord Jesus. I don't fit in this world. I am no good, unfit, useless and I can't handle it anymore." I was crying loudly, begging over and over again, but it was past midnight, no one was around and I'm sure no one heard me.

There seemed to be no other answer to my life. I had met Jesus a year ago and made a commitment to a way of life, but it had not worked. I was not going to abandon that commitment, but since it did not fit in this world I wanted to go where it did fit—home to heaven.

I have no idea how long it was before I came out of that trance-like experience; many blocks later I discovered that I was back at the college.

For the rest of the year I merely went through the motions of doing my class work. I did just enough to earn my credits; otherwise I had already departed. Somewhere in that maze out there I believed there was a way to walk in Jesus' steps, but I had not found it here.

10.

The Wilderness Experiment—The Idiot is Ignored

*M*y Winnipeg educational experience was a dead end. After one year of classes I was as much without direction as when I started. Then I received a letter from my brother Pete. He had just taken a school at Carrot River, Saskatchewan, in the far northland, ten miles short of the end of civilization. It was a two-room log school and Pete wanted me to join him. I could even live with him and his wife and forthcoming child. It was an offer I could not refuse, so, again relying on Pete and coattailing on his credentials, I had a job.

Carrot River was an Old Colony settlement at the far reaches of civilization. The parents of these students had fled to this northern region to escape education, but the school system had caught up to them. A provincial school was built, and the children were required to attend.

The more devout of the Old Colony parents, however, found a way around the law by building shacks even farther north in the bushland and living there during the winters, too far from the schools to make attendance possible. Only in the summer months did they return to their main homes to do their farming.

Despite that, Pete and I arrived a month before the opening of school so that we could, with the school authorities' permission, enlarge the teachers' dwelling. Our plans called for an extension that would double the size of the tiny, two-room house, providing additional sleeping quarters, as well as a living and dining area. With no electricity, plumbing or telephone to install, we had a construction job similar to the farm buildings we had built as teenagers.

When the house was ready, Pete left for a brief period to bring his wife and newborn son back to join us in the wilderness.

The year proved to be a phenomenal success for me, as well as for Pete. Most of the families had known our grandfather who had been a German teacher in one of the villages farther south. A number of the parents of our students had been students of his, attending the German school for three months of each year for three years. This was the only type of education approved by the church, and our grandfather had been considered a good person and a capable and competent teacher. Thus, these parents were thrilled when we arrived. We were one of them.

That year not a single family moved north to the bushland for the winter but stayed on their farms and sent their children to school because they trusted us. When the superintendent of schools, of Mennonite background himself, came to visit, he was astonished at the number of children attending the school. They had, literally, come out of the woods.

Most of these students had never been outside their immediate community, had never seen a town, a telephone, electricity or running water, paved streets or sidewalks. So whenever they had studied their lessons adequately we rewarded them by telling stories—stories from civilization, such as "Life in the City of Saskatoon, or Swift Current, or Moose Jaw." They wanted to know what the rest of the world was like and listened to us by the hours after they had learned their lessons. The classrooms were utterly quiet, and the children's obedience reflected their parents' respect for us.

Late one night, as Pete and I were preparing our lessons by the light of a single kerosene lamp, an old man walked into the house without knocking. He stood in the doorway and solemnly announced, "I have chosen you boys to build the coffin for my wife. She died this morning."

We realized immediately that this was not a request; it was an honor bestowed. We followed him outside to unload the lumber, the lining and the paint into the rear of the classroom building. On the back side of a calendar page he sketched the size and shape of the coffin. She must have been a very large woman, but his only comment was that she had worked hard all the years of her life.

School was dismissed early the next day so that we could build the coffin. We finished at midnight and applied the second coat of paint as the students arrived the next morning. That evening we added the lining, padding, hinges and carrying grips.

The following morning the old man arrived with his truck, unannounced as before, and picked up the coffin. He examined it carefully, pronounced it acceptable and invited us to the funeral that afternoon and then for a light meal at his house afterwards.

We dismissed school at noon since everyone was expected at the funeral. The service was long and the eulogy retold the woman's entire life, emphasizing all the births and deaths that had preceded her. It ended with a final recognition of the "two schoolteacher carpenters who built such a fine coffin."

Sometime during that year, in spite of the success I was enjoying, an overwhelming urge began to rise in me. I needed to get back to college and complete my education. I dreaded the thought of being an elementary schoolteacher for the rest of my life. I could not accept that what I had experienced so far was all there was.

I began casting out in different directions. I considered the University of Saskatchewan, but it was too costly. I had heard through the grapevine that if one attended college in the United States it was rather easy to earn enough money to pay tuition while taking full-time classes. That seemed to be the only way I could complete my education and then come back to Saskatchewan with a college degree. But I knew no one who had crossed the border and entered college in the United States. I seemed insatiably driven, perhaps by the trauma of my early education experiences. I still had a huge unfinished agenda, and it appeared that the only way I could resolve that was to get more education. Secretly I believed that more education would eventually obliterate the unidentified idiot that had caused my earlier failures.

By the end of the school year at Carrot River I had only $400 to my name. With nothing more, and with my parents unable to give me even $10, I still insisted on going back to school. I resigned from my teaching position (the first time I could leave a job of my own accord), claiming that year victorious. I left everything behind, except what I could fit into my suitcases, and traveled into the unknown where nobody knew me.

11.

Across the Great Divide

I received the customary application materials from all the colleges to which I had inquired, along with form letters. But from Goshen College in Indiana I received a handwritten reply. The Dean of Students, Atlee Beachy, wrote to me, telling me he had taken a pack of applications along with him on vacation and, being without a typewriter or secretarial services, he had decided to spend his vacation writing to each of those applicants.

It was apparent from his letter that he had tried to understand the content of my application and my wish to use Goshen College to complete my education. He warmly and personally invited me to come. He even sent me train and bus schedules and offered to meet me at the bus terminal in Elkhart, Indiana. His was such a loving response, something I obviously needed so desperately, that I had to go to the place from which this invitation had come.

I was totally baffled by this foreign country and its strange educational system. The competent students who spoke English with such clarity and ease, coupled with my basic assumption that I was an inferior person, made me feel extremely self-conscious from the minute I arrived. I was ashamed of my inappropriate clothing; I did not know what kinds of mannerisms to use or how to present myself. I avoided being seen in public, apart from going to class, for quite a long time, staying in my room or hiding in the library, diligently studying.

Within a few days I began to see notices posted for one-day or weekend jobs, such as catching chickens or helping to clean out a barn or building. I accepted all I could, found rides out to the farms, and earned my first income. The pay was higher than any I had earned in Saskatchewan and within a few weeks I had earned enough to replace my entire wardrobe. I bought clothes that matched my fellow students' and threw everything else away in shame.

Selecting carpentry jobs over all others, I soon established myself as a carpenter with several local contractors. They let me work when I was able to, and I often took on projects that they did not want to do themselves, ones I could do at night and on Saturdays. Soon I was working a forty-hour week and earning a full-time salary while maintaining a full credit-hour schedule. I discovered I could earn my own living, pay my tuition and carry a full academic load. I believed I could make it in the American system.

I felt increasingly comfortable, also, with the group of Mennonites with which I was now associating. I found similarities between their way of thinking and the Old Colony background from which I had come. These Mennonites were humble and conservative, people whose Christianity was found not only in their words, but in the quality of their personal lives. I felt at home with this philosophy of life. Within a few months I knew that I would never return to Canada to live; I had finally found a community where I could belong.

I studied extremely hard, considerably more than the other students, but I needed to excel and it brought me great rewards. Instructors thought highly of me and I became friends with many of them. I wrote letters back to Saskatchewan filled with wonderful descriptions of my new life and the academic success I was experiencing.

There was one striking exception, however: chemistry. I had enrolled in Qualitative Analysis because I thought I had taken adequate chemistry in high school to be able to handle it. The course was taught by a professor whose teaching style resembled that of my high school chemistry teacher. I was soon inundated with facts and data that my brain was incapable of processing.

I simply could not handle the course. I went to see the professor a number of times, but he was geared much more to preparing medical students for their future careers than he was toward tutoring a stumbling student from another country. He made a deal with me: he would give me a passing grade if I would promise *not* to enroll in his next course, Quantitative Analysis. I promised. I passed with a D average and never came close to chemistry again.

One of my favorite courses was Zoology. It was taught by an elderly professor, S.W. Witmer, who had been on the faculty at Goshen for decades. He was a brilliant man, as well as kind, and formed close relationships with his students. This class required many skills that I knew were my assets. We had to draw diagrams, illustrated from our own dissections, with all anatomic parts named and labeled precisely. Even the printing we were to use was done according to a specific format. Since I excelled at illustrating and diagramming, as well as calligraphy, I received good grades in the course. My success in Zoology even sparked a secret yearning to pursue a career in medicine. But my dream of such a vocation was shattered forever by my encounter with chemistry.

I enrolled in as many literature and English courses as I could. I particularly loved Shakespeare and the chance to analyze all the characters and plots, whether tragedy, comedy or historical drama.

One literature course included works by Chaucer which I found, much to my amazement, that I was able to read with greater ease than the rest of the students in the class. I discovered that Middle English, Chaucer's language, and Low German both originated in the Old Saxon period of history among the Angles, Saxons and Jutes of northcentral Europe. The Angles and Saxons brought their languages with them when they invaded the British Isles, where they evolved into Low English and then Middle English. The language that remained behind in Europe evolved into Low German. Thus, many of the Middle English words that Chaucer used were identical to those in my native language.

Excitedly I noted each one in my textbook and then approached the instructor. He wanted me to explain the correlation that I had discovered since he was not acquainted with the Low German language. Not only could I pronounce the words for him in Low German, but because I knew the native language from which they had originated, I was able to define many words and the implied meanings of others, which he had not understood before. He asked me to explain to the class the correlation between Chaucer's Middle English and Low German, showing them as primitive languages with the same linguistic ancestry.

I particularly recall one sentence in Chaucer which describes an ailing elderly family member whose bed was "on top of the stove." This statement had always baffled the professor until I described the kind of heating system found in many of the primitive village homes. A large, earthen brick furnace, about six feet high and six feet long, was built in the center of the house. The house was designed so that the walls of the furnace were exposed to each room of the house. In one of the rooms the top of the furnace functioned as a shelf where blankets and other items were stored. Because it was a warm place, that shelf was made into a bed whenever anyone was ill. This type of heating system had been used for centuries in northern Europe and Russia and was recreated on the western Canadian prairies. Because my grandparents had such a stove, and I had climbed on the shelf myself, I knew exactly what Chaucer was describing from medieval England.

The opportunity to speak to a class called forth the best of my creativity, insight and thinking. It also proved to me that I could do college work and fed my growing sense that my brain worked, even at a superior level in certain specific, selected ways. At the same time I still experienced the dramatic, completely unexplainable opposite when I was totally incapacitated, as in chemistry class.

Music was highly valued at Goshen College, as it was at all Mennonite institutions, but it was not expected of me. Here there were so many other people making beautiful music that I was not stigmatized for my lack of participation. I attended chapel every day without coercion, relishing the music. It resonated profoundly in my inner being even though I could not make the sounds myself. I simply sat there inhaling the phenomenal strains of the great hymns as they were being sung. I frequently attended musical programs and concerts, letting the waves of music wash over me.

When my first year at Goshen College came to an end I felt successful, having proved that I could do college level work and survive in the United States. But I was at a crossroads. One year of college was all I needed to obtain a permanent teaching certificate in Canada. I could return there and teach for the rest of my life without ever having to take another course.

Yet I had already decided I would not go back. I had made my way here; I had found my element. There was nothing for me back in Saskatchewan.

12.

Greek Will Always Remain Greek to Me

*T*he spring of 1952 found me confused and without direction. I had experienced two enormous failures in trying to teach, having been fired twice and having succeeded only once. Furthermore, I left behind my identification with the Old Colony when I crossed the border between Canada and the United States. What was I to do; where was I to go?

Could I find my vocation in seminary? I did not necessarily want to prepare for the ministry but I had a compelling desire to study. It felt almost hypocritical that as a result of attending seminary the church might call me to so high an office as the ministry. I was reluctant to register.

I paid a visit to the office of Dean H.S. Bender. He looked over my credit hours, saw that the registrar had tabulated all my transfer credits and, calculating the courses I was taking at the time, said, "Why of course you are eligible to be admitted into the seminary next year. Why don't you enroll immediately?"

That sentence gave me both a stamp of approval on my life venture, as well as a visa to stay in the United States for three more years of graduate education. I could now see academic success ahead for me. The registrar's office had counted all the years of my Canadian education and given me more than two full years of college credit. With the year that I had just completed I could now overlap my final year in the Bachelor of Arts program with the first year of the graduate program.

And the Mennonite "Pope" had pronounced his blessing upon it.

Seminary seemed like the place where I could settle my unfinished personal, theological, denominational and intellectual agenda.

The same campus as the college where I had felt so at home now offered me a three-year graduate program to conquer. I would have access to some of the greatest scholars in the Mennonite church who were members of the faculty! Financially I knew I could make my way doing carpentry work. Academically I knew I could carry more than a full load. So I enrolled, eager for a great experience.

I would not be satisfied with the Th.B. undergraduate degree; I wanted the graduate Bachelor of Divinity degree (now known as the Master of Divinity). I aimed for the highest academic and intellectual goals, still needing to prove to myself that I was not an idiot.

Receiving a B.D. from Goshen Biblical Seminary was a highly distinguished accomplishment. Only a few such degrees had been awarded by the school, and all had been earned by scholars who were recognized throughout North America. Now I had the opportunity to join that elite group. Maybe then the nagging doubt about my capacity for normal brain functioning would finally go away.

The fact that the primary purpose of the seminary was to train pastors was only of remote interest to me. I quickly assessed my peasant origins and the reality that I had no famous lineage or name to ease my way into the ministry, and left the future outcome to God or fate. I was here to settle an inner score. This drove me much more than the possibility of occupying a pulpit after graduation.

Little did I know that I would immediately run into a solid brick wall. The graduate program which I had entered required at least two full years of Greek language studies. That was to become my Waterloo.

Dutifully I enrolled in the beginning Greek course. It was assumed that in the first year a student would learn the language, the vocabulary and the grammar. Then the second year would be spent in exegesis, translating the original Greek text into English while developing a working knowledge of the original text. With that background a biblical scholar could always return to the original Greek for study. In fact it was assumed in our other course work that we would no longer use English translations.

So I began my Greek studies only to realize that I could not memorize the Greek alphabet. No matter how hard I tried, or how many schemes I created, I could not retain even the first lesson. My colleagues quickly mastered the first week's assignment and were ready to go on to the beginning rules of the language. Within several weeks we were to know many of the general grammatical rules, all of which floated by me like a puff of smoke.

Several times a day I opened the textbook to the first page and gave my total concentration to the letters of the alphabet: alpha, beta, gamma, delta, epsilon, zeta, on through to the end. Nothing I could do would imprint those twenty-four letters in my brain. I took a Saturday off from my carpentry job to spend the entire day learning that alphabet. I went over the list hundreds if not thousands of times. By the end of the day I could manage to recite the entire list. But Sunday morning I awoke to the discovery that in one night I had forgotten an entire day's work.

I could find no comforting explanation for what was happening. I knew that I had been unable to learn High German in previous years, but I attributed that to chaotic teaching methods. Here I was beginning fresh. I had no unpleasant associations with Greek. So why could I not learn it?

Without any answers, I proceeded to the next page—elementary rules of grammar. We had been told this passage was extremely important to know, so I marked it boldly. But I could not understand the opening paragraph. Not one idea made any sense to me no matter how often I read it. The next paragraph had no more meaning than the first. I noticed that each of the grammatical rules was numbered, and I turned to the end of the book only to discover that I would need to know 603 of those rules to pass elementary Greek!

Next I turned to the vocabulary lists. With intensive concentration I was able to recognize three of the eight verbs on the list. My elation turned to despair, however, when I realized that each verb had to be conjugated, and that I would have to memorize 256 forms of each word and know to which of six principle parts each belonged. As I gazed at the chart my brain turned to noodles and I gave up. It was early enough in the semester that I could switch to another course, nothing was recorded on my transcript, and I lost no tuition money.

I devoted all my energy to the other subjects I was taking and mastered them one by one. Should anyone have wanted to find me I was in the library encircled with a dozen textbooks on the subject at hand. I was a plodding reader and often had to read and re-read slowly, but I had time so I persisted each day until the library closed and then continued in my room until midnight. Living in a funeral home, without any distractions, I was able to master the reading requirements. With great determination I overrode my reading handicaps and convinced myself and the faculty that I had the mental capacity to do graduate work.

The following year I had to enroll in the beginning Greek course again. For one full year I battled that same textbook. I caught on to a few concepts, learned a few more words, and knew I could not give up this time. My textbook was a pathetic sight with all the markings I made. In desperation I underlined, added my interpretations, drew diagrams. On and on I fought what appeared to be an invisible enemy that would not let me learn.

By this time even the first-year students had passed me with ease. The teacher was kind and caring and often called me into his office to go over the previous lesson, but he knew that I did not have a grasp of even the most elementary level of the language. By the end of the year I failed the course.

Then one of the most outstanding Greek scholars in the school heard about my plight and offered to tutor me. I was entering my third year of seminary and making my third try at the same beginning course in Greek. For one entire summer, the first thing every morning, I met Dr. J.C. Wenger on his front porch. Day after day he explained the textbook to me, line by line. He used different colored pens to highlight different items. He wrote his own explanations above the author's while he talked to me at my comprehension level.

I sensed that he cared so deeply about me as a person that no sacrifice was too much for him. He pronounced the words with clarity and emphasis, translating everything. He had me repeat after him, idea after idea, while he marked my textbook. I took that book with me to my carpentry job after our sessions and recited Greek words as I hammered and sawed. Every evening I reviewed the lesson and then returned to his house the next morning. By the end of the summer I passed my course. I still believe that I was given credit more on effort than on accomplishment.

I cannot describe the work I invested in my Greek course that senior year. I still have the card catalog I made of thousands of Greek words. I recorded each word on a card with its exact meaning, the number of times and places it appears in the New Testament, and all its variations of meanings or usage. Even now the cards reek with desperation. I had concluded that if I could not learn Greek I could at least make a reference source to which I could turn when I needed it.

My Greek New Testament offers further evidence that I never flinched from work! I bought a New Testament that had a blank sheet inserted between each printed page. Underneath each Greek word I wrote the English translation, and on the blank pages I wrote the explanations for the text. When I examine this Bible now I almost cry, remembering the vast effort I made to conquer that course.

By the grace of a kind, loving faculty member I was given a passing grade for that year of Greek study. I was then qualified to receive the most distinguished degree of the college and seminary. But I had not yet answered the ques-

tion, who exactly am I? Was I the idiot that could not comprehend the subject that stood at the heart of the seminary
curriculum, or was I the student who could work on two
degrees simultaneously, in addition to holding a full-time
carpentry job? Was earning this degree sufficient to convince
me that I was, in fact, intelligent? Or was I still the idiot?

I had always been torn between two dichotomies. At one
moment I easily outwitted my peers; the very next, I could not
move an inch while they won the race. How could I understand myself? Was there a defect in my brain that emerged
inexplicably to render my mental processes inoperable?

I reached back into my past, searching for some explanation. Was it my premature birth? My parents' illiteracy?
Was it the malnutrition I suffered or the week-long coma I
was in? Maybe this unknown defect was what my elementary
school teachers had detected and tried to beat out of me.

Could it be that a peasant beginning like mine could never
be escaped? Maybe the real error was that I should never
have left the village. Other than my twin brother who somehow had managed better than I had, no one else had dared
leave. So why should I expect to escape and succeed?

But how was I able to earn three college and graduate
degrees in four years when I was hounded for two of those
years by a Greek enemy? Such questions continued to dog my
steps even as I relentlessly pursued my elusive goal.

13.

Seminary—An Invitation to Nothing

*I*n seminary, while I battled the opponent that refused to let me learn Greek, I also discovered allies I had not known existed—a photographic memory and an intelligent mind.

I was taking my first class in church history, taught by the renowned Dr. H.S. Bender. I had heard that this was the course that separated the scholars from the rest of the students. It was a great privilege to take, but also difficult to pass.

To each class Dr. Bender carried a manila folder of notes, then left it closed as he told the history of the church from Pentecost until the present day. This two-semester course included the history of the world as it intersected with the evolution of Christianity as well as other religions.

To my relief I was able to follow this eloquent professor's thoughts, but I found taking notes at the same time required enormous effort. One hundred minutes of continuous bombardment left me completely exhausted after every class.

I was using this course as a test of my ability to do graduate-level work, and I had to succeed. To make sure I did not miss a detail I purchased several voluminous textbooks on church history and read them along with the class work.

Determined and desperate to conquer this subject matter I recorded each major era in my notebook. In tiny script, and often using a single word to remind me of a concept, I could fit one month's worth of lectures on a single page. By the end of the course I had it all on six pages of paper.

When it came time to study for the final exam I reviewed those six pages over and over again, well aware of how difficult it was for me to remember details. When I sat down to write the exam I was astonished to discover that I could see the exact content of those six pages all in chronological order before my eyes. I answered each question as if I were copying directly from those notes. It was so vivid that I actually felt guilty!

After two years of courses, with the transfer credits I had brought with me from Canada, I was awarded a Bachelor of Arts degree from Goshen College. Having also finished one year of seminary training I planned to complete the additional two years that the graduate degree required. Unsure of my future vocation I decided to take all my electives in Elementary Education and thus received a Bachelor of Science in Education degree as well. With my acute fear for my future survival I had to build in all the safety valves that the system permitted.

Now I insisted that my twin brother join me here. I owed it to him. He had bailed me out so many times in the past; now it was my turn to do something for him. He did come, with his wife and two young children, and, as I had done, took a full course load while supporting himself and his family doing carpentry work.

Early in my seminary years, while I was studying in the library, a young member of the nursing school faculty sat next to me at one of the tables. It was perfect timing! She was taking courses while teaching nursing arts and was hard at work studying the English poet, John Milton. She asked for my opinion, and I expounded on Milton's eschatology of predestination and dispensationalism. Dorothy was impressed!

We soon spent hours discussing issues and ideas. She was from a Mennonite congregation in eastern Pennsylvania; I was attracted to her conservative style. We found we shared common values related to church and education.

I told Dorothy all about my peasant background, my nearly

illiterate parents and the limitations of my early education. Much of our time together was spent with me telling her stories in graphic detail about my past.

If Dorothy were to marry me I wanted her to be as fully informed as possible about me. All my difficulties with spelling, reading and grammar I assigned to the defective education I had received and the unique cultural background from which I had come.

Dorothy accepted my explanations fully and accompanied me on a 2,000-mile bus trip back to Saskatchewan to visit my parents whom she received as her own. She discovered she could even understand the Low German language from her knowledge of German and "Pennsylvania Dutch"; she also learned family recipes from my mother. A bond grew quickly, and she was part of the family.

After a year-and-a-half-courtship we were married, took a week-long honeymoon to Niagara Falls and New England, and returned for my final year of seminary.

I had settled one big issue—that of marriage—but another continued to weigh heavily on me: What next? Why had I spent the past three years struggling to get a B.D. degree? Where would it lead? What would I do after I graduated? Of what value were all those A's and a third sheepskin?

I was preoccupied with these questions. One telling picture in my seminary yearbook captures my pain and turmoil. The scene is of a dozen seminarians casually chatting in the classroom while waiting for the professor to arrive. But at the far end of the room is a lone figure—me—separated from the group, silently looking out a window, lost in thought. Only I know that this person was dying inside.

I was extremely grateful for my seminary education. I had met the challenge and reaped immeasurable rewards. I had studied with an expert on inductive New Testament studies, a theologian who had written a monumental work, an Anabaptist historian who retold the story of the church as if he had personally lived through it all.

But something was missing. The experience invited me to

nothing! I was a scholar in the midst of scholars, but I was sinking and no one knew. I had come through a great training center for future Christian ministers. At each graduation much ado was made of those who had been "called" to serve a church. Nothing was said about those who were not called. They just seemed to disappear when they left the school. I gradually realized that I was one of those other ones.

Just prior to enrolling for the final semester I grew increasingly desperate. Then I received a note from the Dean giving me an appointment to report to his office. Surely this was the time, I thought, when he would determine for me my future in the church. He would point his finger to the north or south, to Africa or the Third World, and say, "There, my son, is the land where you are called to serve. Go now and preach the gospel."

I was highly apprehensive as I sat in the waiting room for the culminating moment when all would come clear. Finally I would know the purpose for which I had labored so hard.

A secretary ushered me into the office at the appointed time and I took a seat as I assumed I should. Behind a huge pile of notes, books and letters, a foot deep and covering the entire desk, sat the Pope, as he was called by the students. He was working feverishly and I sat silently, believing that he would soon pause and address the concern that hung heavily upon me. I watched him carefully. Large in stature, both in size and position, he held sway over an entire denomination of several hundred thousand members. He had articulated "The Anabaptist Vision," and in so doing had mobilized many of his fellow Mennonites. Soon he would give me my vision too.

After what felt like an hour he noticed me. He was startled. He had not expected me to be sitting there.

"What do you want?" came his hasty request. Obviously I had broken an important train of thought.

"Why, you called for me. I have an appointment card, see?" I stammered.

"Oh, yes. Didn't my secretary give it to you?" he asked impatiently.

"No," I replied. "Give me what?"

Rummaging around on his desk he pulled out a piece of paper and laid it on the pile nearest me. It was my course schedule, indicating that I could meet the requirements for completing my Bachelor of Science in Education degree as well as my Bachelor of Divinity degree.

After examining it carefully I looked up. I could see only the top of his balding head with a few streaks of long gray hair covering it. He was back at his labor, pen in hand, coining papal decrees.

Just as before, a long time passed before he abruptly glanced up at me and said, "Is there something else you wanted?" Without waiting for a reply he returned to his work.

I whispered something about needing to talk to someone about my future. The year was ending, I told him, and I didn't know where to go.

If he heard me, he gave no indication. After another few moments I came to my senses, walked into the corridor and then out onto the cold campus. My last ray of hope was shattered.

"He doesn't give a damn about me or my future," I muttered over and over again.

My final semester was perplexing. Not one invitation from any church came my way. I hadn't expected any or looked for any, but if there was anything I should have done to make my availability known, I had not been informed. Instead I rehashed my entire life journey, extinguishing any flickering flame of self-esteem. I reminded myself that I was only a stray from a poor Saskatchewan farm who never should have come to these prestigious halls. The farm with all its hopelessness and despair was probably where I belonged, no matter how many degrees I had earned. The dirt on my shoes could never be erased. That must have been obvious to the faculty and my colleagues. No wonder I had heard no "call." No one sent a tramp to a pulpit or to some faraway country where the people probably knew more than he did. I would fade away like other unknowns before me. And with that my soul died another death instead of flaming with the vision I had caught only a few years earlier at this school.

On graduation day Pete and I were each to receive two degrees. In fact the college had issued a news release: "Twins Receive Four Degrees at Goshen College Graduation." Just as my name was called I decided not to go up. "This is a farce," I whispered to myself. But I did not even have the courage to carry out my threat, and I dumbly followed the others forward.

Where was my invitation to live, as the visiting dignitary proclaimed in his commencement address? If it had been there in the midst of all this I had missed it. Others had accepted such an invitation for themselves, but for some reason it had not been extended to me in such a way that I could understand it. In spite of the brilliance that marked the day the idiot seemed to have once more had its way.

At that moment I turned away from the ministry and set my face towards social work. Only later was I to find that the invitation to live was not an intellectual experience, but a relational and emotional one, an encounter of one's whole person with that of another. I was to learn that, not in a church setting, but in a secular one.

14.
My Invitation to Live

After graduation from Goshen Pete and I went our separate ways. He received a National Science Foundation scholarship for a year of graduate education at Ohio State University. His carpentry skills sidetracked him, however, and he established a kitchen cabinet business in Indiana that proved to be enormously successful for him.

Convinced that I was not called to the ministry I turned to social work. We relocated to Dorothy's home area, and I enrolled in a master's degree program in social work at the University of Pennsylvania. Here I was awarded a full scholarship for the entire tuition, as well as a stipend to cover living expenses.

Once again I felt out of my element. With the exception of three summer terms at normal school I had spent my entire life in a Mennonite nest. My high school and college education gave me a world view from a Christian perspective; my faith was central to my understanding of life.

Now I found myself at a university that was decidedly secular. I was in a program involving personality development, psychology and social work. I was encountering a new philosophy of life, a different view of human beings. What was I doing? Was I jeopardizing my faith?

I decided that if I reached a crossroad that forced a choice between my degree or my faith, I would choose my faith. I wanted the degree, and I would do everything possible to maneuver within the program, but I would not sacrifice my faith.

For the first several weeks I remained silent in class. I

claimed a corner chair where I could barely be seen. As the
first month passed I began to realize I could not hide forever.
I made a list of all the students in my section and checked off
each time a student spoke in class. As long as there were
others who had not yet talked I was comfortable. But the day
came when all had contributed except me. I panicked.

I now knew for sure that I was a misfit. "What is wrong
with me?" kept racing through my mind. My anxiety was
crippling, my fear debilitating.

One day after my class in personality development as I
attempted to sneak out unseen, the professor stopped me.
Very warmly she asked, "Could you stop by my office right
away?"

Laura Dowens seemed to be compassion personified, and in
her office I began sputtering that I was not making it, that I
felt like a fish out of water who was totally tongue-tied. She
leaned as far over her desk towards me as she could and said,
"That is what we are here to talk about."

She helped me to voice my greatest fear: that this secular
setting would force me to abandon my Christianity to which
I clung desperately. I was sure the crossroad was just ahead
and I knew which way I would choose, no matter how great
the consequences.

I was so overwhelmed that I broke into a sobbing cry. "I do
not want to abandon this training program. I have a pregnant
wife, due in a few weeks, and no means of support other than
my scholarship." I wept at the bleakness of my future—a
stranger in a foreign country, married to an American, determined not to go back to Canada.

By now I was sure she would label me emotionally unstable,
unfit for the program. Instead she wiped her own eyes and
said, "If you could have only told us sooner, we would have
understood." Then she went on, "You are one of our finest
candidates. You come with the highest academic credentials
and references. Your fieldwork supervisor has great hopes for
you."

I countered that I was too different from the rest of the class with my peasant origin and my religious beliefs.

To this she instantly responded, "Beneath the surface we are all very, very different. It is not a question of differences; it is a matter of accepting our own and others' differences."

Then she read me a quotation which has since become my motto for all relationships, deeply imbedded in my entire being.

"Will people ever learn. . .that there is no other equality than the equal right of every individual to become and to be himself, which actually means to accept his own difference and have it accepted by others?" (Otto Rank, *Beyond Psychology*, p. 267).

She was not yet finished. "Our task here is not to make you over into our image, but to have you claim completely who you are and share that as freely as you can. We want to know about your Christian convictions since they are so deeply a part of who you are. We cannot know you unless we know that side of you, too."

I sat for several moments, absorbing it all. "Then there is no choice to make," I reflected slowly. "I am not asked to give up anything. I am being asked to claim it fully and fully enough to share it freely."

"That is right," she said with absolute conviction.

I left the office in a daze and walked the streets of south Philadelphia pondering it all. I was amazed that at my point of greatest crisis, this professional, this scholar, had not judged me. Instead she had extended herself to me, caring for me to the point of her own tears, allowing herself to hurt for me. Her ultimate concern had been for my welfare.

My whole being sprang to life. I had thought that the invitation to live came from God alone. I had accepted his greatest act of unconditional love as my answer to life. Yet while my soul was alive I had been so crippled emotionally that I seemed lifeless. Suddenly one person had become an instrument of God without fully realizing it. Furthermore, if she could be used in this way, so could I. In accepting this invitation I knew that I would need to extend it to others.

What I found I wanted others to encounter also.

I had just discovered the power of listening with love. I had experienced the revolutionary potential for change that can happen when love creates a relationship. It can, literally, transform lives.

I learned that Otto Rank had authored a book about this approach. In fact, in *Beyond Psychology* he uses the New Testament rebirth experience as a model for the transformation of the human being. Rank builds his psychology around the basic concept that by participating in Christ's resurrection, one can be reborn.

I was totally awestruck! Rank's proposition was surprisingly compatible with my theological understanding. I knew now that I was in the right place. My call had come here, rather than in seminary! I became a model student. I immersed myself in the program so I would be equipped to effect the same change in others that I had experienced myself.

My turnaround was so dramatic that some faculty viewed me as a novelty. In fact I learned later that one faculty member used me and the example of my life in her doctoral dissertation, defending the effectiveness of this master's degree program in bringing about personality change.

During my graduate studies I tried intensely not to reveal my difficulties with written language. My reading, spelling, handwriting and grammar were all drastically impaired. I had no explanation for it, and I was grossly ashamed of it.

Although I could read the material that was assigned, I read so slowly and with such great effort that I could barely meet the minimum requirements. Because I was so easily distracted I needed a totally quiet environment, free from any interruptions or background noise. Nowhere at home or school could I find such a haven of silence. When I was tired even silent surroundings were not enough to keep me on track. I was unable to sustain reading for more than three or four paragraphs before my mind drifted away. Although my eyes still followed the lines on the page, I remembered nothing.

So I made a deal with my wife. Whenever possible she read

to me while I took over child care and household duties. She reads with exceptional skill and speed and enjoys it, and I found that I could listen and comprehend it all even while washing dishes. As a result she knew the content of my education as well as I did, and we could intelligently discuss every issue together.

She came to my rescue when I floundered in the sea of term papers that I was continually required to write. I could not allow any faculty member to see my handwritten material, and I have never been able to learn to type. Fortunately Dorothy learned to decode my atrocious handwriting, and, with her skill in grammar, spelling and typing, together we produced papers that were letter-perfect. Professors would often comment on the precise format of the papers but I remained silent. I could not yet discuss such an unresolved issue.

As part of my training program I was placed in a fieldwork assignment with a child welfare agency. When I was on the job long enough to feel some competence, I was given a case that triggered my energy and commitment. My supervisor was a superb practitioner and we had great respect for each other. I admired her skill and she believed in my potential. I knew she would follow the process carefully and send regular evaluations of my performance back to the School of Social Work where her appraisals were highly valued. I was ready to prove that I knew what to do as a practitioner of the art of social casework.

Yet my agenda in the case included personal, as well as professional, issues. Five young children were victims of a situation in which the parents had each other arrested and were serving alternate prison terms. The parents had declared their unwillingness to keep any of the children and were using them to take revenge on each other. The children needed to be protected from abuse and neglect. With no hope for reconciliation or the establishment of an intact family unit, adoption or foster placement was the only option.

The youngest of the five children were identical twin boys

whom I found naked in their crib, huddled to each other, trying to keep warm in a wet and filthy bed. Being an identical twin myself, and with the vivid memories of my own childhood family circumstances, I responded personally to their plight. In addition I had two little girls of my own at home whom I loved absolutely. In the face of giveaway children, all of my own rescue needs surfaced.

As I proceeded into the case I carefully documented on tape every event that occurred, as well as my decisions involving each child with the appropriate theory supporting my activity. I relentlessly sought out the best possible placement of each child, carefully balancing the individual needs of each one with the need to keep them together as a unit as much as possible. By the time the adoption phase was reached the typewritten record had grown to hundreds of pages.

Because this was such a complex case several associated agencies and many other caseworkers became involved. They all read my lengthy report.

One agency executive told me she took the document home for an evening and could not put it down. She read throughout the night and called me in the morning to say that reading it had been one of her finest educational experiences in child welfare and well worth the loss of a night's sleep.

I believe that all I had learned and believed and felt came together so perfectly in this situation that no price was too high for me to invest in this case. That five children were now in secure, loving homes was my true reward.

I was nearing the end of the program when one afternoon Dr. Roland J. Artigues, a senior faculty member, approached me. Placing his hand on my shoulder, he asked, "Abe, how is it going with you?"

I replied that things were going well. I had completed my thesis and my advisor had told me that it ranked with the best of the graduating class.

"Yes," he nodded, "I just came from the thesis review committee and I heard the same comment."

Acknowledging that he was about to violate university

policy, he went on, "Because I believe that you have no idea of what your academic potential is, I have to urge you, Abe, to come back as soon as you can and get a doctor's degree in social work."

I was baffled and asked him for an explanation. Assuring me that he meant what he said, he told me simply that the field of social work needed people like me to become leaders and educators. My performance had generated excitement in faculty meetings and he thought I deserved to know.

Part of me was so exhilarated that I could have glided home far above the city streets. But another part of me recalled the examination paper I had just had returned with all my spelling mistakes marked and the grammatical errors noted. I received a good grade on the content, in spite of, as the instructor said, the agony it was for her to read it. Such contradictions were still the story of my life.

I received my master's degree in social work, along with more clear signals to push on for a doctorate. Only the fact that others recognized my accomplishments gave me the courage to believe I could do it. I had no predecessors who had paved the way. I had only questions: "Am I intellectually competent?" Every success I realized had a qualifier in it: "That's all the farther I can go." I was acutely anxious about my decision to go on, and I lived with great insecurity.

Because the university required three years of practice after the master's degree before readmission, I had time to decide. Besides, I had a wife and two small children at home to support and it was time I went to work.

15.

The Last Rites for the Idiot

When I completed my master's degree I accepted a key social work position—creating an adoption social service agency. My duties involved formulating and recording all the policies for the agency, as well as doing most of the casework. I had had experience in a division of the Children's Aid Society during my supervised fieldwork, so establishing the procedures was routine, and in less than a month the agency was running smoothly. The work was not sufficient to keep me occupied full-time, so I was able to pursue further graduate education.

The University of Pennsylvania had the right part-time program for me. It was one year of specialized training in marriage counseling at its reputable Marriage Council of Philadelphia. I was readily admitted.

One component of the program was to be my undoing. A major part of the process was for each of us to take turns conducting counseling sessions behind a one-way mirror while the instructor and the rest of the class watched. After each session, every word, movement and action that occurred during the session was discussed and critiqued. As long as my classmates were on the hot seat I performed admirably. I was able to decode hidden meanings, body language and subtle innuendos in both the clients and the counselors.

My classmates often asked me to lunch so I could explain how I arrived at such observations. All I knew was that I allowed myself to enter into the experiences of both the couple and the therapist so that I was experiencing it the way they were. Somehow I was able to intuitively step into their shoes. My contributions during the conferences that followed were merely reiterations of what I had felt being in their positions. I found it easy to do.

Then came my turn in front of the one-way mirror. I turned into a bumbling fool. All my worst fears happened. I blushed to a bright crimson. I could set no direction for the session. The clients felt so sorry for me that they tried to comfort and reassure me.

The dreaded idiot that I thought I had buried long ago lived again. It was a rerun of my childhood when I could not read my lesson, memorize my parts or spell my words in the spelling contest. Not only could the observers behind the mirror see through the glass, they could also look through the mask I wore and see the idiot inside.

At the follow-up conference I was speechless. My classmates felt so sorry for me that no one could have a meaningful learning experience.

The director of the training program took me to her office to try to explore what had happened. I had no reasonable explanation. Was it stage fright or panic? Or was it something more serious? Maybe I was emotionally disturbed or even mentally ill. My situation needed to be addressed.

I was asked to withdraw from the program for a period of time and go into therapy. What I had dreaded so terribly since early elementary school had finally happened. My insane fear that whatever was wrong with me would someday be discovered was coming true. Now everything I had accomplished in life would be totally destroyed.

The director called the psychiatric clinic of the university and arranged for an appointment. My day of doom was upon me. I was in a total state of terror. Such a process of self-disclosure could only end in catastrophe. My hidden demon would be identified, released and revealed for all to see.

I was first seen by the chief psychiatric resident, a student himself. The encounter was as disastrous as I had feared. He

asked question after question and took copious notes. I told
him everything he wanted to know, no matter how personal.
But each session ended with no explanations from him, no
insight, no summary of his observations. He gave me only my
appointment time for the next session and left me stranded
with my vivid imagination and my panic.

Weeks went by. When I asked for feedback he merely noted
my questions. The mystery that he was creating was becoming absolutely intolerable. Finally in desperation I demanded
some word from him. He blurted out that I had an acute
character disorder and was so clever at manipulating my
surroundings that I even tried to outwit the therapy process
to make him appear incompetent. I, he said, had made him a
victim of my pathology.

When I asked him what a character disorder was, he told
me to read a textbook on the subject. He then terminated
therapy, telling me that character disorders were beyond help.

His conclusion destroyed me instantly. In sheer terror I
reported all that had happened to my supervisor at Marriage
Council and she immediately called the Chairman of the
Department of Psychiatry. He asked me to come to his office.

I was met by a warm, fatherly man whose face and entire
demeanor radiated compassion. He listened intently as I told
him my plight. He, too, recorded pages of notes, but he talked
with me, adding his insights to what I was telling him.

In fact we ran far beyond the allotted time. He explained
my life as a series of insurmountable obstacles, not patholo-
gies. He saw my life as a victorious drama, not a defeat.

I began to believe that if anyone could uncover my secret
demon and rout it out, this man could. Session after session
we met. I was eager to tell him everything and he seemed
ready to hear it. He was genuinely intrigued with my life
journey. He pointed out the unique strengths I had mustered
in moving out of a primitive peasant culture into a world of
college and university degrees. He acknowledged and celebrated with me the centuries of cultural change I had under-
gone in my thirty-three years. And he helped me understand

that there would be times, such as those in the observation room, when parts of myself that I had not yet integrated would emerge. Blushing, which had been such a self-destructive part of me, would naturally occur in such settings.

Dr. Peltz granted that there were confusing parts to my story. He saw that in most situations I showed adequate, even tenacious, self-confidence. Yet certain events destroyed every shred of that confidence. He suggested that the psychiatric resident likely became so frustrated by these discrepancies that he picked a label and pasted it on me. But he disagreed with both the label and the method.

By our last session together we had covered my entire life up to the present day. Seeing myself through his eyes gave me self-confidence and self-esteem. We were both aware that I had made him into my ideal father figure and had translated everything he said into ultimate truths.

The experience proved to be healing. I picked up my place in the training program, competently conducted marriage counseling sessions before my critics and observers, and held my own in the follow-up discussions. By the end of the year I received my certificate in marriage counseling.

I had been profoundly affected by my encounter with this man. Not only did I leave my blushing in the therapist's office; I also left behind the idiot. Dr. Peltz had pronounced me well. If a flaw existed at the center of my being, I simply concluded that one existed in everybody else as well. I was a full-fledged member of the human race.

After our final session I walked directly to the registrar's office of the Graduate School of Social Work to enroll in the doctoral program.

16.

A Dyslexic Doctoral Degree

*C*andidates for the School of Social Work's doctoral degree program were required to complete a pre-doctoral academic year. I was given a residency practicum at Norristown State Hospital where an experimental project was being developed to attempt to reach and rehabilitate their most chronic mentally ill male patients. I volunteered to be the social work representative on the team.

The idea was to select the most severe chronic schizophrenic male patients and bombard them with social stimuli until they could not help but respond. The population chosen for this project were men who had been chronic residents of a back ward for several decades. They did not speak and were unable to care for themselves, and it was presumed that they would spend the rest of their lives in this condition.

These men received no therapy. They were herded into a huge day room every morning and left to their own devices. Patients spent their days in whatever pattern each had adopted. Some refused to wear clothes, some sat in the same spot on the floor in their own excrement, some babbled or sang or screamed in states of complete delusion. Others had laid claim to particular rocking chairs in which they rocked from morning to night year after year. At the end of each day they were herded through a shower stall like cattle, and then put to bed.

I was intrigued by the events of life that could do this kind of damage to human beings. I was ready to try anything, at any cost to myself, to see if it were possible to break through an impenetrable barrier that kept people in such a snake pit. For twenty or more years some kind of effort had been made, but these people had not responded. Could our team make a difference?

I embraced the project as my own. To get a truer sense of these men's lives I spent days living in the ward with them. I came at 6:00 in the morning as they were herded out of bed, and I sat with them in the awful stench of the day room. I accompanied the stampede to the dining room where they ate with their hands. At the end of the day when they were driven through the showers I went home. My wife could smell me entering the front door.

Despite the horror of their lives I felt a kinship with these people. It was only by the grace of God that I was not among them. Something had gone wrong in my life, too, and I had no better explanation for my defect than these men had for theirs. My disability, my suffering, enabled me to identify with their plight in an uncanny way.

I was part of a team encounter session in which we all attempted to call forth some responses from these men. I suggested that the men's families be enlisted in the project, hoping that the bonds of kinship might kindle some sparks of recognition. The task turned out to be difficult. Many of the families had long ago given up, had ceased all contact and were reluctant to get involved again. After all, their hopes had been shattered so many times before. But some believed in my dedication and were won over by my enthusiasm.

It became clear that patients responded in direct proportion to the amount of engagement between them and their families and the staff. The families soon realized that they were effective partners in the treatment process. Therapy was no longer some mysterious event that took place in the hallowed privacy of a psychiatrist's office. It became a picnic meal eaten with patient, family and one or two team members. When a patient spoke his first word in twenty years, we all rejoiced. Words led to phrases and then to sentences. We were breaking through!

I began to conclude that the chronic, "hopeless," mentally ill patient was actually socially disabled, the product of a family system and, later, an institutional system programmed for the individual's destruction, not cure.

At the end of our project we reported some startling results to the psychiatric, psychology, social work and nursing staffs. Patients were responding. Some had moved up to higher functioning level wards, and others were even able to return home to their families.

Our bold new approach to treating chronic schizophrenia impressed the staffs. The social work supervisor singled out my contribution to the project. "It is obvious that your dedication was the catalyst that made it happen," she said. "Our profession has never before been recognized as having anything unique to offer to the whole treatment process. Social work will never be the same at N.S.H."

I made a written report of the project for the hospital which the medical staff used in the training of the psychiatric residents. Then I got a note from the superintendent which said, "This is a profoundly moving description of a unique hospital program. It could be presented for publication if Mr. Schmitt could correct his problem with syntax."

I read the note and did not know what the word "syntax" meant, how it was my problem, nor how I could correct it. The article was never submitted for publication. Assuming that the problem was some gross grammatical error, I waited ten years before I risked writing anything for publication.

Each of us in the pre-doctoral class was required to present a client, group, or social situation, illustrating our own academic growth as a social work innovator. Before each presentation I read my fellow student's preliminary report, reliving the situation each described, placing myself in the drama, and analyzing the process from the inside.

Dr. Ruth Smalley, the Dean and instructor of the course, seemed to value my contributions. I remember that she frequently turned to me when a particularly difficult moment came up and said, "Well, Mr. Schmitt, you can usually bail us out in a crisis like this. What do you think is the issue?"

I entitled my class project, "Lazarus, Come Forth." We had given that name to the project at the hospital since we were, in fact, doing what Jesus did when he called the deceased Lazarus back to life. Dr. Smalley enthusiastically commended the clarity of thinking in my presentation, my commitment to the project and the novelty of the idea. In her comments to me after class I began to believe that this was the unique and innovative kind of work she was looking for in a doctoral candidate.

On my final paper about my fieldwork practice Dr. Smalley wrote, "This was so exciting and deeply rewarding for me to read because of the giant step you took in your professional development here. What sensitive, thoughtful and thoroughly functional work! Here you believe in yourself as a social worker (and no wonder!). Because you are rooted in a function in which you believe, which feels right, and *is* social work to you, you are free to respond in feeling to your client. What amazing growth!"

I now know that what happened there was a product of my handicaps. Because I had long ago realized that I could not think in a linear way, I used every effort to expand my more spatial, intuitive process of thinking. Because I could not remember series of facts and exact information, I had learned to experience life situations much like many of my clients did. Ironically in this academic setting I was being rewarded for my compensation.

When the time came to write my exam, the strange phenomenon that had happened during my final exam in Church History at Goshen College recurred. Now as I sat down to select the one question out of three related to professional social work practice on which I would write, I suddenly could visualize the entire answer before me. I could see the exact pages in the textbook from which to draw my answers. For eight hours I wrote feverishly, quoting directly from my sources at times, and filling forty-seven pages in response to one question.

My exam, I was later told, was the most detailed and complete that the committee had ever seen. But I was dumbfounded: how could I have suddenly risen so far above my lifelong problems with language usage and precise data recall? These had always been obstacles for me. Maybe, I thought, my problem all along had been just mental laziness.

The mystery continued. At the end of the year I was one of three pre-doctoral students out of twenty-seven applicants and the only member of my master's degree class to be admitted to full doctoral candidacy.

But a rude awakening awaited me in the doctoral program. I needed to complete a research dissertation. It required an original systematic study and an organized report written according to the rules of professional research. That took me straight to the core of my disability.

During my first doctoral year I accepted an internship at Spring Grove State Hospital in Baltimore, Maryland, an institution recognized nationally for its advanced resocialization of the chronic mentally ill. Patients were treated for their social disabilities rather than psychiatric illnesses. Since this issue was to be the focus of my doctoral training the School of Social Work recommended that I spend a year there and awarded me a fellowship that covered the entire cost, as well as living expenses for my family.

I had become an ardent exponent and practitioner of resocialization. I had discovered how to translate the concept into functioning units in which the crippling effects of institutionalization were minimized and the resocializing process was enhanced. But where in all this was a dissertation?

I began recording all kinds of processes that fascinated me. I documented ward meetings; I selected individual patients and monitored their responses. I brought home bundles of handwritten material that my wife faithfully typed into legibility. Then every few months I mailed a pack to my faculty advisor.

My consultation sessions with the doctoral advisor were

disastrous. She could not comprehend how all this material fit into something that could be called a dissertation. I had no direction, no singular purpose, no outline. It was a full ream of typewritten data documenting my zeal in helping patients; otherwise, she could make no sense out of it.

She was frustrated and angry. I was angry and distressed. I thought her job as my advisor was to transform this into an organized, purposeful study. I expected her to create order out of the chaos. After one particularly bad advisory meeting I left her office and threw a 300-page, neatly typewritten document into the trash can just outside her door. I then asked the university for one year's leave of absence from the doctoral program until I could get myself situated in a salaried position in another nearby state hospital. Once there I would see if I could begin again.

I blamed the bedlam on my faculty advisor. I refused to recognize the flaw that was really to blame. To own it would have destroyed all my drive to complete my degree.

It was during that year that our third child was born. The following year saw the birth of our fourth. With two early elementary-aged children as well, we were inundated with child care. In addition my wife spent hours and hours typing my material, some of which I later discarded in my frustration. How we ever survived that period, I do not know. My discouragement was at an all-time low, but we were both committed to my obtaining the degree. My drive to overcome the obstacles won, and I fought on.

I soon held a key training position at Philadelphia State Hospital, teaching the resocialization process to large numbers of personnel from hospitals throughout the state. A good number of colleagues went on to develop their own research projects, further testifying to the effectiveness of this technique.

Then a godsend arrived on the scene—Dr. Robert Smith, a specialist in psychological research. After wading through the chaos of my material he quickly analyzed where my research had gone wrong. He recognized the significance of the data I

had already gathered, helped me reword my ideas into re-
searchable questions, then showed me how to obtain quanti-
fiable measurements.

With his ability to bring everything into focus I was able to
systematically document my findings with a clear purpose in
mind. As the fog lifted my excitement was unbounded. I
explored and measured the responses of chronic mentally ill
patients to the process I had developed. I always felt Robert's
presence just over my shoulder as I completed the research.
He had made it possible for me to reenter the doctoral program.

From him I learned the form by which such a project should
be written, following the best methods of psychological research, and I returned to the dissertation, full of great enthusiasm. My research advisor at the university gave me full
permission to utilize the consultant services of Dr. Smith; she
must have been greatly relieved that she, as well as I, had
been rescued from the hopeless mess!

After gathering all the data I took a three-week vacation to
write the entire dissertation. I found a quiet hideaway where
I and my material were undisturbed. I arrived early every
morning and worked ferociously. Each day momentum picked
up. I saw the entire project clearly from beginning to end like
viewing a panoramic landscape. All I had to do was describe
it from left to right. Each day was another segment of the
view. I simply had to push my pen fast enough to get it down.

At the end of each day I was exhausted. I carried home the
day's production and Dorothy typed it while I took over the
child care, dinner preparation and housework. After the
mental fatigue I suffered, the physical labor was restful.

I became a recluse. I feared any outside thoughts or con-
tacts would cause me to lose my vision. With singleness of
purpose, in three weeks' time I completely finished and
Dorothy typed the dissertation. It was ready for the committee, and I was fully confident that it would meet their expectations.

All the while that Robert Smith had been helping me he had

been ill, battling Hodgkin's disease. As I made copies for my advisor and the committee, I made an extra one for him. Immediately after I delivered it to him he was hospitalized. He took it with him as his only reading material. The copy lay open on his nightstand when he died. He never knew what a legacy he left in my life. I dedicated my dissertation to him.

My advisor could not believe I had completed the dissertation so quickly. Given my earlier work she was reluctant to let it go to the committee without reading it first and approving it. However, she was far too busy with her own teaching to be able to read it in the next several weeks. I showed her the chapters, explaining the content of each, the methods I used in presenting my arguments and the specific findings. Unable to spot any problems she gave me clearance to distribute copies to all the committee members and arranged a day for me to defend it orally.

My formal presentation began with a flowery introduction from my advisor. Then came the questions regarding my research method and conclusions. Once satisfied, the committee proceeded to discuss my two basic premises: that patients defined and treated as schizophrenic and chronically mentally ill could more accurately be described as socially disabled, and that a treatment process, which I called resocialization, could be effectively used, quantified and documented. My data proved that a significantly high percentage of patients responded measurably to this treatment process.

Having read literally everything that had been written on this still novel concept, and having been so zealously involved in the process, I felt freed to speak with absolute certainty and authority. Committee members switched modes and began asking questions from their own curiosities. One psychiatrist on the panel concurred that my theory was valid.

Then I was asked to leave the room. In less than five minutes I was called back to a standing ovation and welcomed as a colleague. I had earned the final degree.

Dr. Anthony Wallace, Chairman of the Department of Anthropology, spoke of the value of my study to the existing knowledge dealing with the problem of chronic hospitalized patients. He even asked me to remove some statistical computations which he thought were superfluous. The main argument, he felt, was valid enough without them.

I was ecstatic. I ran to the nearest pay telephone and called my wife who joined me in the victory celebration. Next I called Mrs. Smith who said, "Robert would have been so happy to hear this news."

In my exuberance I called all the people I thought might be even remotely interested. Finally, I called my parents in Saskatchewan. Even though their education was meager they were impressed that I had earned a doctor's degree. They found it hard, though, to comprehend why it had nothing to do with medicine.

17.

From Peasant to Professor

*T*he secret fear that something beyond my control would happen, that I would be found out, that all my work would crumble around me, now dissolved. The dread that I had endured all my life seemed conquered forever. Education had been my ladder out of the peasant village and I had reached the top rung. I would henceforth be identified as Dr. Abraham Schmitt; that could never be taken from me.

Less than one year after receiving the degree I was asked to take a joint appointment at the University of Pennsylvania. I was to teach personality development and family dynamics in the School of Social Work, to be responsible for the practice of all the clinical social workers in the Department of Psychiatry, and to supervise the trainees at the Marriage Council. The interdisciplinary position was to build professional development within each of these fields.

I began teaching as aggressively as I had worked as a student. Before long I began toying with the idea of offering a course on death and dying. After all, I was teaching students who were to become helpers of others. Certainly they would be involved with persons facing either their own deaths or the death of a loved one. The vast majority of people in the helping professions had no training in dealing with death, although in their practices they often faced it.

I was fascinated by the subject of death, perhaps because I eluded death at an early age—I was the twin that had "already died or was about to die," and then had suffered a near-fatal illness at the age of eight. In my childhood village death was viewed as a natural part of life. The women, my mother included, helped prepare the body, the men dug the grave, and everyone, children included, participated in the funeral service. When Pete and I built that coffin at the back of the schoolroom in Carrot River and dismissed classes the day of the funeral, we were full participants in this natural part of existence. At Goshen College I lived and worked in a funeral home and learned the American way of death.

So death was more friend than enemy to me. I fully believed that if one allowed oneself to have a collision with death now, to experience the finiteness of life, then one could truly live. I was convinced that people die poorly because they live poorly, and they live poorly because they will not face their own finiteness, which ultimately is death. I wanted to help others encounter death, to "wake before they died," so that they, in turn, could help others face death in a sensitive and meaningful way.

My proposal for such a class raised many eyebrows. "Morbid!" was my colleagues' typical response. Even the title—Death and Dying—caused noticeable discomfort whenever it was mentioned, until I began referring to it as "D and D."

Eventually approved, the interdisciplinary course brought together students from the schools of social work, medicine, nursing and divinity. It became a resounding success, oversubscribed by students, with critical acclaim in the local and campus press.

Philadelphia Magazine sent a staff writer to participate in the class and then write a cover story on the issue of death and dying, based largely on material from the course. While the writer was gathering material for the article my co-teacher discovered this woman was also struggling with her own unresolved grief at the tragic loss of her only child just a few years earlier.

As a journalist she was approaching the issue as a purely academic exercise, but my co-teacher observed to me, "I don't know how she thinks she can do it. With all that denial, the tension she creates is awful."

My co-teacher urged her to come to me for therapy. She did, intending to work her way through the issue intellectually, all the while writing the article as part of her therapy.

Once I invited her into a treatment process she realized that she needed to deal with all the emotions of such a tragic loss. She finally surrendered to the process and permitted herself to cry her way through it.

As a result she became involved in the experiences of others facing grief and death. She was invited to join the staff of *New York Magazine* where she wrote about the much publicized case of Karen Ann Quinlan.

I later received a note from her saying, "Many thanks for getting me unstuck from my grief."

Success began coming to me in other areas of my triple assignment as well. I did not have enough openings to accommodate all who requested my supervision in their Marriage Council training. And I worked myself out of a job in the Department of Psychiatry by training social work supervisors to take effective leadership in the clinics. Thus, less and less was required of me.

No longer was I dogged by the need to prove that I would never have to return to the peasant village that I had fought so hard to escape. Nor was I any longer driven by the notion that I had to keep on climbing academically to prove my worth.

After several years I was more disillusioned by being part of a university faculty than challenged by it. The interpersonal rivalry bothered me immensely. The most influential decisions affecting rank, promotion and seniority were made at night over cocktails rather than at formal staff or committee meetings. Promotions were made, it was commonly said, over the fallen bodies of one's peers or superiors.

This behavior seemed as brutal and primitive as that which went on in my childhood village. In fact it ran completely counter to my Christian faith. This was the collision I had anticipated between my Mennonite/Christian beliefs and the academic system. But by now I felt secure enough to know that I was not diminished by it; the university was. Here was a faculty training others to be healers that, at the same time, was destroying each other. The situation posed an irreconcilable difference that I did not care to try to resolve. If I was naive, I was glad to be. I had acquired a status that I had not really sought. I was at last secure enough to realize that I would always be a peasant, and suddenly I was proud of it.

I decided to work my way out of the university. I had reached the top and found that I did not want to be there. I cared little about the university except for my interaction with the students. In that I could be myself. I risked some unconventional practices like refusing to be addressed as "Dr. Schmitt." I told the students to call me "Abe," which they found hard to do. It was against the school's policy, but I no longer cared. I held informal class sessions which I believed helped students to evolve more uniquely than the common lecture format allowed.

I knew I was going to leave within the next several years, so I decided to be myself, buck the system if need be, and get out without scars and with integrity intact.

Simultaneously I built a house for our family. That became a ceremony in recognition of all I had ever physically built in my life, a way of acknowledging that other part of myself. I had a great psychological need to build it my way and come to terms with myself as an integrated whole person.

I designed the house with an attached office and waiting room where I intended to set up a private practice in counseling. Like the barn which was attached to my village home, my office would enable me to work, as my father had, only a few yards away from my family.

Our four children were now fourteen, twelve, seven and six years of age, and family life was extremely important to me. Although I saw clients in the evenings I scheduled only two per night with a major break between, during which I could return to the family activities.

The two younger children estabished a ritual with me. Each night they would sit, one on either arm of the stuffed rocking chair, while I read to them, sometimes for as long as an hour, before bedtime. As they grew older we read together David's reading assignments for school. Because he struggled with reading as I had, and his younger sister was always willing to help him, the three of us would do his book reports together.

Our two older daughters had a large number of friends and relationships, and it soon became necessary to install a telephone line separate from my office line. I built a recreation room in the basement, furnished with the sound equipment necessary for teenaged tastes in music, and our house quickly became a gathering place for young people.

Our home also became one of the places where a group of seven couples, all graduates of Goshen College, met as often as every week, cementing friendships and providing me with a setting in which I could process issues I was facing in my academic and professional life. This "sounding board" of loyal friends remains an important part of my life.

My counseling of clients was a violation of my contract with the university which stated that I was not permitted to carry on a private practice while having a full-time faculty position. I did it anyway and was deliberately vocal about it at the university. When I was questioned about this possible conflict of interest or depletion of my energy level, I explained that I was simply matching the output of everyone else on the faculty.

When my private practice was large enough that I could earn my livelihood from it, I handed in my resignation. The whole time I was at the university I felt as though I had been swimming against the current. I left satisfied that I had reached my goals, that I had completed my task. I could now settle down with what I had earned. I was at peace.

18.

Diagnosis of Dyslexia

*M*y private practice grew far beyond what I had imagined. On top of that I was often asked to conduct workshops on grief and on marriage and family issues. I found myself writing books based on my own experiences and those of my clients. Dorothy and I led numerous weekend marriage encounter workshops. Every public exposure brought me more and more client referrals.

I was fifty-five years old, my life was full, yet I still lived with the flaw. Why did I still have so much trouble remembering a simple word or a telephone number or people's names, or following directions? Why was I so easily distracted? Why did I become disoriented in so many situations? What about my fear of heights? How was it that some days I went about in a complete fog, my brain barely functioning? Why could I still not spell?

One day a client came to my office and announced that she was dyslexic. She told me that she had been diagnosed by professionals when she was a child and had gone to special schools. She wanted me to understand dyslexia and what it was like for her to live with it. As she began listing her symptoms I felt as if scales were falling from eyes. She could not cite a single symptom that I did not also have.

I made her talk at great length about her disability, knowing that I was finally, for the first time in my life, discovering a name for my handicap.

Yet at the same time I could not fully accept this diagnosis of my problem. It felt too convenient. What if I were using a label to avoid taking responsibility for a defect in my personality?

I was not even familiar with the term "dyslexia." I never heard the word throughout my graduate studies nor at the many psychiatric clinical conferences which I attended. Learning handicaps were considered to be problems of mental retardation or psychiatric in origin. Even in my personal therapy with a renowned psychiatrist the term or concept had never surfaced.

I have since discovered that a large number of clinicians, as well as academic institutions, still do not recognize dyslexia as an indentifiable entity.

By this time I also had a nineteen-year-old son in college who had struggles similar to mine. I assumed that we had a common flaw, something that he must have inherited from me, but I did not know to call it dyslexia.

Then I happened to see a television interview with Dr. Harold Levinson, an expert on dyslexia. On the program he offered a simple test which, he said, could help determine if one had dyslexia or not. I watched, but only to establish once and for all that I was *not* dyslexic. I was growing embarrassed about my personal interest in this idea. I hoped the program and its test would rule me out; then I could stop talking about it.

Dorothy watched with me as a series of elephants crossed the screen at increasing speeds. I saw the figures change from separate individuals several inches apart, to overlapping fig-ures, to a cluster of blurred images, to a ribbon of gray moving across the screen.

When the test was over she said, "I wonder why they didn't speed it up sufficiently to show us what it would look like to a dyslexic. It was too slow; I saw separate elephants the whole time. I could even count them all as they passed."

We then realized that I had experienced the reaction of a dyslexic and she had not.

The program moved to a discussion of other symptoms of dyslexia. I could no longer deny the diagnosis. "The phobia of heights"—what a struggle I had with that. I remembered the time I could not accompany Dorothy and the children up the national park observation tower. Another time I forced myself to ride with them in the glass elevator up the outside of the CN Tower in Toronto only by concentrating my full attention on the carpet on the floor of the elevator, refusing to think about where I was or what I was really doing. "The inability to take a series of directions"—I could not follow more than two directions without getting lost. Dorothy takes all directions whenever we must ask for them. "The complete inability to remember a series of numbers"—I must drive my clients crazy, asking them to repeat their phone numbers several times; no more than two digits at a time, please. Even then I usually reverse two of the numerals.

I began reading everything I could find about dyslexia. Dorothy and I joined the Orton Dyslexia Society and attended their conventions where speaker after speaker described the symptoms of dyslexic patients. Then in group discussions I told my story while I listened to others tell theirs. Our experiences had been the same. Here I was in the presence of my kin, and I felt peaceful, accepted and understood.

Since dyslexia is a syndrome, and a syndrome is a cluster of symptoms, a diagnosis is based not on the existence of one or two symptoms, but rather the presence of multiple symptoms often in varying degrees of severity. So I began making a list of any and all attributes described in the literature that indicate the possible presence of dyslexia in an individual. This list, compiled entirely from the professional literature, now contains 71 items (See Appendix B).

Using my list I then created a "symptom inventory" by which one can grade oneself on a scale based on the severity, intensity or frequency of the symptom in one's own life. One can also discuss these items with a close friend or family member to get an outsider's impression.

The inventory also provides for the exceptions since it is known that, while a symptom may be common in most dyslexics, the exact opposite may be true in another. For example, many dyslexics have some motor and coordination deficits, yet

Bruce Jenner, a diagnosed dyslexic, was an Olympic gold-medal winner.

The symptoms in the inventory are grouped into categories. The first group contains those symptoms which are congenital. They become apparent early in life as developmental lags, but may be outgrown later. Some of these are, "As a child I was known to have been clumsy," or "I had trouble learning to skip or ride a bike," or "Tying my shoes, using a zipper and buttoning my clothes were all hard to learn."

The second level or category are those manifestations that occur as a result of the developmental lags. Because dyslexic children develop more slowly in critical left brain processes, these symptoms appear when the child comes in contact with the academic system. The child is unable to cope with traditional educational methods. Examples are "Learning to read was difficult for me," or "Spelling was one of my most difficult subjects," or "Learning a second language was difficult for me." Some of these struggles may also be apparent later, such as, "I have difficulty with the directions of left and right"; "I cannot remember more than five telephone numbers"; "I am known for my absent-mindedness"; or "Even on familiar roads I get lost."

A third level involves the emotional and personality consequences of having been academically handicapped: "I often thought I was a dumb child," or "People often think of me as being stubborn, inflexible and rigid," or "I have one or more phobias, such as heights, knives, crowds or enclosed places."

A fourth level includes evidences of compensatory mechanisms or abilities; for example, "I prefer orderliness because it gives me great comfort," or "I have an excellent pictorial memory," or "I often use rituals to simplify life," or "Periodically I will solve a problem in an unexpected moment of insight which surprises even me."

When I applied this test to myself I found that I rated seven items as "Sometimes," sixteen items as "Rather often," and forty-five items as "Extremely often." The inventory has helped me, not only in demonstrating how many of these symptoms I have, but also by showing the way in which the symptoms cluster.

Hoping it might be helpful to others I have made the inventory available to clients and professionals. A number of clinicians in the field of dyslexia have found it to be a useful tool, aiding the sometimes difficult diagnosis of this disorder.

19.

The Idiot Disclosed

Now that I had a name for the demon that had followed me all my life I began to look back and reinterpret my life with this new vocabulary.

Dyslexia runs in families and shows up in boys far more frequently than in girls. Studies now in progress are reporting preliminary findings of the presence of actual brain abnormalities visible microscopically. The impairment exists in the left hemisphere of the brain where the major sensory input and motor output areas are located. This, then, results in delayed or erratic development of all language skills.

There can be multiple causes. In addition to its genetic component, dyslexia can also be acquired anytime before or after birth. Lack of oxygen to the brain, a high fever or an actual brain injury can all result in a developmental impairment or abnormality to the left hemisphere.

Every male in my immediate family has some degree of dyslexia. My father had great difficulty in learning language. All my life I heard that Mother was so much better than he was academically. They were in the same class in school and he never ceased to be amazed at the way she outshone the rest of her classmates, including him. His basic assumption was that girls learned easily and boys did not.

As an adult Dad manifested many symptoms of the disability. Whenever he was in the house he demanded absolute silence. He could not read his German newspaper in the presence of any distractions. His attention deficit disorder was as severe as mine. Even at mealtimes he demanded total silence. If an infant could not be kept quiet he simply took his food and went into the only other room where he ate alone.

It was a generally known fact in our village that Dad was lost somewhere in space, unreachable. This, everyone thought, accounted for his inability to succeed in farming and why it was that, if it had not been for Mother's efficient management skills, the Schmitt brood would surely have starved to death.

My dad was seen as peculiar, odd and a loser. We all knew it and made fun of the situation. He came from a large family and had many brothers. I assume that all of them were like him, but because they all moved to Mexico I have no way of knowing.

Whenever I talk about dyslexia and its symptoms to someone from the villages, or to an Old Colony Mennonite or descendant, I hear a sudden "Ah-ha." I know I have found another dyslexic or close acquaintance of one. I have a strong hunch about the Old Colony people. Throughout their entire history they have shunned education. They have consistently moved from country to country, always to the remotest regions, packing up and leaving whenever mandatory education caught up with them. Their own educational system, three months of the year for three years, offers little more than the rudiments of reading, writing and simple arithmetic.

During my years on the faculty of the University of Pennsylvania I became intrigued by the psychological motive behind every historical event, and the historical context as a factor in understanding the formation of individual or group personality. I came to view the Old Colony Mennonites as a group of people who remained homogeneous for hundreds of years because of their separation and isolation from external influences. A common congenital factor rendered the male population unable to learn, while the female population remained unaffected. That fact so threatened male leadership and made the men so fear being regarded as inferior that it led them to reject the entire education process where feminine superiority was obvious. This anti-education theme became the most powerful motive controlling the group's behavior.

I have concluded that Old Colony culture was built by dyslexic men whose deeply imbedded, unchangeable defect was at the core of this people's extreme efforts and resulting hardships as they fled back and forth across continents for centuries, simply to avoid education.

Their stated reason was to protect themselves from the "world" and its evils and to maintain a separate, pure and holy lifestyle. Yet other groups of Mennonites without the learning handicap were able to remain distinct and intact while, at the same time, developing strong educational systems that often served as models for the surrounding communities.

I wonder if the basic reason for the conflict in my boyhood village between the uneducated descendants of the original Old Colony Mennonites and the educated-in-Russia Mennonite immigrants was that the one group was dyslexic and the other was not. My speculations will have to remain just that until further research either substantiates or invalidates them.

I am not the only offspring of my father to inherit this familiar defect. I have three brothers, all of whom are impaired to some extent. None of my four sisters appears to be afflicted, however. Since I have a son with this disability the hereditary chain is firmly established.

I am the most impaired dyslexic in my family. All my siblings struggled in school, but none has the gruesome history that I have. They vividly remember my struggle, but it was not theirs.

I now assume that, in addition to the inherited trait that was passed on to me, my handicap was amplified by a series of circumstances. Possibly my premature birth contributed to it; likely the kidney infection that I developed at age eight with its resulting high fever, causing me to lapse into a coma and not regain consciousness for seven days, caused an additional degree of brain impairment. Upon my return to school it appeared to the teacher that I had learned nothing, and I was put back a grade and targeted as the academic idiot. None of my brothers or sisters ever failed a grade.

After this all of my other symptoms escalated until I was the classroom fool. The attention deficit disorder would not allow me to conform to classroom expectations of quiet concentration when all around me were thirty other people creating innumerable distractions. I was caught between inner protests and outer threats, all while I was supposed to be learning. I could not do it.

Dyslexia is primarily a language-learning deficit. It was most evident for me in my inability to spell, read and speak the English language, the primary purpose of the educational systems into which I was thrust.

Because my developmental process did not keep pace with my maturation, teachers attributed my deficiencies to laziness. No explanation could account for the manual dexterity I showed in building a miniature farmyard or Ferris wheel (the winner in a provincial competition and displayed during a Dominion Day celebration in the nearby English city of Swift Current).

As much as I wanted to leave my language defect behind in the village, it followed me to private boarding high school. If the teacher came into the classroom snarling and spouting facts in rote fashion, with no explanation of the core meanings, my disabilities flared and I failed. Neither could I handle any subjects taught in German, a language I could not learn no matter how considerate the teacher was. But in subjects such as physics, biology and algebra, taught using multisensory methods by kind, enthusiastic teachers, I had nearly perfect grades.

The question of what was really wrong with me was not settled at this school. Even though my beloved principal was convinced of my competence, I was not. My first session of normal school was a near disaster. Here, for the first time, I defined my defect as an emotional and/or mental problem. Only the intervention of a sensitive faculty member kept me from going under.

When I started teaching at Montford all my symptoms came back to haunt me. I was now the teacher, responsible to maintain order and impart knowledge, all the while dealing with my bundle of handicaps. Here, too, I failed.

The next year at Hague the counterfeit teacher was revealed and the dyslexic idiot claimed its victim. Coming from a basically religious background I naturally interpreted my entire problem as a spiritual one. It was a fortunate conclusion for me. Had I decided that the problem was emotional or mental, a setting such as that could have totally destroyed me. There were known solutions in that environment for a spiritual problem, which I gratefully accepted, even as there were people eager to help me in defining and resolving it. Consistent with my way of dealing with life, I pursued repentance with every fiber of my being.

Because living with my inner deformity had been so cruelly consuming, I clung to the church community's solution with a passion of equal strength. I expected everyone else to have as full a commitment to faith. I viewed Canadian Mennonite Bible College as a utopia, demanding perfection and holiness of every student and teacher according to my definition. My hopes did not, nor could not, work, and I crumbled psychologically. My self-concept had been feebly formulated. Dyslexia takes a terrible toll on a developing child's self-concept, especially, as in my case, when it is not identified and the child is blamed, even punished brutally because of it. The frequent failures in my early life and the lack of explanations for them had crippled my sense of self. I should have, for example, been able to enter into my classmates' pranks and fun instead of curling up with my self-imposed wounds.

In struggling to find my identity I was best able to define myself in spiritual terms. Yet I took on the spiritual identity far too absolutely. I tried to simplify life into neat categories— black and white. I could then choose which I wanted and end the struggle. I wanted most to escape the tension between light and darkness. The only solution I could envision was to die and go to a state of perfection, namely heaven. But although I begged for that release it did not happen. In despair and defeat I turned away from Winnipeg.

The Carrot River wilderness school was a no-fail proposition. I had my twin brother to give leadership to the entire venture. I had conquered my difficulty with the spoken language. My other handicaps did not matter in this setting of mutual affection shared among the community, students and teachers. I succeeded even if I did borrow from my twin.

Yet I left that secure setting and took the biggest leap of faith of my life. How could I possibly think I was ready to go to college in another country with only one year of success to my name?

I know that I dreaded staying in that remote setting; I felt doomed to stay there forever. That dread was, I believe, the secret idiot, still uncaptured and untamed, lurking somewhere in the dark. Instinctively I knew that if I remained in that place I would never identify the idiot or ever defeat it. So, against all odds, I fled to the United States.

Perhaps I inherited something else from my ancestors: that the answer to life's problems was to flee. They fled from education and I fled towards it. However different the result, our motivation was the same: the solution can be found in the next country.

In truth, my answer *was* in the next country. The fool I had made of myself remained in Canada. Although the idiot inside came with me, I could, at least, bury it with college and university degrees so that no one else knew it existed. My oddities and quirks were seen by others as evidence of the eccentricities typical of the "scholarly type."

In my four years at Goshen College and Biblical Seminary I earned three degrees. Yet the most important lesson I learned was to compensate for my learning handicaps. Here the right hemisphere of my brain was able to take over for the insufficiently developed left hemisphere. I perfected my photographic memory so that it stored information in a safe place until I needed to present it to a professor who gave me A's for doing so.

Once I was in graduate school I could sidestep the most overt and menacing of the dyslexic symptoms. Fortunately I was married to a person who functioned as well in the left brain hemisphere as I did in the right. All of my reversed letters, my hieroglyphic spelling, the sentences that adhered to no syntax, and the haphazard paragraph order all vanished with the help of my typist-wife. I rescued her from an overdose of child care and household duties, and she rescued me from my specific language disabilities.

Now I could begin to attend to the emotional impairment that had begun with my first contact with education and had escalated whenever I collided with the secret idiot. My chosen field required that I confront my inner being. Social work demands one's entire person. No part can be omitted or hidden. No matter how much that frightened me, I sensed a reward lay ahead, like a light drawing me onward.

Mrs. Dowens, my instructor in personality development, set me on a course of discovery that shaped my professional life. The purpose of our teaching, she emphasized, was not to make everyone alike, but to find the uniqueness of every human being. We were learning two things: to make this discovery for ourselves and to teach those same skills to others.

That awakening totally freed me to grow. My task was to stop being ashamed of being different and to instead accept my distinctiveness. The degree to which I could accept myself was the degree to which I would grow professionally. As I made peace with my differentness I could offer this same understanding to, and celebrate it with, every client. I grew as a clinician as I left the caterpillar of my personal self and metamorphosed into the butterfly of my professional self.

I experienced only one reversal in this process when, while working in front of a one-way mirror, the worm reappeared. I blushed uncontrollably, leading me to seek therapy. I found help from a true professional who listened with respect and admiration as I told the truth of my life. He met me not as a disease, but as a person—exactly what a dyslexic needs.

I had driven myself to get a doctorate in answer to a need far more internal than external. To effectively practice social work a master's degree is sufficient. To go beyond that is unnecessary unless one wishes to teach in the profession. Then a doctoral degree is valuable. Although I did later teach, that was not my goal. I was merely obeying an obsession to prove to my world that my intellect could function well.

Yet here I was struck by the basic truth of my disability: dyslexics cannot organize. My global, diffuse thinking process was unable to handle the linear thought processes required to research and write a dissertation. Yet as soon as this was handled by someone competent in those areas, I was able to complete and defend the dissertation. In fact I could do both easily.

When I reentered the classroom, this time as a professor, the contradictions within me came into full view. Whenever I tried to perform in areas of my impairment—for example, writing on a blackboard—I failed. In areas outside my handicaps, such as conceptualizing the theories of Abraham Maslow, Erik H. Erikson, Sigmund Freud or Otto Rank, I excelled.

Otto Rank and his theories of personality development had the greatest impact on my professional development and my entire career.

20.
Rank and I

*I*t was in the early weeks of my master's degree program that I was first introduced to the ideas of Otto Rank. His statement which Professor Laura Dowens quoted to me about accepting one's distinctiveness relieved many of my fears and set me on the course that was to change my life.

I determined to find out more about the man who thought this way. Otto Rank, I learned, was a German psychoanalyst, a close friend of Sigmund Freud. In fact he was Freud's personal secretary and a member of the inner circle that surrounded the father of psychoanalysis.

During the 1930s two faculty members of the Pennsylvania School of Social Work, Jessie Taft and Virginia Robinson, read Rank's writings and traveled to Paris to learn to know him better. When Rank moved to New York City and set up his own practice of psychoanalysis, these two women became his patients.

Returning to Philadelphia they used Rank's theories of personality development to establish a new focus in the social work helping process, called the Functional Approach. By the time I came to the school in the late 1950s, all of the faculty members had learned Rank's theories, some had been his patients, and the school had become the center for the teaching of functional social work practice.

Rankian followers had great affection for the man and his theories, but his writings were never highly valued. His books were difficult to read, suffering, perhaps, from having been translated from German into English. To my surprise though, I discovered that I did not have the same difficulty that my fellow students had in reading Rank's works. This I attributed to my familiarity with the German language and the affinity I had for Germanic thinking processes. Unlike English writing which is linear, Rank's German writing is cyclical, and its chapters and paragraphs lack introductory remarks or lead sentences. It assumes that the reader will understand the content as it emerges, without explaining it beforehand or summarizing it afterwards.

This style of thinking and writing I understood; it was natural and made sense to me. I was also drawn to his use of biblical terms and references in conceptualizing his theories. When he used the term "rebirth" to describe the capacity of human beings to be drastically transformed by some kind of mystical experience, he based it on Christ's gospel of rebirth and transformation through a life-changing commitment.

This kind of language and understanding made me feel right at home. In fact I was able to grasp these concepts and apply them so easily that my supervisors often asked me to share with the graduate level staff what I had learned the previous week and how I was using it in the practice of social work.

As I progressed through the doctoral program I continued to comprehend more fully, and be committed to, the Rankian theory. As time went on all of the original faculty members who had learned directly from Rank either died or retired, and within a short time after my graduation I was the single voice adamantly proclaiming Rankian ideas.

It was only natural then that I was invited back to continue teaching this theory and its application to social work. Taking Rank's stages of personality development I created a chart that graphically illustrates his two primary emphases, union and separation, in the developmental process (See Appendix C).

According to this concept, union and separation are dialectic forces that operate on an individual throughout one's entire life. Beginning before birth, when a child experiences complete psychological and physiological union with its mother, this process continues as a series of unions and separations.

The birth process is the first separation when the child becomes a physiologically separate individual. Throughout infancy the child remains in union with the central parent figure until the first assertion of the child's individuality is made at about two years of age. Childhood is characterized by a continuation of union with the family until adolescence is reached and another major separation occurs.

In each separation of the developmental process persons establish their own individual identities, while in each union or connectedness with another they discover their value or self-worth.

So throughout life these journeys go back and forth until death, the ultimate separation, and then eternal life, the ultimate union. My right-hemispherical thinking allowed me to conceptualize this entire process into a chart showing the back and forth pattern of these movements. Because the zigzagging reminded some people of an EKG strip, the chart became known as "Abe's cardiogram." It was reprinted and used on many occasions. Fellow faculty members asked me to deliver this specific lecture to their classes, using my chart to illustrate the movements of union and separation throughout life.

Although Otto Rank died in 1939 an association was formed to carry on his work. In 1972 I was asked to lecture at the annual meeting of the Otto Rank Association. (The presentation was eventually published in their journal.) It was at this meeting that I met the writer, Anais Nin, who was also there to give a paper since she had been a patient of Rank's. The impact that Rank made on her life she recorded extensively in her published *Diary of Anais Nin*. She and I compared notes throughout the day about how her personal life and my academic experience had both been transformed by this man.

Several years later the editors of the *Comprehensive Textbook of Psychiatry*, the standard work used by most departments of psychiatry in their residency training, asked me to write a section on Otto Rank which was published in the second and third editions of this volume.

When I left university teaching I took Rank with me into my private practice where I translated his theory into marriage counseling. I created what I called a Model for a Maturing Marriage, postulating that marriage, like life, is a growth process. It is not the blurring of two personalities into one, but instead an opportunity for growth, utilizing union and separation as fulfilling and enhancing experiences rather than personally or relationally destructive ones. So, briefly, how do Rank's understandings bring light to troubled marriages?

I see difficulties in marriages as a need for a major rebirth process. Whenever one or both partners express a degree of separateness or individuality it appears to cause a major disruption in the relationship. Many couples cannot see in that the potential for growth, nor are they willing to pay the price for such growth. Many marriages come to an end as a result.

I call my therapeutic approach to marriage counseling "Conflict and Ecstasy." My primary task in treatment is to enable two people in a relationship to trust intimacy. When this happens, both can discover their individual self-worth and experience separation creatively so they are able to affirm their identity within and through the marriage. Again I created a chart (See Appendix D) showing these zigzagging movements within a marriage, and I use it with couples I counsel.

When I can help a couple interpret these movements of their marriage in a healthy way, they are able to find new meaning in their relationship, new experiences of each other and new freedom. Then they have no fear in intimacy for each person retains his or her identity and a new closeness is possible. Yet separation is possible only if the bond between them is strong enough. Conflict is seen as a necessary phase in their growth, while, at the same time, they accept and value each other's unique identity. Individuals can move toward each other in the union of a lifetime, yet simultaneously experience themselves as distinctly separate. Here in marriage, as in life, is the establishment of the two truths, union and separation, the dialectic of growth, making it possible for the human personality to evolve to the full height intended by the Creator.

21.

Dyslexic Fathers/Dyslexic Sons

*T*hree days ago I received a telephone call from Saskatchewan telling me that my father had just died. Having visited him less than one month ago, I am unable to return for the funeral.

I have written a eulogy which is being read at his funeral today. I have also been pondering my relationship with my father and, in turn, my relationship with my son.

My father and I had a kinship beyond the normal family connection. I believe he sensed that whatever was wrong with me was also wrong with him. We had an understanding between us that was different than between him and my other brothers.

The illness that hospitalized me at eight years of age affected him deeply. It was diagnosed as a kidney infection, but someone at the hospital told him that its probable cause was a vitamin deficiency. Because we lived mainly on meat and potatoes and he was an unsuccessful farmer, Dad blamed himself for being a poor provider and the one responsible for my near-fatal illness. He was nearly overcome with guilt and spent the rest of his life making up for this to me.

When my learning handicaps became more apparent after my hospitalization, Dad added this to his burden of guilt. Having experienced learning difficulties himself, he intensified his attention to me. Although he could do nothing about my problems at school, he seemed to do everything he could to enhance the relationship between us. This became so extreme and evident to everyone else that my brothers decided Dad's relationship to me was like the biblical patriarch Jacob's relationship to his favorite son, Joseph. They even began calling me Joseph.

Once we received a shipment of clothing, the kind that was sent to impoverished farm families during the Depression. The jacket that was assigned to me was a multicolored one which immediately sealed my identity in their minds. Now I became known as "Bunta," the Low German word for multi-colored. This nickname stuck for many years, a continual reminder of my status as the favored son.

Even after I moved far away my relationship with my father retained a tender quality. Whenever he called he expressed deep feeling for me and always inquired first about my health and that of my family. He was greatly relieved to learn that we were all well. Next he needed to know if I was still "making it," if I was earning enough to survive. Once these two issues were settled he soon ended the conversation, satisfied.

Now I, too, am the dyslexic father of a dyslexic son. I feel that same affinity for him that my father felt for me. As an infant David was robust, healthy, a bundle of activity and pleasure. His activity level soon turned into a problem, however, when it took him twenty-three months to learn to sleep through his first night. His hyperactivity made living with him extremely difficult. He exhausted both Dorothy and me to such a degree that I needed to take a year's leave of absence from all graduate studies. I simply could not care for this boy and study at the same time.

As our son grew older I knew there was something different about him. He was precious, he was bright, charming and sensitive, but there were definite indications that he was not like other boys his age. Once he started school his learning difficulties became immediately apparent. Dorothy and I made many trips to school and had many conversations and conferences with his teachers. I took the position as his protector and defender from anyone who would try to harm him.

In one serious confrontation David was falsely accused and harshly punished for instigating a commotion in his class-room. When he reported the incident to me, distraught at being punished so severely when he was innocent of any wrongdoing, I immediately walked the short distance to the elementary school to take issue with the teacher. After I had confronted her, firmly defending David's honesty and inno-cence, she admitted to me, in tears, that she was having difficulty controlling her class and that she was already on probation because of it. She begged me not to go to the principal. She acknowledged her error in dealing with David and agreed to apologize to him for the harm she had done. I insisted that she call me if she ever had any question about his behavior. I lived only two blocks away and was readily available to discuss the matter with her.

The remainder of the year was uneventful; this teacher continued in the school for many years and always greeted me graciously whenever we met.

Obviously I had an intense need to protect my son from the same kind of harm that was done to me. I was so intimately involved in his struggle that long before I knew the name for it I could not separate my son's difficulties in learning from my own.

It was almost as if I were raising a prototype of myself. I lived through all he was experiencing—from being vastly different from the other children to the difficulties he had with reading and spelling. Intuitively I imagined what was going on in his life, and I responded as I wished someone had done for me.

In my therapy practice I have dealt with many dyslexic children and their parents. While a number of fathers have been able to respond sensitively and tenderly, others have displayed animosity toward their children. These fathers are devastated by their children's handicaps, and they react with anger and avoidance. These dyslexic fathers are distressed by their dyslexic sons. The situation puts them through too much replay of their own experiences. Yet, if they can make peace with their own past and accept themselves, they can know a relationship of great depth and tremendous intimacy with their sons.

My protectiveness of David continued until he reached adolescence when he wanted more distance. Just as my father had allowed me to leave home and attend boarding school, I permitted my son to detach himself from me. He became secretive, hiding his day-to-day affairs from me. It was only through his report cards that I knew in what subjects he was struggling or excelling.

In his twenties he, like I, moved far away from home, this time to the opposite side of the continent. Yet our relationship remains close. He calls me frequently about any matter and readily confides in me. Our intimacy and high regard for one another is due, I feel, to the fact that we know deeply each other's struggles with the same handicaps.

On this day, as my father is being buried, I am deeply aware that the bond of a dyslexic father to his dyslexic son is one of my dad's greatest gifts to me.

22.

Living on the Right Side of the Brain

*I*just received word that the workshop planned for tonight was cancelled due to a lack of enough registrants. The workshop coordinator apologized over and over for having to cancel, especially, she said, after I had put so much time into preparing my presentation. After insisting that I would not accept any payment for my time I hung up and laughed. I had not spent one minute getting ready for the workshop, nor had I any intention of doing so. The truth is that I am unable to prepare.

As a person whose thought processes are based in the right hemisphere of the brain, I have no mental functions capable of organizing or outlining such an event. The only preparation I can do is to first imagine the experience of the event and then picture the overall impression that I intend to leave with my audience. I may think of some issues I might address or some examples I might use, but what actually happens depends on the way I experience the content as the event takes place.

I accept only topics with which I am intimately acquainted. It may be a subject on which I have written, delivered speeches or taught in graduate school. The issue may be one through which I have guided many people in the therapy process. It may even have involved my own family. I simply trust that when I get to the occasion I will experience the content in such a way that I can invite my audience into the venture so that they will become involved in it too. I try to be as fully alert as possible and then trust the experience for the rest. I simply take a nap and go.

The right and left hemispheres of the brain provide each individual with two modes of consciousness. Left-hemispherical thinking is scientific, focused, directed, linear, verbal, rational and concrete. Right-sided thinking is intuitive, receptive, artistic, diffuse, nonlinear, sensuous and spatial.

Recent studies have shown a physiologic basis for this difference in brain functioning that varies from one individual to another. Because our western culture has favored the characteristics of left-sided functioning, our educational system reflects that bias and is heavily weighted against those individuals whose physiologic makeup has granted them attributes of creativity, imagination and fantasy.

People with congenital or acquired dyslexia often have left-sided handicaps that are so severe that most of their mental processes are delegated to the right hemispheres of their brains. As a result fifteen percent of the population function directly opposite to the standard methods of education and the accepted, "normal" ways of thinking. Thus, many of these people believe they are defective. Helping dyslexic clients understand and accept themselves as different, not inferior, is one of the most helpful things I can do.

Until I took ownership of my right-hemispherical function, I was baffled by my style. In the presence of left-brained persons I felt inferior. I sat in the classes of professors who had their notes perfectly outlined from beginning to end. Each lecture was a precise segment of a whole. For every subject there were subtopics, with sub-subtopics. Every concept had exactly three or four points within it.

I diligently took notes, reproducing outlines exactly, but I could not understand how subjects or concepts could permit themselves to be divided up as perfectly as a pie. For me there were all kind of notions that did not fit into that pie. If I suggested one a professor might insert my idea as a sub-subpoint in subject area B.1., but I could not comprehend how or why it was done that way.

When I became a professor there were students who came
to my classes with their notebooks and pens poised, expecting
an organized presentation which they could dutifully record.
At the beginning of the class they might note a few items; then
they would sit, waiting and waiting for the next point, but it
never came. Finally they would put away their pens and close
their notebooks.

My method was to create an experience with words. I was
teaching Theories of Personality Development, a subject
which I genuinely loved and lived. Without books or notes I
would create an event in which the students could participate
and *experience* the content.

Some of the more compulsive, left-hemispherical students
objected to my style. One student came up to me after several
weeks of classes and, showing me a single page with scattered
notations, protested that I was so disjointed she could not
make sense of my class.

Considerably more often students expressed gratitude for
what happened to them in my class. They were using my
course, they said, to become clinicians. I was modeling that
role for them while teaching the subject matter which they
needed to know.

There are risks in this type of teaching and workshop
leadership. Some days I am in a mental fog and nothing can
bring me out of it. At those times I am unable to create the
atmosphere or conditions for learning by experience. These
are the days when I desperately yearn for a neat set of notes
or a well-crafted outline. Since I cannot produce such saving
devices I have developed my own strategies. I divide the
participants into small groups, have them discuss an issue
from a previous session and report back to the entire group
later. I spend this time in oblivion; my brain is switched off.

Because the focused linear side of my brain is under-devel-
oped, I cannot be involved in more than one item or event at
a time. To shift gears, to move from one issue to the next,
requires a very deliberate effort. On occasion in my faculty
office at the university I was faced with one student sitting in

front of me, three more waiting outside the door, several faculty assignments on my desk that needed to be in the typist's hands before noon, and a class to teach at 1:00. The telephone had already rung once and could ring again at any moment.

Unlike my colleagues, who appeared to thrive on such challenging stimuli, I could not handle it. My brain simply short-circuited and shut down. This was another factor in my decision to leave university teaching and pursue private practice where I could be more in control of the demands on my mental functioning.

Now I see clients on a precisely regulated schedule each day without changes. I have two time slots each morning, three in the afternoon and two in the evening. Between each client I have a thirty-minute break during which I go through a deliberate mental exercise of disengaging and then re-engaging.

I need to use that same mental exercise whenever I am interrupted by a telephone call during a session with a client. I must set aside the client, walk out of the room, then re-engage for the next issue. Returning to the client I reverse the process. Whenever possible I now switch off the telephone while I am seeing a client, for even the chance of its ringing during that time is more than I can bear. I have accepted my right-sided functioning and I try to structure my life accordingly.

Global thinking is a characteristic of right-sided functioning that has enabled me to step back from details and to view the larger context. With a deficiency in sequential memory, a left-sided function, I cannot remember facts as many people do. But I can translate what I hear into larger, logical concepts. These I remember for they fit into everything else I know. It is like studying all the skeletal and muscular parts of the body, then turning to a canvas and painting the human figure.

When new ideas are presented my entire perception changes. Thus, for me, learning is not simply gathering more information; it is personal transformation.

A professor-friend of mine is writing his autobiography as I complete mine. He, as a person with highly developed left-hemispherical functions, is producing a thoroughly organized, well structured chronology of the facts of his life. Yet he is having difficulty citing illustrations for fear that they will not fit properly into the chronological data.

My story, on the other hand, is full of flashbacks, generalizations, drama and broad descriptions. He tells me I paint pictures as I write. Yet my work lacks the neat orderliness of an unfolding story; for that I need the help of another.

I am struck by the contrast: two people with similar academic careers, both trying to tell their stories, each lost in separate hemispheres.

23.
Creative Sublimation

I have become a voracious reader. I read nearly everything I can get my hands on. My professional library holds hundreds of books, mostly in the fields of personality development, psychology and marital interaction, as well as specialized issues related to my areas of interest. I read the daily and Sunday papers from front to back, weekly magazines and numerous periodicals.

Reading is still work for me. Yet my need to learn and to know is insatiable so I force myself to read. One of my nicknames as a child was "Curiosity Schmitt." In the Low German language this was said in a derogatory way, usually by my uncles when they saw me approaching, knowing I would ask question upon question about anything and everything they were doing. I never stopped with "What?"; I pushed further to "Why?" I had to understand the inner meanings of life and the world around me.

Later I realized that I could find answers to some of my questions in books. No matter how difficult the task of reading was for me, my curiosity grew ever stronger. Now my friends advise each other, "Don't leave a book or magazine on the coffee table in front of Abe if you want his attention."

Dyslexia has been defined as defective reading.[1] Developmental dyslexia is a failure to profit from one's reading instruction in spite of having adequate intelligence and educational opportunity.[2] Reading is a complex process involving visual perception, sensory memory, attention, control and the processing tasks of selecting, coding, decoding, storing and retrieving information.[3] All of these processes occur in the neuroanatomy of the brain. Neuroanatomical deficits, the widely accepted cause of dyslexia, result, then, in the impairment of the tasks necessary for reading.

Language is basic to communication, and reading is essential for communication other than speech, so any deficits in one's ability to read have a great effect on the individual and, ultimately, society as a whole.[4] Symptoms of defective reading vary greatly, but commonly include reversing letters, words and concepts, omitting and/or repeating words and phrases, and comprehending poorly what one reads.

My own symptoms vary from day to day. On bad days when my symptoms are at their worst I experience a constant mingling and mangling of words, phrases, lines and sentences as I read. My eyes seem to pulsate as the words go in and out of focus. The page looks like a television picture during a storm when the antenna sways back and forth in the wind. I read in spurts as the page clears and then blurs again. I feel as if I should put my hands at the edge of every line to keep the print from floating away. I must grab every word and hold it in place until I finish reading it; otherwise the letters scramble or the word simply vanishes altogether. Some words do just disappear and I read on as if they never existed. When this happens I come to the end of a sentence or section and realize that what I read did not make sense. Then I must go back and read it all over again, hoping this time to catch what I missed before.

Any noise in the environment can interrupt my concentration while I read. Even the starting and stopping of the refrigerator or a vacuum sweeper running in an adjoining room catch my attention, interfering with the job at hand.

With my wife I have developed a collaborative style of reading. If I really want to know the content or the author's position but I am unable to tackle the entire book, I give it to Dorothy. She reads it, underlining crucial passages and writing notes and cues in the margins, directing me to, or away from, certain passages as applicable. Then she returns the book to me and I, by reading only the highlighted sections, have the information I need. Many of the books in my library are doctored up in this way.

At other times Dorothy discusses a book with me, reading selected passages aloud. My global thinking processes help me grasp the content and its implications for me and my practice. I can then translate what I have "read" into clinical skills.

On good days when I am at my best and there are no distractions I do a form of speed-reading which permits me to grasp the content of a paragraph or section by gliding over the surface without tangling with individual words. Apparently I use words or groups of words to trigger a series of mental flashes, thus allowing me to grasp the concept as a whole without having to read every word correctly.

This works well until I am asked to read out loud. Then the words become gibberish. I avoid such situations whenever possible because it embarrasses me and others. I sputter and spit out words, completely eliminating some, inventing others, as my eyes try to follow the text, while in my brain wires crisscross and circuits short out.

Once while conducting a weekend workshop I revealed the worst of my reading handicaps to an audience of over a hundred people. It was during the Saturday afternoon session when, because I was running out of creative steam, I tried to read something I had previously written. I hoped the passage would stimulate dialogue and rescue me from the mental fog that was rapidly rolling in.

For ten minutes I struggled to read. Although I knew the content, the words that I heard myself saying did not make sense, even to me. I felt the extreme discomfort of the audience and, in despair, I surrendered. The moment was unredeemable; I had no clever devices with which to cover my tracks. So I simply told the audience that I needed sleep, that my brain had preceded me to bed. Humiliated to tears I faded into oblivion. After a nap I returned for the evening session and continued the workshop as if nothing had happened.

Fortunately that did not occur at a promotional event for

my first book, *Dialogue with Death*. The publisher invited me to deliver an address on the subject of the book to the company's entire staff and sales personnel. I decided to read the opening chapter of the book as an introduction to my speech. I was well rested and energized by the excitement of the event. Since the book had not yet been released I knew that no one had a copy in which to follow along. Furthermore, the content was so familiar to me that I would not get lost if my words did not match the text exactly.

I read the first several lines word-for-word, but I sensed a restlessness from the audience. My brain switched to automatic pilot as I delivered the words from my heart and not from the pages of the book. The session ended with a standing ovation.

Afterwards the editor in chief remarked, "I have never heard anyone read an entire chapter before an audience and get away with it as you did."

Books and I have made strange bedfellows. Sigmund Freud said that the human psyche loses nothing without replacing it with something else. This unconscious psychological mechanism is called sublimation. In my case I lost the ability to learn language, and I replaced it by spending the rest of my life with words—reading, teaching, speaking, counseling and writing books.

After the publication of one of my books a newspaper reporter visited my office to interview me. As she probed into my style of writing I showed her my journal, one of many that I keep at arm's reach all over the house and even in the car. I told her how I take one wherever I go, that I must record whatever stirs or startles me, externally or internally.

Since in her vocation she depends on words she was both understanding and curious. "Why are you so obsessed with manufacturing words?" she asked me.

At the time I had no answer; I did not yet know about my loss. I was only aware of a great urgency within me to work with words, to play with words and to make words work for me.

A psychiatrist friend calls this "a creative sublimation"; that however great my loss in one direction, I was able to make up for it in the opposite direction. What had been my loss has become my gain.

---

[1] John Money, "Dyslexia: A Postconference Review," in *Reading Disability, Progress and Research Needs in Dyslexia*, ed. John Money (Baltimore: The Johns Hopkins University Press, 1962), p.9.

[2] "Dyslexia, The Language Disability that can Be Overcome" (Baltimore: The Orton Dyslexia Society, 1982), p.7.

[3] Robert C. Calfee, "Memory and Cognitive Skills in Reading Acquisition," in *Reading, Perception and Language,* ed. Duane D. Drake and Margaret B. Rawson (Baltimore: The Orton Society by arrangement with York Press, Inc., 1975), pp. 55-61.

[4] Roger E. Saunders, "Dyslexia: Its Phenomenology," in *Reading Disability, Progress and Research Needs in Dyslexia,* ed. John Money (Baltimore: The Johns Hopkins University Press, 1962), p. 35.

24.

Imprisoned by Words

*T*he word "dyslexia" literally means "impaired words." The prefix "dys" indicates faulty or impaired, and the Greek root word "lexis" refers to speech, words or vocabulary. Faulty speech, impaired words, mixed-up vocabulary—this summarizes well my most obvious handicaps.

Letter reversals, often a diagnostic indicator of dyslexia, plague me. As I write, reversals appear almost one per sentence. It is as though that part of my brain controlling letter order and spelling stalls momentarily or short-circuits, and during that instant I write "whis" instead of "wish." Sometimes I lose the middle of a word. I mean to write "no one," but a bleep in my brain occurs at that moment and "ne" appears on my paper. It is as if my mind sees the ending of the second word before finishing the first and omits the letters in between.

I easily confuse "was" and "saw." I know the difference between the two; perhaps the fact that I use them so often has worn out that particular brain connection.

It is a strange sensation to be writing a word and suddenly get stuck on a particular letter. I may write three or four "i's" all at once before I can stop. It often happens when I am writing my name. One morning recently I tried to endorse a check. As I began writing, three "A's" appeared before I could stop myself, and when I got to my last name, I wrote "Schmmmm." This happens so frequently that I have an instant corrective strategy. By dotting one of the humps I create an "i," and by heightening the next two and crossing them I make two "t's." I draw a line through any remaining humps as an extra flourish to my signature, a true dyslexic autograph.

Not only do I reverse words and letters, I have great difficulty remembering or reciting sequences of numbers. Telephone numbers are especially troublesome because they are
an important link in my keeping contact with my clients.

Recently a distraught person called, explaining the circumstances of her life, asking if I would accept her for counseling.
Just then our second telephone rang. I put the first caller on
hold, only to discover that the second call was long-distance
and equally as urgent. I returned to the first caller to get her
phone number so that I could call her back. True to form, I
forgot to ask for her name. She gave me her phone number; I
carefully wrote it down and told her I would return her call as
soon as I finished the other.

Already my head was spinning. I disconnected the first
phone to prevent any more calls from coming through. The
dread of its ringing again was too much for me to handle at
that point. I returned to the second caller and dealt with the
problem at hand.

Now it was time to return the first call. I dialed the number
which I had written down, only to get a recording telling me
that the number I had reached was not in service. I had mixed
up the digits. I had also broken my own cardinal rule by not
reading the number back to the caller before hanging up. I
mean to always do that, especially when there is a crisis
situation involved, with the intense confusion that that creates.

I unplugged both telephone lines and made a cup of coffee
to give me some time to unravel my mangled brain. I had told
the person that I would call her back. I knew she probably
would not call me again because she had been apprehensive
about my accepting her as a client. I had not yet told her that
I would see her, nor had I offered her an appointment. She
could easily assume that my failure to return her call was my
way of rejecting her and her call for help.

Just then Dorothy returned home. She dialed the number
herself in case I had reversed the numbers as I dialed (a

common occurrence). The recording proved it was, indeed, the wrong number. Then came the careful process of elimination. Knowing the name of the town from which she had called, I established that the first three digits were correct. That left four digits to unscramble. Assuming that I had heard the first one correctly I wrote down the five remaining possible combinations of digits. My wife dialed the first two, and they were both out of service. The next was answered by a male voice who emphatically stated that he had not called our number and he did not need a doctor! The fourth try was correct and I gave her an appointment.

Had I incorrectly recorded the first numeral, the number of possibilities would have increased to twenty-four, a monumental task to untangle. Had I reversed the prefix, it would have been impossible to trace that call.

My speech also suffers from this unpredictable brain functioning. My family has been most subjected to my halting speech and my disjointed phrases. Patiently and impatiently they have listened to me sputter, stutter and pause for great lengths of time between words or ideas. Often in exasperation they have finished a sentence for me just to end the frustrating wait.

Yet I have spoken before countless audiences, addressed distinguished colleagues and conducted many workshops and conferences, all with little or no evidence of my handicap.

These discrepancies, the "tide effect" as I call it, are realities I have come to accept. The severity of all my symptoms can vary from day to day, from hour to hour. It feels like a tide that rises and falls, even like waves that wash in, sweep over me and then recede. Unlike the tide, however, I cannot predict the rising and subsiding of my symptoms. Often it seems that if a sudden demand is placed on me, such as giving a speech or testifying in a court hearing, I can rally to meet the challenge. My thoughts are lucid and my speech is eloquent and clear. My impressed audiences do not know that afterwards my brain may have shut down so completely that I do not know my way home.

Sometimes it is not the words themselves, but my ability to recall them that is impaired. This symptom is called word retrieval deficiency. I call it word slippage but it feels like forgetfulness. It is with me always. Every time I open my mouth there is a high probability that I may lose my key idea, my main purpose for talking. I may lose the name of the person I am addressing.

For most of my life I had no idea why this happened to me. The experience of it has ranged from frustrating to embarrassing to devastating.

There are times when I cannot recall the name of a simple household item although there is a photographic image of it in my head. I describe its size, shape, color and location until my wife supplies me with the correct name for the item.

At other times a client sits in silence as I take a short gasp of air and search for the key word or point I want to make. Many clients dismiss this particular mannerism as one of my peculiarities. I wish sometimes that people knew the struggles dyslexics have to communicate, the ever-present likelihood that their brains will go into complete disarray.

I am often vividly reminded of my humiliating experiences as a teacher when I could not call my students by their names. This particular disability became especially embarrassing for me as a faculty member in a graduate school. I taught two or three moderately sized classes for at least a full year, sometimes two, yet I could not remember any of the students' names. To make matters worse, the subject area was human development and emphasized the uniqueness of every human being. What is more unique to anyone than his or her name?

Once or twice a semester a bewildered student would remain after class to upbraid me. There was no excuse whatsoever that I could not call her by name. This was the second year that she had taken classes under me. My failure to call her by name was a complete violation of all the psychology I taught. Addressing her correctly was a test of my recognition of her distinctiveness and I had failed.

What makes this so baffling to me and others is that I have

not forgotten who these people are. I remember infinite attributes about them. I can recall details about clients that
they may even have forgotten. I can see their exact posture
as they sat in my office, their exact facial expressions; I can
recollect the emotion that predominated during a session and
even the phases of the healing processes. It is as if these
persons were once my most intimate friends and this intimacy
always remains with me. I can immediately plug into the
meaning of the lives we shared together in the office—but I
cannot remember their names.

Now that I have learned that this is a symptom of dyslexia
I live with it much more comfortably. Now I have an explanation to offer those who cannot understand why I have
forgotten their names.

"Look here, my colleague, my client, my friend, I am dyslexic. That does not mean what you may think it does. I have
an excellent memory. My head is working well, except in
specific areas where it plays tricks on me. It will bleep out
your name, but it will not bleep out you or anyone else. I have
a great capacity to listen to your entire being, and I will take
you into my being and keep you there for a long, long time.
You are, and will remain, precious to me, but you must
remember that when I press the retrieval key I cannot use
your name to do it. Most people you have ever known use your
name as the reference for storing all the information about
you. I cannot. That does not mean that I do not care about
your distinctiveness; I do.

"You see, I have printed a picture of you in my soul with all
the information you have given me. Each time you tell me
more I add more details to the picture and it becomes more
fully complete. Ask me to recreate that picture and I will, but
please don't ask me for your name."

I am reading in the quiet of my living room and a car drives
past. My mind leaves the page and follows the sound. I am
listening to a client in the office and a dog down the street
begins to bark. I no longer hear the client's words as I consider
a confrontation with the neighbor.

As a dyslexic child I could not control my distractibility, and I was strapped for it. As a dyslexic adult I still must deal with this attention deficit disorder. Sometimes I can make a simple change in the environment and eliminate the distraction. If I am sitting in a lecture hall and a heating fan takes my mind away from the words of the speaker, I move to a different seat. At other times, especially if the level of distraction is too high, I suddenly switch off.

Walking into a crowded social setting is like walking into a hailstorm. I face a barrage of stimuli, both simultaneous and intense. I have no selection process by which to sort it all out. I feel a pull in every direction. Every person requires that a connection be made. To protect myself from the onslaught I become totally engaged with one person and completely absorbed in that conversation. Then everyone else vanishes and the person with whom I am talking and I are sealed off from the crowd. When this ends I quickly find another encounter, equally intense and exclusive. I am completely unable to engage in another conversation at the same time.

I have a defect in my data-processing function. I need more time to switch from one episode to another, from one source of information to another. As soon as too many events occur at once something in me switches off. I fade away. I depart the immediate event, spaced out. At this point I usually flee to some quiet place, some place where I can be alone and recoup.

I know that it appears to others that I am running from them, that I am avoiding them, that I am a snob. It is true that I am preoccupied, but not with great ideas or issues. I am simply coping with the problem of unraveling the mental confusion and clutter that such a setting triggers. I really do love to socialize and I love to converse. If I could only take each person, one at a time, with opportunity between each to reorient my brain, I would have the time of my life!

Strangely enough, on another occasion, in the same setting, I can be the life of the party, pulling puns, making witty remarks and sharing in the laughter. Anyone attending both events could not account for the contrast. Neither can I.

Some mornings my brain refuses to awaken. My body arises but my head is empty, my brain is gone. I struggle to think; I shake my head to see if I can get it going. I order my head to keep operating and keep prodding it to make it work. Fortunately not all my mornings are like this. Some days I am so alert that I can write dozens of pages before anyone else gets up. Yet all my life I have awakened to some hazy mornings; morning fog, I call it.

Such mornings often occur if I am particularly tired, if I did not sleep well the night before, or if the previous day or weekend was especially taxing. On mornings like these I cannot even remember if I have shaved or brushed my teeth two minutes after doing so. I forget what I am to do next and stare into the closet, completely dazed. Jarring myself I say, for example, "Get dressed for church." Half a minute later I must remind myself again, "Church." My entire dressing process becomes tediously deliberate with repeated reminders to myself to keep at it. Before leaving the room I must stop and examine my clothes. "Did I put on matching socks? Are these the clothes I intended to wear?"

It seems to me that if in a dyslexic brain specific parts malfunction, then the processing of information is more complicated. Messages must find alternate routes of passage, and simple mental operations become much more difficult, especially if the individual is tired or under stress.

Because I so often grope through this haze in my head I have ritualized every early morning activity. I shower, shave and brush my teeth in a prescribed, routine manner. I lay out all the items I will need in their proper order and put each one away after using it. That way I know that I have completed each task.

Breakfast, too, has become completely ritualized. I use the same bowl, same spoon, same cup, all found in the same place every morning. I eat the same kind of cereal in the same exact amount. If the people at that cereal company knew the years of devoted loyalty that I have given them, they would use me for publicity. I have eaten this very product nearly every morning of my adult life. I do like it, but definitely not that much! Years ago I made it part of a routine to get me through this early morning murkiness. With it I know that I have eaten breakfast, and it feels right.

I follow a similar deeply imbedded pattern as I make a cup of coffee. With each step carefully programmed I do not need to think. The ritual simply takes over. I have formed a groove in my brain and everything just happens automatically as I follow it through.

If the fog does not lift after breakfast I go through the motions of what appears to be normal living, but I am only remotely connected with what I am doing. If it is a morning when I have no clients scheduled and nothing demands my immediate attention I sit down with a cup of coffee and allow my thoughts to float freely through my mind. I flit lightly from subject to subject, at perfect peace. I am only vaguely aware that the hours are passing until I get a call for lunch. What have I done so far that day? I have drunk a cup of coffee.

On another such morning I attend a workshop, but I am insulated from all the events that flow past me. I know what is happening on the outside, but it does not touch me. It is as if a pane of glass separates me from everything around me. The lectures may be inspiring, but I am too spaced out to be moved by them.

Behind the glass, though, I am fully alive. I am thinking, processing and organizing my inner life. My mind picks up any thought and pursues it to endless depths. The intuitive, creative and imaginative part of me is vibrant with energy. My eyes catch sight of a vase of hardy mums on the platform. Instantly I am planting the flowers in my yard, creating patterns of flower beds in vast array within my head.

A sudden burst of laughter from the audience jars me back to reality, but too late. I have missed the joke even though my eyes were focused on the speaker the entire time. Sometimes at that point an idea or illustration from the lecturer may filter through. I take it like a gopher smuggling food into its burrow and savor it inwardly until I emerge again.

The workshop is over and as I prepare to leave I am greeted by a number of people. I respond with a smile, but I utter no sound. Not until I have walked away do I realize that I must have appeared rude. Now I recall the pleasant people who went out of their way to acknowledge me, and I did not return a greeting.

There is no possibility that people can understand my behavior. I do not act that way deliberately, nor do I choose to be rude. At times I am simply lost in the fog of my dyslexic brain.

25.
Music: Dissonance and Desire

Music has always been inside me begging to be expressed, but I have been unable to give it form. All my life I have lived with the tension between my yearning to create music and my complete inability to do so.

When I was young I listened for hours to my friend Pete strum his banjo, to Uncle Bill play his guitar and harmonica, and Henry his violin. Every Saturday night I curled up next to the radio—for it was then that the station from Nashville, Tennessee, came in best—and listened to the Grand Ole Opry. All week I lived for Saturday night, to be absorbed by Roy Acuff and his violin, the Carter Family and their songs and ballads. The songs were of life as I knew it, filled with tragedies; heart-wrenching stories of lost love, death and remorse. "Broken-Hearted Lover," "Lonesome Valley," "I Have No One to Love Me" and "Will the Circle Be Unbroken?" resonated with my deepest feelings. I was totally engrossed in every word; my body vibrated with each note.

When the program ended I blanked out and went into a fantasy, trying to relive the experience of being swept away by the words and music I had just heard.

I wanted so badly to sing. I wrote out the words to songs, as many as I could remember, then ran out into the farmyard and tried to sing them. I simply had to reproduce the music that affected me so profoundly. But the sounds that came out of my throat were nothing like the music that was in my head. I tried over and over again, but it was totally useless.

"Why can't the music come out?" I would cry to myself. "Why am I being beaten at school for not singing when I want to sing; I want desperately to sing! It must be my fault. My throat makes no music so it is all my fault."

As I grew older I listened to records and attended concerts, and the music carried me away to heights of glory. Violin music, especially, has always moved me deeply. I have never played the instrument, but it seems to play in harmony with the music of my soul. One Sunday morning I listened to a soloist while my mind accompanied him on the violin. It made his singing even more beautiful.

Sometimes in church when I feel at my very best I can sing, but the hymn must be utterly familiar and the melody simple. Because I cannot memorize I need to read the words. Because of my poor eye coordination I have difficulty following the lines. Additionally, because I cannot read smoothly I am unable to stay with the rhythm of the music. So with the amount of effort I need to make in order to read, follow the beat and know what kind of a sound to make with my voice, it is usually better that I remain silent.

That allows me to listen to the people singing around me. When persons nearby sing particularly well I make a point of thanking them for helping me worship.

They are often surprised when I tell them what has happened; they are not sure they actually *can* sing that well. Yet to me it was beautiful, and I am grateful for people who make music when I cannot.

26.
Conflict and Ecstasy: A Dyslexic Marriage

I recently asked Dorothy what it is like being married to a dyslexic. She, without hesitation, stated, "It's like living with a disaster waiting to happen!"

"I never know," she elaborated, "what kind of instant impulse reaction you may have. It is always possible that you will say the exact opposite of what you mean to say without even knowing that you said it. I usually know that it is not what you meant to say, but if I try to correct you, you become annoyed and upset. You don't realize that I have heard something other than what you intended to say."

Twenty years ago I wrote an article based on the model for marriage counseling that I had developed. Entitled "Conflict and Ecstasy: A Model for a Maturing Marriage," it was published in a national journal and reprinted in several others. I have since made reprints available upon request and have distributed over 9000 copies of the article. Repeatedly I have received letters and responses from individuals, couples and therapists, telling me that the article was helpful and meaningful.

I believe the article has been effective because it describes exactly what Dorothy and I have lived through in our marriage—a lot of conflict and a lot of ecstasy. Most of that mix is directly related to my dyslexia.

Dorothy and I experienced ecstasy when we discovered how much we complemented each other. Because of the severity of my handicap I needed help in major areas of my life. When

she could provide that help we both felt good and experienced
the uniqueness of our relationship. Likewise, when I could
give her what she needed, we also felt a sense of fulfillment.

I came to Goshen College at twenty-four years of age desperately lacking stability. I had a tremendous sense of being
lost; I wanted to put down permanent roots somewhere.

As Dorothy's and my relationship developed I believed that
I had finally been found by someone who was willing to marry
me and to stay permanently married. I was euphoric. She
would fill the void in my life and provide the security that I
needed so badly. No longer would I have to compete in the
often vicious game of dating and courtship. I had played that
game poorly, but at last it was over. I was settled for life.

Even in the smaller matters of daily living, Dorothy was the
answer. I needed someone to type my term papers for class;
Dorothy was a typist and a champion speller and could spot
all my errors and even read my atrocious handwriting. I could
not (and even today cannot) manage money or a budget, or
run a household. That, too, Dorothy has handled with skill
and efficiency since the day we were married. At twenty-two
years of age she had shouldered much of the responsibility for
her mother and household after her father's death. She
naturally took up the same role in our home and handled it
with equal ease.

Dorothy had no desire to pursue a career although she
graduated at the top of her nursing class. She received her
R.N. license, then practiced only one year before being invited
to a collegiate school of nursing to teach nursing arts while
she simultaneously completed her bachelor's degree. After
our children were born she ceased employment and became
the primary care-giver at home. I wanted to be out in the
world finding and establishing myself both academically and
financially. Those were the roles we preferred, and we slipped
into them.

During the first ten years of our marriage we were exceptionally poor financially. We had both grown up in poverty so
we accepted it easily, even interpreting it as an appropriate

Christian lifestyle. Our week-long honeymoon set the stage for our frugality during those early years. In a 1951 Chevy that Dorothy had purchased from her own earnings we drove to Niagara Falls, then through the Finger Lakes and Lake Champlain areas in New York State and on to Vermont before returning to eastern Pennsylvania, at a total cost of only one hundred dollars.

We often relished the fact that we knew how to live on very little income. In fact we now recall that period as one of our happiest, for, as we struggled to survive, we grew closer together each time we succeeded in the struggle.

One day Dorothy came home with a bag of groceries, having bought each item on sale, thus saving several dollars. We celebrated that as a major victory. Another time I saw a swivel rocker that the owners could not sell because a bolt was missing.

"I have a bolt like that at home," I said to myself. I paid five dollars for the chair that we still use today.

Dorothy remembers going to an auction shortly after we moved to the area where we now live. We had no furniture and she hoped to get a bargain. A kitchen set was brought forward, and, as the auctioneer stepped up on one of the chairs for a better view of the crowd, he broke right through the seat. No one wanted the set after that.

"That didn't bother me," Dorothy told me later. "I knew you could fix it, so I got the whole set for five or eight dollars."

On the matter of child-rearing we found ourselves both complementing each other and in conflict with one another. Dorothy saw herself as the disciplinarian, the one who set the rules and boundaries. She set many because, to her, life was an orderly, disciplined process. She wanted our children raised in that kind of framework.

My need was to protect the children from all evil and harm, to treat them with a lot of love and tender care. I did not want them to be wounded as I had been. So for every bruise, or even potential bruise, I ran to their aid. Sometimes I even felt I had to protect them from bruises that I thought Dorothy had inflicted.

Dorothy, in turn, saw me being much too soft with the children, so she imposed more rules to make up for my lack of doing so.

Other conflicts in our marriage have occurred when my dyslexic symptoms have erupted, usually at the most unexpected times. Those are the moments when she feels she is living with a "disaster waiting to happen."

Conflict is inevitable in a dyslexic marriage. Many marriages in which one partner is dyslexic are in turmoil and often end in divorce. Many men, unable to perform a role which they see as customarily male, such as money management, question their whole masculinity. They may demand control when, in fact, they are incompetent to handle it. Problems also arise if the wife of a dyslexic husband is unwilling to take over some areas of responsibility and views the husband's incompetence as immaturity. These are common dynamics and contribute to the divorce statistics among dyslexics. Much turmoil and anxiety can be avoided if both members of such a marriage understand the symptoms and how they affect the people involved.

One of the most valuable contributions to our marriage has been Dorothy's eagerness to understand and learn all she can about dyslexia. She not only has a dyslexic husband but also a son with the same disability. Dorothy has read all the books I have (usually because she has read them to me!) and together we have attended conventions. She insists on understanding the symptoms so that when bizarre ones do occur she knows they arise from the disability and are not all voluntary.

Dorothy says that the discovery of my dyslexia was "like a light going on. It answered a lot of things that we have not been able to understand."

When I asked Dorothy to elaborate on some of my symptoms and how they have affected our marriage and our family life she quickly pointed to my drive, my need to create, my "binges" as she calls them.

"It's like an adrenaline high," she says. "Once you get

started on an idea or project you can go for days, weeks or months! There's no stopping to take a breath; what you're doing takes precedence over everything and everybody."

I remind her that a whole book can come out of one of those highs, or a dissertation written in three weeks' time, for example. She then suggests that I know no happy medium. "There are either the highs, the binges, when you take nothing else into account, or there are the lows when you don't feel like doing anything."

Dorothy has also had to deal with dyslexic rage, another component of the disability. It is usually triggered by confusion, or the threat of confusion, and erupts suddenly as it did when I was child and was taunted into a fight. I am aware that when I am very close to the precipice I need only a slight push from Dorothy—maybe just the mention of the fact that I might have done something the wrong way—and I go over the edge.

She is often embarrassed by my inability to sit still in public meetings, church or group settings. Once I reach my endurance point and have had enough I get up and walk out, leaving her sitting alone, wondering what has happened, often having to account for my behavior to the rest of the people there.

"Whenever confusion enters, you exit," Dorothy tells me.

While my pictorial memory has often been an advantage to me, Dorothy feels differently. I have stored inside my head memories of everything that has happened in our marriage. I have thirty-seven years of instant replay.

"And to me you recall only the bad ones!" Dorothy chides.

My dyslexic symptoms have affected not only Dorothy but our children as well. Some they dismissed by a casual, "Oh, that's just Dad." Other behavior has become the butt of family jokes. My obsessive journal-writing has often been the object of jest, as is my need to carry many pens.

Once at a group event I was standing in line, writing in my journal, oblivious to the crowd around me. One of my daughters, farther back in line with a group of her friends, called out to me, "Hey, Dad, how many pens do you have with you today?"

"Enough," I answered as I showed her several in my outside coat pocket and then opened my coat to reveal a few more in the inside pocket. She and her friends were duly entertained.

Dorothy believes that the greatest impact my dyslexia has left on our children is that I was so often lost in another world, unavailable to them.

"Even when you were home, you were gone, spaced out, especially when you were on one of your binges," she said.

Now, as adults, our children often say they did not know me. As they have read portions of this story they have been shocked at the truth behind their father, yet they are happy to have discovered the missing pieces.

One daughter said it well: "Dad, you needed to write this book, and I needed to read it."

27.

My Peaceable Kingdom

*B*ecause I function primarily in the right hemisphere of my brain I experience a great deal of conflict in trying to live up to my own and society's left-sided expectations. Fortunately I have found several means of escape from this conflict, places where I can synchronize my inner being with the needs of my right-sided existence and find peace. One of these is through mirror-writing.

Many young children, when first learning to write, form some of their letters backwards. As they mature and practice writing they usually correct that impulse by the end of first grade. In children with dyslexia, however, those reversals may persist, even to their writing entire words and sentences from right to left. This is commonly known as mirror-writing, for the words appear as they would if reflected in a mirror.

At a national convention on dyslexia one lecturer stated that the ability to write backwards is a rare, but diagnostically significant attribute of dyslexia. I went up to him afterwards and showed him a sample of my own. He asked me to demonstrate it for the rest of the people who had gathered around us.

When I am writing backwards, or even upside down and backwards, I get a sense that I am writing the way I was meant to. I learned the traditional method because it was expected of me, but it has always felt against my grain. When I follow my natural inclinations I move from right to left. My handwriting becomes more legible and even, and I experience a sense of rightness and an absence of frustration. I am at peace with myself.

While mirror-writing satisfies only me, I have found another escape that allows others to benefit as well—woodworking. In the villages among which I grew up, woodworking was a highly esteemed craft. I began learning as an early elementary student when half of each Friday afternoon was devoted to woodworking. Our teacher had created a small shop in the basement and we used only simple hand tools, but Friday afternoon was the only good part of my entire school week.

This was the era of fretwork, the creation of intricate and delicate designs in thin sheets of wood using only a coping saw. Because of my manual dexterity I became skillful in the use of these hand tools. I went on to acquire some power tools and make several pieces of furniture.

I put woodworking aside as I gave more and more time to academics. But suddenly, five years ago, all my activities came to a sudden halt when I had to undergo open heart surgery. During my recuperation I needed to keep myself occupied with something different than academics and therapy, and I rediscovered woodworking in the form of clock-making. I began by making simple wall clocks, then went on to schoolhouse clocks.

By the time I resumed my professional counseling practice I had fixed upon an absorbing hobby—creating clock designs by making adaptations from originals and adding my own innovations. I expanded into desk and specialty clocks that commemorated noteworthy events such as a retirement. I developed memento clocks and trophy clocks. Then I tried a grandfather clock and, without using a design or model, found tremendous pleasure in making it.

Since that time I have made twelve grandfather clocks and hundreds of other varieties. Dorothy creates faces from counted cross-stitch, a skill she learned as a child, while I make the frames on a lathe.

Now my most restful, peaceful place is my shop. When I walk into my shop, or even *think* about going there, my level of stress is immediately reduced. I have so convinced my cardiologist of this that he is setting up a woodworking shop of his own.

When I am there I have mental peace, as if I have come home. I am in a setting where I belong. It is a sense of being at one with my brain instead of being in conflict with it. During so much of my educational journey I was at odds with my head. Now when I yield to my true nature I experience a stillness that confirms this is the way I was meant to be.

My shop is truly my peaceable kingdom. There are no words in my shop; there is no talk. Occasionally the telephone on the wall rings and I am in touch with the outside world. But as soon as I hang up I am lost again in my wordless space.

In quiet and perfect stillness I select a piece of wood and work it with my tools. Totally absorbed in what is happening I move it from one tool to the next and watch a clock emerging. I use no kits. I start each clock with only a general notion of how it will look and make modifications as I go so that it is a continuous creative process.

Every hand tool has its own place on the wall, and I return each to its proper spot when I've finished using it. Every week I clean and vacuum the entire shop. I remove extra pieces of wood and make sure every tool is clean and in its place. Then I survey my kingdom and pronounce it good.

I accept no time frames in this world; I impose no deadlines. I always tell a customer, "I will call you when it is done." Clock-making is timeless.

Clock-making has given me a new identity, a new way to relate to people. No longer do people back away to a safe distance as they did when they learned that I was a professor, or that I am a psychotherapist or marriage counselor. No more nervous laughter from people, nor apologies for having dropped out of school, nor for having just been divorced. No more the glib statement, "Thank goodness, I have a good marriage."

Now I can talk to people about clocks, about wood. They tell me that their grandfathers made clocks or that they have shops, and we talk about tools. I am no longer a person lost in his head but someone who has hands and can use them skillfully.

My peaceable kingdom, whether it is in mirror-writing or in clock-making, is a place where I can stop making words the way it is expected of me; where the conflict between who I really am and what I have been forced to be finally ceases. When I listen to and follow my true nature, then I am at peace.

28.

A Dwelling Designed
for Dyslexia

*I*magine how an individual with dyslexia would design and build a house. I did exactly that, although when I began the project in the spring of 1969 I had no idea that there was a name for my cluster of personality quirks. I selected the building site, the design and the construction method without consciously knowing that I was trying to alleviate or minimize my affliction. I always gave myself other explanations for what I was doing. As correct as my rationales may have been I realize now that they were efforts to help myself and others understand what I was doing.

I did most of the work on the house myself during an eighteen-month period while I was on the university faculty. I went at the project with a ferocious intensity that I now recognize as a response to that ever-present fear at the center of my character—I needed to build a monument so that everyone (myself included) could see that I was not a defective human being. I had done carpentry work all of my life, but in this community no one knew that. This house would be both a haven and a message that as a carpenter I was not defective.

I spent the winter prior to the construction carefully designing the house. I did not hire an architect; this house was to come from the design in my head. In my imagination I created each section of the house, visualizing exactly how each floor would fit on top of the other, how the stairways would be placed and how the entire design would function.

It was absolutely essential that each of our four children

have a room of his or her own. Privacy was an important issue
in these plans. In fact the whole house was designed so that
most areas could be closed off from the others. My reason, I
told everyone, was that a house should not echo noises from a
stairway, television or loud children. The real purpose was to
protect myself from *any* noise. I carried this to the extreme:
the plasterers wondered why the inside walls and ceilings of
a house needed insulation. My alibis convinced all doubters:
I did, after all, have a lifetime of practice at rationalization.

I wanted a simple house, I explained, because of my basic
belief in simplicity. Actually I was trying to minimize my
disorientation in buildings and places. I have been lost so
often, even in restaurants, and I was not going to lose my way
in my own home. My house is simple to the point of being
bland. I often look at it now and think about the extras that
would have improved its appearance. But I was answering
my needs at that time, even though I did not know their
names.

I have an obsessive need for precision. Anything that is not
exact causes me great distress since I must mentally keep
correcting an error. I would not allow my house to do that to
me. It was to give me peace and tranquility from my inner
demon. If it were possible to build that quality into a house,
I would do so. After the floor joists were in place I measured
the entire house from corner to corner to make sure that it was
square to within a quarter of an inch. In fact every measure-
ment in the house had to be exactly square, level and of correct
dimensions. My dyslexia-driven, desperate attempt to keep
life under control dictated even the details of the house. For
me orderliness is vital; anything less can set off total inner
chaos.

In fact this entire house, from the disarray of my study to
the tidiness of the living room, from the chatter of my office to
the tranquil wordlessness of my shop, reflects the enigma of
my life and being.

29.

A Dyslexic Dream

*T*he process of writing this book has consumed so much of my conscious, daytime energy that my unconscious sent me a status report recently in the form of a dream.

For many persons dreams clarify, through symbolism, what is happening in their lives. This seems to be especially true for dyslexics who function primarily in the right side of their brains, the source of dreams. I have such clear vivid dreams that I depend upon them for direction in life. (I believe this so strongly that I have written a book on that subject: *Before I Wake—Listening to God in Your Dreams*, Abingdon Press, 1984.)

My recent dream gave me graphic representation of what it is like for me, a dyslexic, to write a book.

In the dream I find myself in my room at college. I know that I am near the end of my college career because I remember previous years and classes, but I do not know how many I have completed or how many I have yet to go.

My overriding problem is that I have lost my schedule book and am frantically searching for it throughout the dream. In my mind I have a photographic image of the day's page, but I cannot determine from it where I am to be at 12:00 noon, nor the class I must attend at 1:00. That both events are crucial for the completion of my academic requirements makes my desperation to find the book all the greater.

As I root through a suitcase I am startled to find a number of textbooks I thought I had lost. I examine each one and recognize their value to me. Here is the book on Chaucer, my zoology text and my books on church history. I instantly recall the content of each one and the great pleasure I had in studying them.

I am puzzled as to why they were not put away on the bookshelf, until I notice that the shelf is already jammed full with many more books scattered around on the floor. The disorder bewilders me greatly—if I had the time I would arrange them.

Becoming increasingly frantic about finding my schedule I dig through more suitcases and boxes. The mess gets worse and worse. Now I discover valued, but wrinkled, clothing being ruined by neglect. I had forgotten I had these clothes, and when I try to hang them up I find that the closet is just as overloaded as the bookshelves. The clothing inside is wrinkled from being packed so tightly.

I still must find my schedule book amidst all these distractions. By now a long line of students is trooping through my room. The people step over my boxes, books and clothing as they pass. I am overcome with shame and despair as I survey the scene and feel utterly hopeless as the clock strikes 12:00 noon. With that I awake, tremendously relieved that it was only a dream.

I recognize the symbolism and message of the dream. The room in shambles is my library where I work on this book. My bookshelves are filled, with even the spaces above each row crammed with more books. Surrounding me as I write are twenty-one piles of papers, file folders and printed materials on the subject of dyslexia. They cover my desk; they overflow onto the sofa and floor.

I know I must organize my environment just as I desperately need to organize my life to cope with my constant dread of confusion. The schedule I am so desperately searching for in the dream is the orderliness that I require to write. As in the dream I will never find it. What is the 12:00 noon deadline? The dread I feel that the time will come for me to produce a manuscript and that I will still be wallowing hopelessly in my materials piled all over the room.

The unique content of each of the textbooks in the dream

represents my dyslexic symptoms. I recognize each of them at a glance because for the last ten years I have been describing them in thirty personal journals. The subject matter of my journals is not organized. I write in any journal that is lying near me on any subject that may occur to me. I can open any journal and immediately recognize the item I've described. Knowing I have written this all down gives me the same pleasure that studying those textbooks did.

I am an obsessive journal writer. I must record everything that happens to me, every thought or feeling I have. It cannot be mine, cannot be safe or permanent, until I write it down. Once it is recorded I am relieved of the dread that I will forget it or lose it when my mind plays one of its tricks on me and goes blank.

Dyslexics dream dyslexic dreams. I have had many, on nearly every symptom with which I have struggled while awake. Each is vivid, horribly confusing and never resolved. In that they are like much of life for me—something to survive, not resolve.

30.

The Gift of Dyslexia

When I began my private practice I set several specific conditions. First of all I would practice alone, in my home office, with Dorothy as office manager. I would not create another institution. Secondly, my relationships with clients had to be authentic, clean and clear. I would not play games. I have always asked my clients to call me Abe, and I address them by their first names. I have found that degrees, rank, wealth or prestige all make very little difference when a person is hurting.

My private practice has proved successful far beyond my imagination. At times my client load has been as high as seventy persons, so that I have had to see people on alternate weeks. Why?

A few years ago several individuals who had all previously been my clients told me they each sensed that I could enter into their individual life experiences with phenomenal intensity. They wondered if I had personally suffered in such a way that I could know the pain each of them had experienced. How could I have such infinite faith in the human person that I could trust they would each find the way back to health, no matter how total the collapse?

Years later when I discovered my dyslexia I was able to go back to my childhood and relive the years of my development. I discovered the true pain of my past, as well as my enormous drive to overcome it. I found, too, faith in the power of caring.

While I was building my house with its adjoining office I gained an unexpected insight into what my role has been in the lives of others. My six-year-old son was playing nearby with a friend. The child knew that part of the house was to be a doctor's office and he asked David, "What kind of a doctor is your dad? Does he take care of sick people?"

"No," David replied, not realizing that I could overhear their conversation. "He's not that kind of doctor. My dad is a doctor of feelings."

What my son intuitively understood about me is the best definition of who I am, both clinically and personally.

One particular client who was aware of my dyslexia and some of my past said during one session, "Abe, from the first time I met you I felt an unexplainable mystery about you. Your sensitivity to my hurt is so authentic that I concluded you must have been hurt like I was. Everything I say to you, you already comprehend, even beyond what I am able to explain. When you take what I have said and play it back to me, I feel as if you have lived my life to the same depth I have lived it.

"You have, in fact, suffered as much as I have. Your handicaps have become the greatest gift you could give your clients.

"You may have a hearing problem, but you are the keenest listener. Your brain may not work in certain ways, but you are the most perceptive person I have ever met. You are able to intuitively sense, experience and reach out to others, then bring it all together into a whole. Yet you do not impose any of yourself onto the process. I feel as if I am doing it all, that I am discovering my own way, and, in the end, that I have healed myself. You are only the catalyst that made it possible."

There is no reason I should take personal pride in such a statement; in fact, I am made more humble by it.

I have not made the therapeutic process into a scientific technique. Furthermore, I am unable to write a case history on a client. Rather, I see the process as an art form with myself as the artist and my clients as the media. When a client and I meet I usually forget the greeting as I immediately focus on who this person is. (I've heard my clients say, "Abe is a therapist who never greets you!")

I begin to create a painting by taking in the person's face and eyes, the way my client cries, or laughs, his or her unique mannerisms. Each session adds more depth, color, light and shadow to the painting. Verbally I paint and repaint this picture over and over again. The painting is the client's, not mine.

Once therapy is completed the picture remains in my mind. Years later a tone of voice or a reminder of the theme of a particular painting can instantly bring the entire canvas to my memory.

I truly believe that, for every person, life can begin again and again and again. That thread has run through my entire life; that is the hope I want to instill in others. We are not made to stay the same. We can change, we can be reborn, we can start over. I am optimistic that everything is possible, that every obstacle in life can be conquered. I have a sense of possibility and hope, that the present can be transcended and the future, glorious.

To every client I say, "Nothing should ever stop you. You can master it, you can get on top, you can be victorious." I do not have to add, ". . .because I did it." It is simply present in everything I say and do. That is the gift of dyslexia.

Appendix A

On October 4, 1991, Dr. Abraham Schmitt was provided with a thorough intellectual assessment utilizing the Wechsler Adult Intelligence Scale, the Revised form. Dr. Schmitt had requested the assessment as he indicated he had been curious throughout his life about how he might test formally on an intellectual assessment measure. He explained that he had suffered from an acute dyslexic condition throughout his life and he was curious about the impact which the dyslexic condition might have on his intellectual assessment.

Dr. Schmitt was a willing and cooperative subject obviously displaying a clear-cut interest in the assessment process. He worked with diligence on the tasks and frequent digressions occurred during which he requested information about the specific subtests which constitute the Wechsler Scale.

The Wechsler Adult Intelligence Scale is generally accepted within education and psychology as being the standard measure of assessing intellectual capacities. It takes approximately 90 minutes to administer and spans a gamut of skills and abilities which have been shown to contribute to that which we generally understand to be "intelligence." It provides a basis upon which shorter intellectual assessment measures are normal and by which they are measured. It is an extremely reliable instrument holding up well over testing occasions within the lives of individuals and providing a reliable barometer of intellectual functioning throughout the adult life span. The 1981 revision of the Wechsler provided a substantial update and made many of the items more contemporary and relevant to the experience of individuals living today.

The I.Q. or Intelligence Quotient number derived from an administration of such a measure indexes an individual's functioning in comparison to the abilities of the overall population. Numerous studies were undertaken on the Wechsler in order to ensure that it could discriminate validly among different strata of intelligence among people. An average performance on the Wechsler would result in an I.Q of 100.

A score 15 points lower or higher stands at approximately the 33rd to 84th percentile respectively, meaning that if one registers an I.Q. of 115 on the Wechsler one's performance exceeds that of approximately 84 percent of the adult population. A score of 130, the border between superior and very superior ranges, exceeds the performances of approximately 98 percent of the population. Dr. Schmitt's Full Scale I.Q. on the Wechsler Adult Intelligence Scale-R was 138, falling at approximately the 99th percentile or within the top one percent of the population.

Two groups of subtests contribute to the overall Wechsler I.Q. and each of these provides its own intelligence quotient based upon the skills sampled. Six subtests highly loaded for verbal skills contribute to the derivation of a Verbal I.Q. and five subscales based more upon performance aspects of intelligence result in a Performance I.Q. Dr. Schmitt's Verbal I.Q. of 126 falls within the superior range of functioning and his Performance I.Q. of 137 moves well into the very superior range. The discrepancy between the performance on the two subscales is not significant at such rarified levels of performance, although it is interesting to note that individuals with learning disabilities such as dyslexia generally perform better on the Performance Subscales of the Wechsler than they do on the Verbal.

It is clear to this examiner that Dr. Schmitt has employed a dedicated and diverse set of compensatory strategies in order to prevent his learning disability from interfering with his overall life accomplishment, in general, and professional achievement, specifically.

Ironically, of course, a facet of his motivation to take control of his life's direction and achieve at such high standards may, in fact, have been provided by the frustrations which he experienced with certain aspects of the limitation imposed by his dyslexia. From discussions which we have had, Dr. Schmitt has made it clear that he was determined to move ahead educationally and professionally despite the difficulties posed by processing problems in rote memory and short-term concrete sequencing. Employing what might be described as a "photographic memory" and a clear appreciation for the visual-gestalt, Dr. Schmitt has explained to me how he prepared for tests during his school years and how this accommodation led him to "experiencing the world" in a manner probably more inherently holistic and complex than is the norm for those of us who are more highly dependent upon discrete and somewhat minimalistic memory functions and cognition, ones which tend to frame our understanding of events and motives in a rather rigid, lockstep "cause-effect" manner.

Dr. Schmitt's accomplishment, if measured from perspectives educational, professional and, most importantly, personal, appear to owe a great deal to his differences of perspective, his inherent high levels of intellectual capacity and his ability to arrive at a rapid phenomenological appreciation of the structures and interweavings of the human dilemma.

It was a privilege to be afforded the opportunity to serve as the administrator of the Wechsler Scale for Dr. Schmitt and also to have been asked to write this brief commentary.

Robert J. Wieman, Ph.D.
Clinical Psychologist

Appendix B
Dyslexia Symptom Inventory

The following items have been discovered to be present in people diagnosed as dyslexic. Each person has different symptoms and these vary in intensity. Some may not be present at all. In some people, the exact opposite symptom is present.

As you read each item, circle the number that most nearly describes you:

1 NEVER
2 HARDLY EVER
3 SOMETIMES
4 RATHER OFTEN
5 EXTREMELY OFTEN
6 THE EXACT OPPOSITE IS TRUE

1.	My development was delayed in learning to crawl, sit, stand or walk.	1 2 3 4 5 6
2.	I was late in learning to talk.	1 2 3 4 5 6
3.	Tying my shoes, using a zipper or buttoning my clothes was hard to learn.	1 2 3 4 5 6
4.	As a child I was known to have been clumsy.	1 2 3 4 5 6
5.	I had trouble learning to skip or ride a bicycle.	1 2 3 4 5 6
6.	I was a hyperactive child.	1 2 3 4 5 6
7.	Learning to read was difficult for me.	1 2 3 4 5 6
8.	Spelling was one of my most difficult subjects.	1 2 3 4 5 6
9.	In school I was easily distracted by noise and other classroom activity.	1 2 3 4 5 6

10. I was often called an "underachiever" or
    told that I was not working up to my
    ability.   1 2 3 4 5 6

11. In the classroom, teachers thought that
    I was not paying attention, staring out a
    window or "lost in space."   1 2 3 4 5 6

12. I had an overactive fantasy life.   1 2 3 4 5 6

13. Teachers seemed to think that I was lazy, or
    too stubborn to learn what was difficult
    for me.   1 2 3 4 5 6

14. I often thought that I was a dumb child,
    or that there was something wrong with
    my head.   1 2 3 4 5 6

15. Learning grammar never made sense
    to me.   1 2 3 4 5 6

16. Learning a second language was
    particularly difficult for me.   1 2 3 4 5 6

17. It was extremely difficult for me to
    memorize poetry or parts for plays.   1 2 3 4 5 6

18. When it came to physical education and
    sports, I just couldn't make it.   1 2 3 4 5 6

19. I found it difficult to learn to type.   1 2 3 4 5 6

20. While reading I will frequently see the
    wrong word, which may be very similar to
    the correct one; for example, "white" for
    "wheat."   1 2 3 4 5 6

21. I often lose my place while reading.   1 2 3 4 5 6

22. I read more fluently in total silence.   1 2 3 4 5 6

23. Reading orally before an audience is
    extremely difficult for me.   1 2 3 4 5 6

24. When I read while tired, or at a low ebb,
    words have a way of floating away. It
    takes extra effort to hold letters or words
    in while reading.   1 2 3 4 5 6

25. I tend to reverse or omit letters when I write.   1 2 3 4 5 6

26. My writing is cramped or illegible.   1 2 3 4 5 6

27. I often print my letters rather than write.   1 2 3 4 5 6

28. It is a habit to write most things that I wish to remember.   1 2 3 4 5 6

29. I am persistently forgetful. When distracted I forget what I intended to do. I am known for my absent-mindedness.   1 2 3 4 5 6

30. The names of simple objects, towns or things escape me very frequently.   1 2 3 4 5 6

31. Remembering peoples' names has always been a problem for me.   1 2 3 4 5 6

32. When I am given a series of instructions, I find them hard to follow. I either forget some, or mix up the others.   1 2 3 4 5 6

33. I have a problem repeating the exact order of words in a sentence I have heard. To copy verbatim from a tape recording is absolutely impossible.   1 2 3 4 5 6

34. I cannot remember more than five different telephone numbers.   1 2 3 4 5 6

35. It is impossible for me to remember my social security number.   1 2 3 4 5 6

36. When using a telephone directory, I keep it open because I may forget the number while dialing.   1 2 3 4 5 6

37. I have difficulty with the directions of left and right. It helps to think of my right and left hand to check out my directions.   1 2 3 4 5 6

38. When exiting a parking lot, I have difficulty knowing which way to turn, even if I entered at the same spot.   1 2 3 4 5 6

39. Even on familiar roads, I may get lost.   1 2 3 4 5 6

40. I have a loose, wordy, rambling speech
    pattern.   1 2 3 4 5 6

41. My speech lacks smoothness. Under
    pressure I tend to hesitate, halt and
    sputter.   1 2 3 4 5 6

42. Under extreme pressure I may say the
    exact opposite of what I mean.   1 2 3 4 5 6

43. I frequently mispronounce words.   1 2 3 4 5 6

44. The same story, told on different occasions,
    tends to vary significantly. People think
    I am stretching the truth, or even lying.   1 2 3 4 5 6

45. Even in ordinary conversation, I tend to
    deliver speeches—markedly different from
    others' conversational manners.   1 2 3 4 5 6

46. While talking, I habitually use my hands
    in gesturing.   1 2 3 4 5 6

47. If I try to carry on a conversation while
    others are talking near me, I experience
    confusion.   1 2 3 4 5 6

48. If someone talks to me while I am
    watching television, I experience acute
    agitation.   1 2 3 4 5 6

49. In a crowded, noisy place I tend to
    withdraw, then act "spaced out."   1 2 3 4 5 6

50. Confusion drives me crazy.   1 2 3 4 5 6

51 I hear all background noises which others
   appear not to notice.   1 2 3 4 5 6

52. I prefer orderliness because it gives me
    great comfort.   1 2 3 4 5 6

53. I am an extreme perfectionist in selected
    areas.   1 2 3 4 5 6

54. I have a yearning to be alone. While
    others would feel lonely, I feel peaceful.   1 2 3 4 5 6

55. People often think of me as stubborn,
    inflexible and rigid.   1 2 3 4 5 6

56. I often use rituals to simplify life; for
    example, I prefer to eat the same breakfast,
    use the same bowl, or dress in an exact
    order very day.   1 2 3 4 5 6

57. When I am idle, I tend to drum my fingers. 1 2 3 4 5 6

58. I prefer rocking chairs and may swing my
    foot, even to the annoyance of others.   1 2 3 4 5 6

59. I have one or more phobias, such as
    heights, knives, crowds or enclosed spaces. 1 2 3 4 5 6

60. At times I am plagued by obsessional
    thoughts, parts of songs, words or phrases
    which I am unable to dismiss.   1 2 3 4 5 6

61. With eyes closed, I have difficulty moving
    my outstretched arm to touch my nose in a
    smooth fashion.   1 2 3 4 5 6

62. I am a notorious procrastinator.   1 2 3 4 5 6

63. I function best under an absolute deadline. 1 2 3 4 5 6

64. I am unable to accurately identify the time
    when something happened. I may say
    "yesterday" when the event occurred some
    days earlier.   1 2 3 4 5 6

65. In trying to learn music, it is uniquely
    difficult for me to read the words and
    notes simultaneously.   1 2 3 4 5 6

66. I have an excellent pictorial memory. At
    times it is as if I see a photograph of past
    events or places.   1 2 3 4 5 6

67. I have very vivid dreams.   1 2 3 4 5 6

68. Periodically I will solve a problem in an
    unexpected moment of insight which
    surprises even me.   1 2 3 4 5 6

69. My symptoms appear more intense at
    certain times of the day, on certain days,
    weeks or months. They come and go in
    random waves.   1 2 3 4 5 6

70. I have relatives who have many of the
    same problems I have.   1 2 3 4 5 6

71. The net effect of these symptoms causes a
    strain in relationships with other persons
    close to me.   1 2 3 4 5 6

(Dyslexia is not easily diagnosed. To better understand
how to interpret the results of this survey see pages 110-
114, Chapter 18, "Diagnosis of Dyslexia.")

Appendix C

The Birth of the Creative Personality of Otto Rank

by Dr. Abraham Schmitt

The Familial Phase

← THE TRAUMA OF BIRTH OF THE INFANT

UNION WITH MOTHER →

(2 yrs.) ← THE TRAUMA OF BIRTH OF THE WILL

UNION WITH FAMILY IDEALS →

(adolescence) ← THE TRAUMA OF BIRTH OF IDENTITY

UNION WITH HUMANITY, CIVILIZATION →

The Societal Phase

← THE TRAUMA OF BIRTH OF THE HERO

UNION WITH THE WORLD, CREATION →

The Artistic Phase

← THE TRAUMA OF BIRTH OF THE ARTIST

UNION WITH THE SPIRITUAL, IDEOLOGICAL PHILOSOPHICAL REALITY →

The Spiritual Phase

← THE TRAUMA OF BIRTH OF SOUL

RECONCILIATION WITH LIFE & DEATH →

ETERNAL DEATH - (ULTIMATE SEPARATION)

ETERNAL LIFE - (ULTIMATE UNION)   ← (an act of the conscious will)

– SEPARATION – (Difference Affirmed) Life (Birth) Fear Overcome

UNION – (Likeness Experienced) Death Fear Overcome

Appendix D

Conflict and Ecstasy: Model for a Maturing Marriage